Teaching Music

Teaching Music

MANAGING THE SUCCESSFUL MUSIC PROGRAM

Darwin E. Walker
South Dakota State University

Schirmer Books
A Division of Macmillan, Inc.
New York
Collier Macmillan Publishers
London

Schirmer Books
A Division of Macmillan, Inc.
866 Third Avenue, New York, N.Y. 10022

Collier Macmillan Canada, Inc.

Library of Congress Catalog Card Number: 88-17463

Printed in the United States of America

printing number
1   2   3   4   5   6   7   8   9   10

Library of Congress Cataloging-in-Publication Data

Walker, Darwin E., 1936–
    Teaching music : managing the successful music program / Darwin E.
Walker.
        p.   cm.
    Bibliography: p.
    Includes index.
    ISBN 0-02-872721-5
    1. Music—Instruction and study.   I. Title.
MT1.W28 1989
780'.7—dc19   88-17463
                                                                         CIP
                                                                         MN

Contents

Preface

If music educators are less successful in their careers than they could or should be, they are not necessarily deficient in musical skills. That lack of success can often be traced to their inability to deal successfully with the day-to-day organizational obligations that confront all music educators. This book is offered as a means of anticipating and alleviating administrative problems in music education in as practical a manner as possible.

Prospective music educators in upper-level college music-education classes and practicing music educators will find the information included in this book to be extremely helpful in their efforts to manage effectively the numerous noninstructional functions of a successful music-education program. Many of the chapters will also be beneficial to musicians not directly associated with music instruction in the public schools. Church musicians, for example, will find all of the managerial chapters helpful in their profession. The chapters on philosophy development, public relations, music testing, motivation and discipline, scheduling, budgeting, fund-raising, music rooms and equipment, should hold a degree of interest for private music teachers as well as some professional musicians. Graduate students in music education will also find this book to be a valuable supplemental text and research source.

A sincere attempt has been made to present the material in accessible language, and practicability has determined the book's scope. Far too often, books associated with music education discuss problems without offering solutions or indicate that the reader should adopt a particular concept without offering examples of the implications of that concept. The intent of this book has been to provide numerous examples as rationale for the recommendations made. When discussing the "goal and objective" process, sample goals and objectives are offered; when discussing philosophy, a sample philosophy is provided; when discussing the importance of press releases in public relations, a detailed format for a press release is presented; when discussing the budget process, a detailed sample budget is included; prices and addresses of where to order music aptitude tests are included in that chapter; sample class schedules, contests and festival formats, library filing systems and equipment, parents' group constitution, and music-room specifications are just a few of the many practical examples given. Great emphasis, in other words, has been placed on the *what, how, when,* and *why* of administering a music education program.

To facilitate use of this book as a text by college and university professors and their students, a "Suggested Activities" section has been provided at the end of most chapters. Because it is a music-education book, this work will fulfill the needs of a music-education methods class that involves both choral and instrumental students, and it will also stand alone as a required text for either a choral-methods or instrumental-methods class.

No teaching area in all of education requires the degree of administrative skills that must be developed by a music educator. It is intended that this book go a long way toward developing the noninstructional skills of prospective and practicing music educators in this country.

DEW

Acknowledgments

I take this opportunity to express my deepest appreciation to my teachers, students, and colleagues, who through the years have all had a profound influence on the information found here.

I owe a very special debt of gratitude to Dr. John Berggren. His faith in me as a young music educator provided me with numerous opportunities for personal growth in the profession. His musicianship, knowledge, and friendship served as an inspiration for me in my formative years as a music educator. Thanks, Jack.

To Jeanne Lesinski and Marilyn Eighmy, for their preliminary editing and technical assistance in the preparation of this manuscript, I offer my appreciation and gratefulness.

Finally, this book is respectfully dedicated to my wife, Marlenna, for her faith in me, for her assistance and advice, her support, patience, and understanding, without which this book would not have been possible.

Teaching Music

The Music
Educator
as an
Administrator

1

The Role of the Music Educator

A well-kept secret in educational circles is the amount of organizational time it takes to operate a quality music-education program—in even the smallest school system. This chapter deals with the many noninstructional, administrative tasks confronting young music educators as they begin their teaching careers in today's schools.

There are as many types of administrative assignments in our school systems as there are classifications of administrators. By the time a music educator graduates from college, he or she has been exposed to a wide spectrum of educational administration and leadership. From the university president or chancellor to the variety of vice presidents and deans, music executives, department heads, and academic advisors, the music educator has had the opportunity to observe a broad spectrum of educational administration. Add to that the multifaceted administrational web to which the music educator was exposed as a student at the public-school level, and the diversity and quality of observed administrative functions becomes immense.

Through this exposure, the music educator has gained insight into how the educational administration system is structured and how it functions. What he or she does not understand, however, is the multitude of nonmuscial functions that need to be performed on a daily basis simply to make the program work. Far too many young music teachers become completely overwhelmed by the myriad of adjunct activities demanding efficient organization and administration. They would much rather be teaching private lessons, conducting rehearsals, and teaching music classes than administrating a program.

For many, the development of organizational skills becomes "on the job training" because this aspect of teacher preparation lacked the necessary depth at the college or university level. They welcome and thrive on the challenge of developing and operating a smoothly running music-education program in their schools.

Others become totally engulfed in the many administrative tasks confronting them and stumble through their early years as music educators, completely unaware of how a well-organized music-education program functions. The teachers who fall into this category often leave teaching after a few years, citing poor pay, unruly students, or poor working conditions as the reasons for their departure, when in fact, it was their own lack of ability to deal effectively with the day-to-day noninstructional obligations of the profession.

The third category of young music educators includes those who graduated from a school system where the music teachers administered an organized, well-balanced, efficient music-education program. Such a program develops quality general music skills and offers musically satisfying, stimulating, and exciting performance opportunities for the students. There is an old saying in education, "We teach as we've been taught." This adage is never more true than when applied to music education. Students who have graduated from successful school music programs will possess a distinct advantage as music educators, having experienced the benefits of efficient musical administration on the part of their public-school music teachers. In their teacher training programs prior to student teaching, all three categories of prospective music educators can benefit from a thoughtful, and above all, practical approach to the development of basic administrative skills.

As part of the preparation for this book, the author personally interviewed over one-hundred music educators, and when asked what aspect of their actual teaching experience did their undergraduate training least prepare them for, an overwhelming number responded with answers associated to some type of program administration.

The Music Educator as an Administrator

John F. Kennedy, in his 1961 State of the Union message, said, "The capacity to act decisively at the exact time action is needed has been too often muffled in the morass of committees, timidities, and fictitious theories, which have created a growing gap between decision and execution." The music educator needs to develop the managerial skills that will enable him or her to promote decisive action when it is needed and avoid the administrative pitfall of making plans and decisions then falling short of success when converting those plans and decisions into action.

A good administrator is often thought of as a person who "can really get things done." What this translates into for the music educator is the ability to identify, maintain and utilize resources, the ability to develop a workable system that will focus energies on music-education objectives. In other words, administration is not an end in itself when measuring program success but rather a means of achieving goals and objectives associated with a quality educational experience.

The role of the music educator as an administrator includes determining the type of program, defining the nature of experiences to strive for, developing a philosophical foundation for the program, establishing teaching patterns, and creating an educational environment. All of the above responsibilities can best be accomplished through an organized and thoughtful examination of the requisite administrative skills. A basic premise, stated simply by Robert House, must be accepted: "Administration facilitates the teaching process."[1]

It is assumed that when a music educator graduates from college, he or she possesses the necessary musical competency to be a successful music educator. Knowledge of music history and theory has been tested and personal musical ability has been measured through four or more years of applied instruction, probably culminating in at least one recital performance. These same potential music educators, however, will at best face several difficult years in the teaching profession, unless at the undergraduate level they are adequately prepared, both mentally and academically, for the administrative challenges that will confront them the very first day they walk into music classrooms and rehearsals.

The discussion of the music educator's administrative functions that follows provides further insight into the need for the development of the abilities so necessary to administering a music-education program as we know it today.

The Music Educator and Administrative Functions

On the subject of school administration, Stephen J. Knezevich has written a highly respected book geared primarily toward graduate students.[2] He lists sixteen upper-level administrative functions. What follows is a statement and explanation of each function in Knezevich's words, along with this writer's application of each function to music education.

FUNCTION NUMBER ONE: ANTICIPATING
What future conditions may confront the institution?

The music educator must plan far in advance for anticipated enrollment in performing groups, proper instrumentation in instrumental ensembles, section balance within choral ensembles, and overall enrollment in the music program in light of possible declining enrollment school-wide. The general music teacher must anticipate what changes may affect his or her program and investigate the latest teaching models and techniques that may be employed in the music classroom in future years. The instrumental music educator must look at grade-school enrollment with an eye to recruitment for the instrumental music program. The choral music educator must focus on continuity in the total choral program, which may often be adversely affected by low male enrollment, due perhaps to the adolescent voice change and competing electives in the school curriculum. Anticipating future facility and equipment needs, along with projecting future concert wear replacement, are additional far-reaching concerns of the music educator.

Accurate record-keeping of student participation in annual school music events, cost per pupil figures, student/teacher ratio, as well as the constituency served by the program can be of great assistance should the school district consider making staff or program reductions. Annual records that include figures indicating program growth, strength, and expected growth patterns should be kept.

Proper anticipation of future conditions facing the music-education program can do much to prevent organizational problems from becoming a disproportionate preoccupation, placing a physical and mental drain on the time and energy of the music educator.

FUNCTION NUMBER TWO: ORIENTING
Ensure that objectives are generated and then used

Any successful program, in or out of education, must include the setting of definable and achievable goals and objectives. It has been a widely accepted policy to treat the terms *goals* and *objectives* synonymously. For the purpose of clarity in this book, an educational goal will assume a distinct meaning from an educational objective.

Goals in music education are to be considered long range in scope, broad in direction, and can be regarded as general in nature. An educational goal is a desired outcome for a student or for a program. Examples of goals in music education could be "All graduates should be able to read music," or "All students should have the opportunity to experience making music on instruments." Both statements demand some type of support strategies or techniques in order to be realistically achievable.

An *objective* in music education can be defined as an accomplishment that is short term in scope, is easily verified and specific in direction, and when properly implemented supports progress toward goal achievement. In other words, specific objectives support and facilitate attainment of broader, long-term goals in music education.

The establishment of goals and objectives is closely tied to a music educator's philosophy. The development and articulation of a philosophy of music education will be presented in Chapter Twelve. What will be dealt with at this point will be the setting of short-term, annual objectives, which are such a vital part of administering a music-education program.

The setting of realistic goals and objectives is one of the most important ingredients in any successful music-education program. The key word here is, of course, "realistic." Objective-setting for general music classes, as well as all performing groups, can involve colleagues, school administrators, and the students participating in those classes and ensembles.

Of a more personal nature are the objectives that the teacher annually sets for personal pedagogical improvement. The setting of these objectives is often done in conjunction with the teacher-evaluation process administered each year by the building principal. The music teacher is usually asked to state in writing the objectives for the year and is then asked the following year if those objectives and goals were met and if so, how. These can include far-reaching program objectives, as well as annual personal objectives.

It must be kept in mind that specific objectives set by an experienced teacher can, and perhaps should, be quite different from those set by a first-year music educator. Also keep in mind that specific objectives such as "increase concert attendance" or "increase communication with my fellow music educators" will generally be welcomed by school administrators and will be realistically achievable.

Five personal objectives that could be set by a middle-school general music teacher follow:

1. Incorporate music of other cultures into the classroom activities.
2. Improve computer literacy.
3. Include more singing as a part of the general-music-class offerings.
4. Increase the number of fretted instruments for classroom use.
5. Become more active in a leadership role in the state music-education association.

Examples of the objectives a high-school choral director might write could include

1. Improve sight reading by spending a few minutes of each rehearsal reading new material.
2. Attempt to improve the choir's unaccompanied singing by programming at least one additional unaccompanied selection of each concert.
3. Increase solo participation at music contest by twenty percent.
4. Visit middle-school choir rehearsals at least once a month for continuity purposes.
5. Recruit more tenors and basses for the choir by starting an all-male ensemble.

If a high-school band director elected to establish a set of objectives for the year, five examples might be

1. Establish improved criteria for evaluation and grading purposes.
2. Organize monthly, systematic cleaning and inspection of all instruments in the high-school band.
3. Increase the concert publicity and promotion.
4. Increase participation of instrumental students at summer music camps by twenty percent.
5. Develop better computer literacy by attending at least one workshop dealing with the use of the computer in music education.

Note that all the objectives set down by the three music educators are specific, easily monitored, and reasonably easy to verify.

The danger that music educators often encounter in setting objectives is being too general. For example, one instrumental teacher's objective might be "Make the band play more musically." Understandably, that is a most noble and worthy objective; however, it lacks specificity. How will the band come to play more musically? What elements of a musical performance require the most work to achieve that goal?

An objective written by a junior-high choral director might be "Improve students' attitude toward chorus." Again, such a general objective is difficult to monitor and verify. The key to writing worthwhile objectives is to be practical, direct, and specific.

Another guideline the music educator must observe when establishing goals and objectives is to keep them educationally sound. They should be educational objectives, educational goals. Beware of setting goals and objectives lacking an educational foundation, such as "Win the Tri-State Jazz Festival" or "Raise $15,000 for a trip to the Macy's Parade."

Other than personal goals, those goals that deal with the music-education process itself are more often than not established as part of the school curriculum through the committee work of all the music educators in the school system. Music educators are encouraged to secure a copy of any formulated educational goals and, if not in agreement with them, to work through and with music colleagues for mutual change. Progress does not always result from change, but progress is not possible without change.

The importance of setting quality and educationally sound goals and objectives simply cannot be overlooked as a valuable tool in the administration of a music-education program.

FUNCTION NUMBER THREE: PROGRAMMING
Generation of alternatives or strategies that can be use to reach an objective

Now that specific objectives have been established, the next administrative task is to plan the means to achieve those objectives.

The first hypothetical objective of the previously mentioned middle-school general music teacher was to "Incorporate music of other cultures into classroom activities." After having decided upon this objective, the music educator should develop the approach(es) he or she feels would best achieve that objective. For example,

1. When rhythms are being studied, use American Indian, Latin American, or other music of diverse cultures.
2. Study the pentatonic scale with Orff instruments and use music of the Orient.
3. When studying jazz, incorporate the African "call and response" technique.
4. Invite foreign exchange or university students temporarily residing in or near the community to visit class.
5. Plan a unit on folk songs from different countries.

The first objective listed by the high-school choral director was "Improve sight reading by spending a few minutes of each rehearsal reading new material." Four steps the choral teacher could follow to achieve that objective would be

1. Purchase a choral sight-reading group method book.
2. Sing with syllables during a portion of each rehearsal.
3. Count and clap rhythm patterns.
4. Devise interval and pitch matching studies.

The band director who was concerned about evaluation and account-ability listed as the first objective of the program "Establish improved criteria for evaluation and grading purposes." Five steps to assist in achieving that objective are

1. Use of music achievement tests to determine musical progress.
2. Administer written tests based on music in the folder.
3. Develop means of allowing extra credit for participation in musical activities in addition to band work.
4. Search for a computer program to aid in record keeping.
5. Develop an improved and more organized rehearsal atmosphere to allow time for the evaluation process.

As the year goes on, the music educator will develop substeps in conjunction with the strategies supporting each objective. Through this organized approach to setting goals and objectives, the music educator creates an administrative setting that promotes success.

FUNCTION NUMBER FOUR: ORGANIZING
Focuses on creating the structural framework . . . required to satisfy demands of objectives

As mentioned earlier in this chapter, the organizational framework required for music educators to properly and efficiently run their programs is vast as well as diverse.

Take, for example, the beginning teacher who is placed in charge of a school's music program, grades five through twelve. In addition to daily class and rehearsal planning, this teacher will more than likely be completely in charge of curriculum decisions as they affect the general music portion of the program, what books or methods to use throughout the program, the procurement and spending of funds, organizing the dispersal and collection of band and choir music and maintaining control over the instrument inventory, which of course includes the repair of instruments. Additionally, this teacher is in control of the lesson schedule and sectional schedule, the concert scheduling of two high-school choirs, one high-school band, two grade-school bands, and two annual general music programs. This particular educator may also be involved in fund-raising projects—along with the dispersal of the money raised—schedule students for the annual solo and ensemble and large group contest, host a music festival in his or her own school, organize a music booster organization, and design a new uniform for the band. The music educator will probably want to be involved in community activities, such as directing church choir, acting as member of the local Optimist Club, and assisting in the Scouting program, all the time being solely in charge of public relations for the music program.

It should be perfectly clear at this point that this music educator must have well-defined and specific goals and objectives and must function in a well-organized instructional atmosphere in order to achieve a high level of cohesiveness and continuity in the music-education program.

The previous example was, of course, a fictional one, but certainly possible, demonstrating the need to organize the "structural framework required to satisfy the demands of the objectives."

FUNCTION NUMBER FIVE: STAFFING
Assigning human resources needed to pursue an objective and fulfill program demands

Normally, a young music educator is not in a position to delegate responsibility to other full-time music staff members for the simple reason that he or she is likely either to be a part of a one- or two-member music department or to be an assistant in a large school system.

A very important part of working with "human resources" can be the degree of involvement the music educator has with a parent support group. Properly organized, motivated, and inspired parents groups can relieve a great deal of the organizational pressure a music educator feels, from fund-raising to the assigning and cleaning of concert wear.

Student volunteer workers can be assigned many routine tasks, such as record-keeping, library management, roll-taking, and ushering and dispersing programs at concerts. Qualified student assistants are often put in charge of sectional rehearsals. Students can contribute greatly to the positive, organized environment of the rehearsal room by helping with general housekeeping chores, bulletin boards, etc. Students can be vital cogs in the promotional machinery for the choral or band program. Almost all junior and senior bands and choirs have members who are on the school newspaper staff. They can become liaisons between the performing group and the school and local newspapers.

At least one student in every musical group has a parent who is an avid amateur photographer. Enlist his or her help in taking photos of the group, both posed and candid, in rehearsal and in concert settings. (Note: In concert setting, not during the concert.) Young people love to see pictures of themselves, and a rotating photo display is a motivational factor, as well as a public relations vehicle.

This same principle applies to parental help in videotaping performances. At least one music parent with a room full of equipment is eagerly awaiting an invitation to apply newly acquired video skills.

The usual use of parents at after-concert receptions and as chaperons on trips are two other very common applications of "human resources" to the music program. The bright, enthusiastic, and resourceful music educator will find many more.

The community at large is another source for "human resources" in support of the music program. Community members who play an instrument are often eager to accompany solos and ensembles at contests and recitals. Others in the community may be able to help locate specialists in a certain style of music or they may wish to assist in a general music class project. Even the smallest community can provide a wealth of human resources. If the objective, for example, is to increase attendance at summer music camps, local service organizations and music clubs can be sources of scholarship funding.

In one's own school, nonmusician colleagues can be of great assistance to the music educator. For example, the foreign-language department can provide foreign-language expertise in choral music; the art department can help with posters; and the drama department can be a great help in staging a concert or general music class performance.

The above are only a few of the many examples of "human resources" available to the music educator in the school and community. The imaginative and secure educator will use many of them and seek out additional ones to assist the day-to-day organizational functions of the music program.

FUNCTION NUMBER SIX: "RESOURCING"
This unusual word is used to describe the process of acquiring and allocating funds

This function is so important that Chapter Three of this book is devoted entirely to the topic. In fact, the securing of adequate funding for the program is undoubtedly the most important and challenging noninstructional function of any music educator. A teacher who is well-organized provides the taxpayers with a quality "product" and develops a thought-provoking and well-researched budget document, which will often be rewarded with generally sufficient fiscal support for the program.

In order to write a quality budget document, music educators need to develop an understanding of the total school budget procedure. They should be familiar with potential funding sources, possess the necessary business skills and vocabulary to be successfull in securing adequate funding, and demonstrate strong philosophical bases for any requests. They must be able to predict future needs, determine revenue potentials, and stand behind their requests with ample support material.

Music educators can also seek funding for their programs outside the school district. The most common such source is the parent support group, as presented in Chapter Ten. Other outside sources that can be explored are service and music clubs. Another source of revenue can be rental fees from school-owned instruments and concert wear. Some schools presently charge a flat fee per student for participation in the music program.

The final and least desirable option for funding outside the school district is the music students themselves, through their own fund-raising efforts. There is a school of thought, supported by sound philosophical theory, that music students should not be involved in raising money for their own programs. The consensus of music-education opinion on this topic is that if the program is worthwhile and is a part of the school curriculum, the school district should support it. As mentioned earlier, this subject will be pursued later in this book.

At this point in the discussion, it is easy to determine how important and even controversial "Resourcing" can be in the administration of music education. The role of educators and how they influence this process is of undeniable importance in today's educational environment.

FUNCTION NUMBER SEVEN: LEADING
Stimulating or motivating personnel to action and toward objectives

This particular function is perhaps one of the most important of the entire list of sixteen functions. Anyone who is in charge of a program, be it an entire two-hundred-teacher school system, a major corporation, or a school music program, must, in order to be successful, possess or develop basic motivational skills. Everyone can think back to their years in the public school system and recall several teachers and administrators who they really admired and, more than likely, for whom they did their best work. Those teachers and administrators were individuals who possessed a high level of natural or learned motivational skills.

The reason this function is so important to the music educator is that a music-education program inextricably involves performance. When individual or collective performance is an integral part of *any* academic program, the ability of the leader to motivate the individuals involved in the program toward their highest performance level is of the utmost importance.

Personality plays an integral role in motivation. This country's greatest political and military leaders are individuals with strong and charismatic personalities. A shy person will generally find it very difficult to lead and motivate individuals toward goals and objectives.

A discussion of this topic appears in Chapter Two; however, it is appropriate at this point to briefly present several techniques that can be developed and used in administrating music-education programs.

First of all, motivation of individuals involved in a music program is not possible without a positive approach to discipline. This does not mean one should become overly strict; it means that an environment must be created in which motivational techniques can succeed. The ability to deal in positive rather than negative terms can be the key ingredient to success in motivating personnel.

In a music-education program, there are a number of built-in motivational opportunities available to the instructor. Music contests can highly motivate students and teachers alike. Yet music contests are also an area of music education where the opportunity for conceptual abuse is always present. For example, some music teachers use "fear of failure" rather than "musical achievement" as the major motivational element when preparing their students for music contests. While this approach can be effective, it is also educationally unsound. The level of program motivation that is derived from contest participation must be carefully measured and monitored to maintain its compatibility with the overall objectives of the program.

In addition to concert performances, awards, point systems for those awards or for grading purposes, and wall charts denoting progress to a particular goal are some of the available means of motivating students. The process of evaluation and grading, while primarily intended to measure student progress and achievement, is often an important motivational tool. For that reason, a thoughtful and organized approach to the evaluation of music students is currently a point of national concern.

The most abstract forms of motivating personnel involve the creation of personal pride within the class or group. The ability of the teacher to take interest in the outside activities of the students, make the students understand their uniqueness, appeal to their sense of adventure, promote group identity, and create and sustain a positive environment for success are all important functions of the music educator as a motivator.

Finally, the teacher who is well prepared for a class and/or rehearsal is a teacher who can then anticipate change and who is in a position to successfully motivate students toward worthwhile musical and personal objectives.

FUNCTION NUMBER EIGHT: EXECUTING
Day to day operating functions that command attention
of all administrators

The manner in which an administrator handles the routine operations of a program can serve as a predictor of success for that program. Personnel need some daily predictability in their lives. The music educators who cannot settle into some type of daily routine in classroom work or rehearsal approach will find themselves with a group of confused and potentially unmanageable students.

In addition to the daily academic preparation for class and rehearsal, the music educator is involved in communication and public relations with peers, parents, administrators, and the community, as well as with such other routine tasks as hall duty, attendance, progress reports, and meetings. Despite the hectic atmosphere of most schools and the myriad activities for which the music educator is responsible, the key to success lies in his or her ability to create a functional, routine atmosphere which students can come to rely on and which, in turn, becomes a part of their daily lives. The music educator who is poorly prepared and unpredictable has failed at an important administrative procedure.

FUNCTION NUMBER NINE: CHANGING
a) Identify something to change to
b) Introduction of innovation
c) Management of change to produce maximum benefits

The management of change is most certainly not a daily function and perhaps not even a weekly or monthly function; however, the ability, upon demand, to manage and administer change in a logical and positive manner can most certainly serve as a principal indicator of the success or failure of a particular program.

Change for change's sake in a music program is a tremendous waste of physical and mental energy on the part of students and teachers alike. This type of change generally occurs when there has been a turnover of teaching staff in the program. Often newcomers initiate change to "make their own mark" on the program. Such alterations are often made without any profound thought about the positive or negative implications of the changes, the degree of previous success of the program, or what portion of the program is being changed. Such unfounded changes are simply an incorrect action of the part of the individual charged with the responsibility of administering the program. In fact, this type of approach often results in confusion and eventual failure.

Change, to be successful, must follow a patient and thoughtful procedure. It must be introduced carefully, not haphazardly, to prepare the individuals involved. In addition, one must possess or develop the skills necessary to articulate, in writing, the proposed change. In music education, the gathering and dissemination of information regarding the change to school administrators, students, parents, and other individuals potentially affected by the change is a primary requisite of the process.

During the early stages of change, close monitoring should take place and the results should be communicated to all those involved. Constant evaluation of new innovations by the participants is desirable. For the music educator the participants would include other teachers as well as the students directly involved.

In music education, programs often change because of the management process. Failure follows the introduction of innovation when the levels of success are not monitored, recorded, and managed. Far too often the innovation is blamed for the failure, when in fact the mismanagement of that innovation is responsible for the lack of success.

Taking this process one step further, let's follow a hypothetical program innovation through the three steps presented as part of this function. Perhaps a junior high school instrumental music educator would like to structure a lesson schedule for all one hundred students involved in the program. School administrative policy prohibits students from missing academic classes on a regular basis for that type of activity.

After a great deal of reading, investigating, and related research, our teacher decides that a rotating, semiprivate lesson schedule could be the solution. The first step has been accomplished: the teacher has identified something to change to!

The plan, along with written support materials based on research, is presented to the building principal. Being a progressive young administrator, the principal informs the music educator that if the classroom teachers support the plan, it will have the support of the principal's office as well.

A meeting is scheduled with the classroom teachers affected by the proposed change. The rotating-schedule plan is carefully explained, questions are asked, and the teachers give their reluctant approval on a nine-week experimental basis.

A letter is then mailed to the parents of students involved in the junior-high-school instrumental music program outlining their participation in the project and asking for their support and assistance in reminding their students about the correct day and time of the lesson as it rotates through the schedule.

Finally, a meeting is held with the students involved in the program. Student responsibility for the success of the innovation is carefully and thoroughly discussed, and the students are excited about accepting the challenge of their role in the new project.

With the rotating lesson schedule in place and functioning, the teacher monitors the feelings of the classroom teachers toward the project, seeking advice on what, if anything, could be done to improve the process. The success and ultimate acceptance of the project depends greatly upon the attitude of the classroom teachers.

Communication with the students and their parents continues at regular intervals during the trial period. Flaws are determined and adjustments made. The building principal is kept informed on the progress of the project. At the end of the nine-week experimental period, a follow-up meeting with the music educator, affected classroom teachers, and building principal results in a positive vote to retain the rotating lesson schedule on a permanent basis. The change was identified, introduced, and managed, resulting in the project's success.

This scenario could perhaps be construed as an oversimplification of a difficult procedure, but it should be remembered that the rotating schedule process presented above is only an example of how the system works. A detailed explanation of the use of a rotating schedule in music education is presented in Chapter Five.

When initiating change or innovative procedures, the degree of communication, patience, research, and organization surrounding the project can ensure its success or failure.

FUNCTION NUMBER TEN: DIAGNOSING-ANALYZING CONFLICT
Conflict or problem diagnosis and subsequent analysis are relatively new competencies

This function is considered new to the educational administration field, but it can certainly be considered "old hat" to the music-education profession. From the early 1800s individuals in this country interested in furthering the cause of music in general, and more specifically music education, have been dealing successfully with conflicts and a variety of recurring problems on an almost daily basis.

Perhaps the best way to begin the discussion of this function is through the examination of a possible problem, one that is a startlingly real problem in music education today—the decrease in participation in the band program between elementary, junior high, and senior high schools.

Let's say that a band director has diagnosed that there is a dropout rate of forty percent between the students involved with the beginning band program and those entering the high-school band at the ninth-grade level. The diagnosis has been made as to the conflict or problem; now analysis of the potential causes must be undertaken.

A variety of causes could be uncovered, some of which could lead to other conflicts or problems. This band director is in charge of the entire band program, grades five through twelve. The following list includes several of the causes that he or she determines could be contributing to the unusually high dropout rate.

1. Lack of band rehearsal time for the bands in grades five through eight.
2. No private or semiprivate lesson time in the grade-school program.
3. Increased pressure on students to make an early choice about whether or not they plan to attend college. Increased requirements for college entrance pressures students to include more math, science, and foreign-language courses in their ninth-grade schedules.
4. Band meeting before the school day.

There could, of course, be several additional factors involved, but for the purpose of discussion four causes will suffice. The resolution of those four choices will be presented as part of Function Number Eleven.

There are many other problematic situations that occur in music education that can require examination and resolution. Poor attitude among these students involved in the high-school choir could prompt the choir director to formulate a list of potential causes. Poor attitude toward pep-band participation could cause the same effect. The elementary teacher could be faced with "problem diagnosis" because of parental questioning of an evaluation and grading system. A middle-school instructor could face inquiries from parents and school officials alike over the attempt to create a "by audition only" choir at the sixth-grade level. There are numerous situations in music education that require the careful diagnosis and analysis of a problem by the music instructor to honestly determine choices that will eventually lead to the problem's resolution. This is a simple fact! When one person administers a program, sets much of the curriculum and many of the schedules, secures and allocates funds, and performs the other difficult tasks asked of a music educator, it is to be expected that the level of conflicts and problems surrounding the program will increase directly in proportion to the amount of responsibility required.

FUNCTION NUMBER ELEVEN: DECIDING-RESOLVING
Focuses on resolution of choices. It can be a conflict-laden or conflict-free decision situation

Let's continue to look at the case of the band director with the dropout problem mentioned in the last section. Preliminary examination of the four diagnoses indicates that numbers one and two hold some potential for improvement without causing havoc within the system. Choice number three generally must be taken at face value for what it is—a fact in educational life that must be accepted and dealt with as professionally as possible. Choice number four has a solution, but it will take time to implement.

Therefore, the wise music educator would do well to concentrate on choices one and two and see what, if anything, results from that effort. For example, the teacher could request from the building principal an extra thirty-to-forty minute rehearsal period, citing the statistics resulting from the dropout research. Part of the time could possible come out of the students' lunch time; the rehearsal could start a few minutes before the regular school time; or the band time could be treated as homeroom time. Choice number two could possibly be solved through a rotating lesson schedule, a plan carefully worked out with the classroom teachers for class release time, or some other innovative technique designed to the satisfaction of all parties. Again, it should be understood that the choices determined and the solutions recommended are simply examples of what *could* transpire in a given situation, not necessarily what approach *should* be followed in that situation.

Too many music educators are likely to spend their time complaining about the negative effects choices three and four are having on their programs and completely overlook the solvable first and second choices. Remember, when going to a principal or any other administrator with a problem, always be prepared to offer potential solutions to the problem. If potential solutions cannot be offered, then perhaps the problem doesn't exist. Administrators tend to see teachers who discuss a problem without providing potential solutions as complainers.

There are many other administrative choices that confront a music educator that, while they don't necessarily result because of a conflict, greatly influence the direction of a particular program. For example, much curriculum decision-making is the responsibility of the music educator, as is a certain degree of the scheduling process. What athletic events to perform for and whether or not to participate in music contests are two more important choices confronting the music educator. What evaluative system to use, the number of annual performances, and the style of classroom control are other choices that need to be made.

As the reader progresses through this book, the choices should become more clear and the decisions easier to make. Successful music educators learn to accept and to live with decisions that are no longer within their control. If individuals cannot accept that premise, they should be prepared to accept the likelihood that impossible problematic situations will constantly and severely inhibit the entire educational process under their supervision.

FUNCTION NUMBER TWELVE: COORDINATING
The administration has the responsibility to unify the activities of various components and to focus the function of discrete units onto the objectives

The music educator is generally responsible for more than one "unit." In many smaller communities one person is in charge of the entire music program. In even larger school systems, where the responsibility is divided among several music instructors, each person works with more than one group. The band director may have a concert band, jazz band, and a marching band. The choral director will probably have two choirs, a swing choir, perhaps a madrigal group, and a music-appreciation class. The individual in a one-person music program could be responsible for all the groups listed above, plus some type of program for the elementary grades. The total responsibility for the successful focusing of the components toward objectives is an overwhelmingly difficult administrative task.

The music educator must work with and coordinate a wide variety of objectives. There are different objectives for the band and for the choir. The upper-level general music program's objectives need to coincide with those established for the lower elementary grades. The total music program must be focused toward meeting the goals and objectives set down by the school district. Parent groups have their own bylaws, and there are other objectives established by the Music Educators National Conference (MENC) and other state and national associations.

It is well within the domain of the music educator to provide leadership in coordinating all of the components of a music-education program that fall under his or her supervision. Continuity of objectives throughout the program is the ultimate goal.

While the responsibility for that type of leadership may appear to be awesome, a music educator who accepts the role of an administrator will handle the coordination responsibility with little or no conscious effort. It is, at best, difficult to offer a pedagogical approach toward handling this function. Usually it just "happens" under the direction of a dedicated and well-organized teacher.

FUNCTION NUMBER THIRTEEN: COMMUNICATION
Concerned with design of information channels . . . supply relevant information in the form most useful to various points in the system . . . provide for the information flow (up or down, in or out of the system) essential to the other functions such as unification, motivation, decision making

America's large corporations long ago realized the value of communication as a basis for building a constituency for their products or services. They call it *public relations* and almost every company, large or small, has a specialist or a staff of specialists charged with the responsibility of communicating to the general public a particular image or philosophy.

Successful school administrators have also recognized the necessity of open communication channels to their constituencies. School boards rely heavily on the information provided by school administrators to aid them in the planning and decision-making process. Taxpayers, parents, staff, and students are all interested and affected by the information provided by administrative communication channels.

The music educator must develop the information channels that will allow the broadest possible dissemination of information in the most effective manner. This integral part of administering a music-education program will be developed in detail in Chapter Nine.

Anyone who has been involved in music education for any length of time has seen the type of person who does a superior job of communicating, of "selling" the program, though the program itself is substandard. On the other end of the spectrum is the individual who either lacks the basic communication skills necessary to promote the program or who has no interest in "selling" music education. Neither situation is acceptable as a model for administration of music education.

The music educator as an administrator must develop useful communication channels throughout the entire system, as indicated in Figure 1.1.

Communication with administrators concerning upcoming events, schedule concerns, and funding takes place on an almost daily basis. Parents can best be informed as to the activities pertinent to the program through a parents organization. Monthly newsletters, parent-teacher conferences, and

Figure 1.1. Information flow.

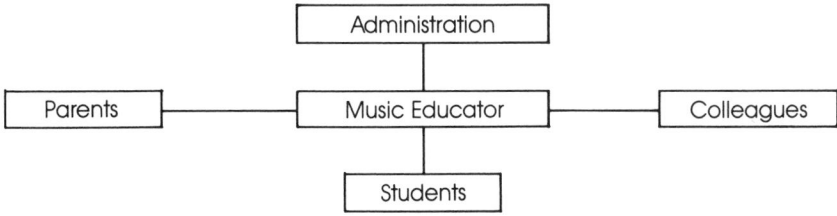

personal contact on the telephone are several useful methods. Colleagues can be kept abreast of necessary information on a day-to-day, personal basis, through regularly scheduled teachers' meetings, as well as the daily announcement bulletin. Students should receive their noninstructional information on policy and the calendar both verbally and in writing.

The music educator can communicate with students, colleagues, parents, and the public in general through both the school and community news media. The instructor who says "I can't get any publicity" or "I can't get anything in the paper" is failing to implement the most basic communication and public relations skills. Communication in the administration of a music-education program assumes incredible significance when it is realized how strongly it influences all the other functions in music-education administration.

FUNCTION NUMBER FOURTEEN: "POLITICKING"
Administrators must function with various internal and external power configurations related to the institutions

The politics related to the administering of any successful program can run the gamut from insignificant to overwhelmingly important. In music education that importance level largely depends upon the size and scope of the program and how many teachers are involved in the instructional process.

For many music educators, "politicking" is perhaps their least pleasant administrative function. The individual who finds the politics involved in music-education administration unpleasant to the point of distraction will find it difficult to adjust to any situation involving compromise.

Politicking for the music educator involves two well-defined levels, *internal* and *external*.

The internal level involves the school administration, including the school board, superintendent, and all principals. It also includes other instructional staff in the school system, the students, and even secretaries, custodians, and lunchroom or cafeteria staff. The external levels include parents and the general public, as well as other school music programs and state and national associations.

Experienced and successful music educators will tell you that they have, from time to time, used their performing groups to do a little politicking in support of the music program. An example would be sending or taking an ensemble to a local service club as part of the club's weekly program when you are soliciting funds for music-camp scholarships. Bands are occasionally asked to meet a plane of a visiting dignitary, and choirs include the superintendent and building principal on the list of homes to visit during their annual Christmas carol tour. Many bands, choirs, and orchestras across the country have had a school official, the mayor, or some other influential resident serve as guest conductor or narrator for a concert program.

This type of activity is certainly permissible and is an acceptable means of gaining support for the entire music program.

Several key points need to be made:

1. Music educators must work comfortably with all the internal and external influences on the program. They may not always be in agreement but must function *with* those various influences.
2. The ability to get along with people is an all-important ingredient of this function.
3. Politicking is *not* necessarily public relations.
4. The ability to see the other side of an issue, as well as flexibility in dealing with others, can have a positive administrative impact on the program.
5. Compromise is not a sign of weakness. It is often the exact opposite.

If a music educator can accept these five premises, the politicking function of administering a quality music-education program will be a positive influence on that administrative process.

FUNCTION NUMBER FIFTEEN: CONTROLLING
Monitoring progress toward objectives, keeping organizational activities locked onto objectives

Earlier administrative functions dealt with establishing objectives and the means and methods involved in implementing those objectives. Without subsequent progress monitoring, the music educator will have difficulty achieving his or her objectives. Far too often, worthwhile and well-thought-out goals and objectives fail because no monitoring process was used. A means of measuring progress needs to be established.

For the general music classroom teacher, written tests, achievement tests, and close observation are often tools useful in monitoring progress toward goals and objectives. At the high-school level, written tests, music achievement tests, and music contests and festival participation may be used to measure specific progress.

Personal "How am I doing?" interviews with the administrators and colleagues can be helpful. Often student input can also be of great value. Improved record keeping and pre-testing and post-testing at all levels are recognized means of monitoring progress toward objectives.

The monitoring process is not one of those daily, weekly, or even monthly functions of an administrator in music education. It can, and perhaps should be, occasional to the point of being casual, but evaluative means must always be in place.

A word of caution: do not let performance pressures override the monitoring and achievement of educationally sound goals and objectives. In the music education profession, there is ample opportunity to lose sight of established goals and objectives. The conscientious music educator/administrator is alert to this danger and makes a determined effort to see that it does not happen.

FUNCTION NUMBER SIXTEEN: APPRAISING
Administration requires the courage to assess or evaluate final results and to report the same to his constituency

In music education, appraisal is accomplished in a variety of ways. There is self-examination through a variety of audio-visual media equipment. Perhaps because it takes courage to look closely at one's self to determine if objectives are being met, critical self-evaluation is one of the least used means of appraising the final results of objectives.

The appraisal and reporting process can be accomplished through contest or festival participation. It takes a certain amount of fortitude to place performance groups in a contest setting for subjective evaluation. If a music educator chooses this method of appraisal, he or she must also be prepared to share the results of such an appraisal with a wide constituency.

Music educators can and should bring in outside consultants to assist in the appraisal progress. An educator from a nearby college or university can spend an entire day working with music students at all levels and will then be in a position to report what has already been done and what needs to be accomplished. The "needs to be accomplished" can most certainly serve as the basis for the next set of objectives.

No one meets all of his or her objectives all of the time. Failure to completely achieve objectives is not in itself a failure. Of greater significance is that the attempt was made, the means to meet the objectives was determined, and progress toward achieving the objectives was monitored in some manner. Positive growth for students, the music educator, and the entire music program results from this effort.

Finally, although it does not take courage to appraise success, this part of the appraisal process cannot be overlooked. A music educator in an administrative role should be aware of all facets of the complete program and should consistently build on success.

The Music Educator as a Leader

Leadership in the school and community

Because of the nature of working with performance groups, the music educator often finds himself or herself cast in the role of a leader in school-associated activities. This role should be readily accepted if not actually sought because many of the administrative functions previously discussed rely on the acceptance of the music educator as a leader.

Keith D. Snyder, the author of a 1965 text dealing with music supervision, carries this thought one step further:

> It must be clearly understood that the leadership process cannot be outlined in neat, sequential steps. Since it is a process, the nature and detail of that process will vary from situation to situation and from group to group. The leader must see the complete objectives of education and his special area with crystal clarity and be able to show others how these goals may be attained. He must also be able to manipulate the setting so that the goals may be attained. Creative thinking and prudent action are demanded, as well as the ability to apply general principles to specific situations.[3]

The leadership process is difficult to describe; it cannot be tied up in one neat little package. There are many intangibles, not the least of which is personality, which are important factors in developing leadership qualities and being accepted as a leader. Still, an individual who can articulate clear and concise goals and objectives and who can proceed in a logical and creative manner toward their attainment should have no difficulty in being accepted as a leader by his or her peers.

Community leadership involves participation. To increase visibility, a music educator might become involved in a variety of nonteaching organizations, such as service clubs, fraternal organizations, social groups, bowling or golf leagues, and church choirs. By serving as an officer or board member of at least one organization, the music educator can assume a leadership role. A teacher who associates only with other teachers in a community is in danger of leading a very dull and unenlightened existence.

Through these community leadership activities, the music educator can generate enthusiasm for music, not only on the part of the youth but also on the part of adults. If people know you as a human being, they are more likely to support you in your programmatic needs.

Personal qualities of a leader

There are strengths and weaknesses to be found in any recognized leader. But, although individual music educators may differ in their approach to leadership, several qualities serve as a common thread among those who are successful.

Enthusiasm. The most easily identifiable attribute contributing to the success of a music educator as a leader is the level of enthusiasm brought to the position. The enthusiasm generated must be genuine and have as its foundation a solid footing based on educational objectives and sound philosophical judgment, as well as confidence based on educational training.

Energy. It takes a tremendous amount of energy to lead and administer a music-education program. The individual with an energy level sufficient enough to allow him or her to initiate and meet objectives will be accepted as a leader. As with enthusiasm and other personal qualities, the energy level must be contagious; it must "rub off" on those students and others who work with the energetic music educator.

Integrity and trust. Students and colleagues alike must be able to trust the music educator, knowing that decisions made and policies established will be fairly and consistently administered. They must have confidence in the fact that promises made will be kept. Students in particular have a low tolerance level for broken promises.

Friendliness. While not necessarily becoming a close friend of the students, the music educator who leads well will develop a friendly approach toward his students and others around him. This friendliness must be sincere and genuine. Again, students are quick to discern any degree of friendliness that is not authentic.

Teaching ability. All other personal qualities of a leader are worthless unless accompanied by high-level teaching skills. The music educator who is a successful leader is also an outstanding teacher. One can be a good teacher and lack leadership qualities, but it is impossible to be accepted as a leader without also being a good teacher. If one can develop the level of teaching ability to the point where successful instruction results in fewer orders being issued and greater cooperation taking place, the ultimate balance between leadership and teaching has been achieved.

The five personal leadership qualities presented above usually exist in every individual administering a successful and respected music-education program. Such administrators may possess other qualities as well, to a varying degree, but enthusiasm for their work, a high energy level, an uncompromising feeling of trust, a professional level of friendliness, and superb teaching skills are the common denominators that create and maintain program excellence.

Styles of Leadership

At this point, four types of leadership styles will be discussed. It is possible that a larger, more detailed list could be presented, but the four types of leadership that follow are widely accepted as the styles most common to education.

Readers should not be misled into thinking that they can memorize the traits associated with a particular type of leadership and simply go out and be that type of leader. It is the intent of this book to guide readers toward understanding their leadership roles, and to provide them with sufficient administrative concepts to support the development of their own eclectic leadership styles.

Undoubtedly, as each of the four leadership styles is presented, examples based on past experiences will readily come to mind. Definitions of the four styles of leadership are freely paraphrased from Knezevich's book *Administration of Public Education.*[4]

Anarchic

The anarchic style of leadership grants total freedom to an individual or group of individuals to make decisions without the leader. The leader does not offer direction or participate in the process in any manner. In this type of leadership, the principal role of the leader is to provide pertinent materials, remaining apart from the process and participating only when called on. The leader lacks interest in the decision-making process and rarely offers comments on activities of the members. After a decision has been made and a course of events begins to unfold, the leader makes no attempt to interfere or become involved in any way. In actuality, anarchy is a "leaderless" social situation.

The anarchic style of leadership has no place in education administration, let alone in music education. In a situation of anarchy, the power belongs to the people, and the struggle to bring structure or order to a probable chaotic situation is all but impossible. Education without order is not acceptable in a democratic society.

Democratic

Although the leader participates in the formulation of policies in the democratic style of leadership, group action or decision making is also involved.

In this style, the group determines what the tasks are and how to organize and accomplish them. The leader also participates in the process. Objective in praising or criticizing, he or she does not allow personal feelings to impede the group's process. Allowing those who will eventually be *affected* by the decision to be involved in *making* the decision is called participatory administration. This leadership style promotes excellent group productivity. Personalities shaped by democratic participation are more mature, more capable of objectivity, and less aggressive than those products of other leadership styles.

The democratic style of leadership in music education certainly assists students in learning to make decisions. However, many music educators *think* they use the democratic style of leadership when they don't in fact give up that amount of control. Music performing groups generally have a panel of elected officers as well as several board members who serve the director in a variety of ways. What they do varies, from assuming complete involvement in the decision-making process as it affects the total performing group to acting as a communication link between the director and the group. They may serve as an advisory board to the director, or they may just be a token panel with few or no responsibilities.

Autocratic

The autocratic leader determines policy, makes all decisions, and assigns tasks to members without direction from or consultation with the group. The leader is personal in his praise or criticism of members of the group but remains aloof from the group. There are no group-inspired decisions. The leader declares what shall be done, when it shall be done, with no reason offered as to why it should be done. Group members have no choice but to accept these decisions.

Far too often this type of leadership is followed "to the letter" in public-school administration. It also has its proponents and followers in music education, particularly where performing groups with a rigorous competitive performing schedule are involved. The autocratic style of leadership in music education is not as prevalent today as it was when individuals in charge of music ensembles came from a military background. This style was further perpetuated when teachers were trained at the college level by third, fourth, and fifth generations of teachers immersed in the military tradition.

Manipulative

In the manipulative style of leadership, the leader makes his or her desires known and then appoints a committee to consider those desires. In reality, the committee is appointed only to approve the proposal, not to deliberate over it. The committee, without much thought or discussion, automatically endorses the proposal. This system works best when leaders reward those who support them and refrain from rewarding, or actually punish, those who do not support them.

This is one of the dominant styles of governing in a nondemocratic society. It still thrives in some of this country's public school systems. In music education, this style is infrequently found intact. Music educators sometimes appoint a committee to make a decision, knowing full well what the decision will be, but also knowing that group support for the decision will be stronger if the decision comes from a committee of members from that group. This practice cannot necessarily be considered a negative aspect of leadership, unless carried to excess. A good leader knows when to apply this aspect of manipulative leadership.

A variation of manipulative leadership occurs when the leader appoints a committee and lists several options. The committee is restricted to those suggested options and is asked to debate the advantages and disadvantages of each, select an option, and report the results to the leader. This semimanipulative technique is frequetly used by leaders who picture themselves as "democratic style" leaders.

Many teachers, music educators included, use the manipulative style of leadership more than they care to admit. Because students frequently make decisions they feel will please the teachers, teachers must be careful not to abuse this administrative privilege.

The young music educator must understand that the development of a leadership style comes with teaching experience. In an actual teaching situation, mistakes—with resulting adjustments—can guide the music educator toward a personal style. He or she will gradually learn to be effective and produce educationally sound results.

The chapters that follow will provide a foundation for individual styles; however, the key to success is flexibility. A leader can be likened to a catalytic agent, a unique ingredient that stimulates a desirable interaction between two or more factors. In music education a catalyst translates potential into reality.

Summary

In music education the administrative tasks can become an almost overwhelming noninstructional responsibility for the young music educator. Only through the development of basic administrative skills can the music educator become an efficient contributor to the musical growth of his or her students.

There are sixteen administrative functions that need to be considered by any music educator. They are the same functions believed necessary to administer a total education system but can be applied specifically to the music teacher as well.

It is necessary to develop both long-range goals and short-term objectives. Strategies must be developed to implement these, and a monitoring process must be put in place that will verify the level of success in achieving them. This monitoring system is perhaps the most important ingredient in attaining one's goals and objectives. It is also the most frequently overlooked aspect of that process.

The music educator needs to have the ability and fortitude to identify, analyze, and resolve existing or potential problems. Many individuals are proficient in the identification of problems, but fewer are adept at analyzing them, and fewer yet can anticipate and resolve problematic situations.

The role of "politics" in music administration should not be confused with public relations in music education. The music educator who is a good communicator will not find public relations for the music-education program a particularly difficult task.

Music educators must provide leadership in both the school and community. Students and the public alike respect and appreciate educators who are active in community affairs and who can provide leadership outside an academic setting. The personal qualities of such a leader are enthusiasm, high energy level, trustworthiness, friendliness, and a confident and able teaching style.

Suggested Activities

1. Reflect on *any* teacher you may have encountered during your public-school education and (a) list five qualities about that teacher you most admired and (b) relate those qualities to the four leadership styles.
2. Develop a set of short-term objectives for a situation in your present educational setting, and list the steps for the implementation of those objectives.
3. Identify something to change in your present educational setting and follow the procedures presented to initiate and complete that change.
4. Prepare questions and interview three music educators regarding their approaches to any two administrative functions. Each music educator interviewed should respond to different functions.
5. What five administrative functions do you see as the most difficult to achieve or implement and why?
6. Identify a potential problem in music education and list probable causes and potential solutions.
7. Summarize three articles in periodical literature relating to any administrative function.

References and Suggested Reading

House, Robert. *Administration in Music Education*. Englewood Cliffs, N.J.: Prentice-Hall, Inc., 1973.

Knezevich, Stephen J. *Administration of Public Education*. New York: Harper and Row, 1975.

Snyder, Keith D. *School Music Administration and Supervision*. Boston: Allyn and Bacon, 1965.

The Teacher
and the
Student

Motivation and Discipline in Music Education

P erhaps no other facet of teaching is of greater concern to future music educators than is their ability to control classroom situations—in short, discipline. Will their students respond in a positive manner under their leadership? Will those students perform as desired, when desired? Charles R. Hoffer cites a study that asked this question of prospective teachers, "What gives you greatest concern or worry as you plan for your first teaching position?" Nearly 2,500 out of 3,000 students responded, "Discipline."[1]

There are more words in print on the subject of discipline than any other single topic in education. Whether it is called "classroom management," "classroom control," "behavior management," or some other contemporary educational term, the subject remains the same. Classroom *discipline*, an old-fashioned term not often mentioned in certain educational circles, is a key ingredient in the effective organization and administration of any school music program.

Maintaining good classroom discipline is a critical element affecting a music educator's success or failure. Frederick J. Swanson points out that of all the college graduates entering the music-education profession each year, some will do a superb job, some will *think* they're doing a superb job, and others will unfortunately be sad failures. The last category often leave the profession after one year because their students are "unruly," "discourteous," "uninterested," and "unteachable."[2] In reality, those teachers more than likely had all the necessary musical skills but lacked expertise in another one of those important noninstructional skills, motivation and classroom discipline.

Motivation and discipline in music education are often-ignored areas of study in music methods classes. Those topics are often vaguely referred to in passing, but no presentation is made of concepts, models, and approaches that can aid a young music teacher in his or her daily instructional life. Any survey of recent graduates in music education will likely reveal how limited their backgrounds are in this respect. College and university instructors in music-education methods must accept the responsibility of more adequately preparing their students for the responsibility of classroom leadership.

An entire book could be devoted to the subjects of motivation and discipline in music education. What will be offered in this chapter will be a summary of recognized procedures for achieving a positively managed classroom, a classroom that is alive with meaningful activity and students who are alert and eager. Good discipline does not happen overnight, nor can it be haphazard or hit-and-miss in nature.

Understanding the Terminology

Motivation and *discipline* are two terms with diverse meanings, but the existence of one in a given situation is nearly impossible without the other.

It is most difficult to maintain a disciplined classroom unless the students are motivated in that direction. It is equally difficult to motivate students toward a specific goal if they are not in a disciplined environment.

Motivation is a most important concept in explaining student behavior. The term *motivation* can be defined as the total of all forces that cause a person to expend energy doing one thing rather than another. Arousing student interest, kindling group spirit, and encouraging student action are all forms of motivation.

Discipline can be described as the conduct that results from training. It involves learning to act in accordance with established rules, in a manner that is socially agreed upon as appropriate in a given situation. Good discipline is evident in situations where students exert an optimal amount of energy in trying to learn what a teacher is attempting to teach rather than wasting energy on other, nonproductive activities.

A teacher may be considered a good disciplinarian when he or she has learned to use the forces of motivation to keep students moving toward their academic goals.[3]

Motivation

There are several natural motivational factors that come into play when working with teenagers in some areas of music education. Students involved in elective music performance groups or classes are already motivated to a certain degree or they would not be there. Thus motivation of performance groups is of a different nature than the type of motivation necessary for students involved in required general music or performance classes. Peer pressure to conform, which is such a prominent part of teenage life, can be used in an advantageous manner in motivating students toward elective performance participation and subsequent achievement, but that same pressure to conform can be an obstacle in motivating students in mandatory classes.

If music educators can develop an association between music and the type of person that students admire, motivation has taken place by appealing to teenagers' need for a positive self-image. Music educators, through their own actions and through external influences, can establish role models to serve as motivating forces. External influences could include such things as pictures and stories of famous people who are exceptional musicians but who are better known for other professional accomplishments.

Teenagers have a strong need for a sense of belonging. Music groups serve this need as well or better than any other aspect of public education. Once again, however, general music classes or other mandatory music offerings do not have such as advantage and must base their classroom motivation on the intrinsic needs of the students.

Motivational factors

A partial list of factors, both external and internal, that can influence a music-education program is offered at this time. Research is somewhat sketchy in confirming the degree of motivational success achieved by some of the factors on the list, but common sense dictates that all items will provide some element of motivation for music-education students.

Fear/desire. Some music educators feel that there are only two true motivational elements in education—fear or desire. Fear as a motivating factor is extremely effective. One need only consider the many acts of fear-initiated heroism that have occurred in times of intense stress. Fear of failure strongly affects human behavior and perhaps never stronger than during the pre-teen and teenage years. Music educators who base their instructional approaches on fear can achieve dramatic and immediate results, but groups that work in a fearful atmosphere tend to perform "in spite of" rather than "as a result of" that fear. When students are motivated by desire, limits are removed and a whole new level of creativity is opened to them. Building a desire to learn holds long-lasting and far-reaching benefits for students, teachers, and entire music-education programs.[4]

Music contests. Competitive and noncompetitive contests contain the motivational elements of both fear and desire, and there is no question as to the motivational implications created by contest participation as it affects both teacher and student, a subject dealt with to a greater extent in Chapter Eight. Something does appear to be wrong, however, with a system that makes it easier to motivate students to be better than students who attend a neighboring school rather than to be the best *they* can be.

Awards. Awards or rewards for the accomplishment of a specific set of objectives is a part of American life. Some type of awards system can provide motivational benefits for school music performing groups, as well as music classes. Awards provide an opportunity for recognition of those students who achieve some degree of excellence in their work and provide some incentive for students who can be considered underachievers. Very often awards are based on some type of point system, whereby students earn and collect "points" toward an award through rehearsal and concert attendance, as well as extra effort and participation in contests, festivals, all-state events, and so on.

Testing and grading. Tests and grades both hold some potential for motivating students toward musical success, but gradually, due to a lack of definitive criteria for evaluation, such measures fall short of achieving the degree of motivation that takes place in other academic classrooms. Also, no student will be held back a year in school for "failing" band, but that situation certainly could occur if a student fails to pass a math or English class.

Performances. One of the reasons students become members of music organizations is because of the performance opportunities. Young people are natural exhibitionists, and they should be placed in group and solo performances as often as the practical limits of the music program permit. The placing of correctly spelled names of all student participants in concert programs can be considered a motivational aid. Inviting alumni to participate in a performance upon occasion can be a source of motivation for student participants, as well as a positive public-relations effort.

Student involvement. Involving students in establishing motivational goals and objectives for music groups and music classes is simply good program administration on the part of the music educator. In addition, the establishment of student committees that support a performing organization gives a music educator an opportunity to work with a variety of music students in an advisory, noninstructional capacity. Music educators are often more successful in motivating a number of small groups toward a common objective than they are at motivating a single large group toward that same objective.

Photographs/recordings. Students like to see themselves, and photographs, movies, or videotapes of performances can serve as an incentive for excellence. Recordings can serve the same purpose. If a recording is made using quality equipment, cassette tapes of a concert can be professionally reproduced rather inexpensively. A cassette recording of their own performance can provide a lasting sense of pride for student participants. That sense of pride translates into MOTIVATION for the future.

Group spirit. Students are also motivated through group spirit, which appeals to their need for a sense of belonging. Group spirit and identification can be enhanced by such things as T-shirts, identifying emblems, jackets, and similar items. Some type of uniform is necessary for performing groups for the same reason. The importance of developing spirit and identity within a group simply cannot be overlooked as a valuable motivational aid.

Compliments. Successful teachers can motivate learning through their positive and friendly attitudes, as well as through their personalities. A mark of a good teacher is that he or she knows when to offer a compliment. Such teachers realize that compliments only motivate when the person receiving the compliment is aware that it is deserved. As will be discussed later, young music educators are cautioned against using false praise in lieu of constructive appraisal of student efforts.

Tim Lautzenheiser, a noted lecturer on motivation in music education, feels that students cannot be *given* motivation, but that they can *choose* to be motivated. It is up to the teacher to set the example and create an educational environment whereby students feel good about themselves. When students feel good about themselves, they perform accordingly.[5]

Teachers need to look constantly at themselves and determine what motivates them toward program excellence. If it is anything less than providing an understanding of music as well as creating an excitement of learning about music, perhaps they need to rethink that aspect of their work. Self-evaluation can be a threatening experience for insecure individuals, but it is a necessary ingredient in employing musical, along with social and phychological, motives for the music-education program.

Discipline and Behavior Modification

The behavorist approach to classroom discipline is derived from the work of B. F. Skinner, whose material was first published in the 1930s and involves training children rather than educating them. Skinner's theory is based on the assumption that people relate to pleasant situations and reject unpleasant situations and that they are likely to repeat a behavior pattern if the consequence of that behavior is pleasant, and vice-versa. Such action can be influenced by what is known as operant conditioning and the use of positive or negative reinforcement in conjunction with specific behavior sequences. Music educators use operant conditioning much more than they might think. For example, if a musical group automatically becomes quiet when the director steps on the podium, they have, at some point, been conditioned to do so.

When a teacher uses the "counting" method in controlling a classroom situation, the response to counting "one," "two," or "three" is a result of operant conditioning. Students are aware of some type of consequence or group punishment if the teacher reaches count three, and therefore teachers using this method rarely get past count one. The counting system, with accompanying variations, is a popular approach to classroom discipline based on the behavior-modification method.

Assertive discipline techniques can also be considered related to behavior modification in that they spell out very clearly for the students what type of behavior is expected and consequences, both positive and negative, that are associated with that behavior. Such an approach to classroom discipline is clearly defined in writing, with copies provided to both students and parents.

Behavior modification has had a profound influence on classroom discipline techniques in all areas of education.

Preventive Discipline

Avoidance of discipline problems is the key to preventive discipline and is most successful when the students themselves are involved in establishing goals and objectives of classroom behavior. Many educators feel that such involvement on the part of students in constructing their own classroom atmosphere goes a long way toward creating a positive learning situation. Students are less likely to break the policies or rules that they have established than they are to violate procedures established for them by an "outside" source—namely the teacher. Further discussion on preventive discipline techniques appears later in this chapter.

Three Common Approaches to Discipline

It may be noted that the following discipline approaches parallel somewhat the descriptions of leadership styles offered in the first chapter.

Authoritarian. An authoritarian teacher compiles strict classroom rules and regulations that are enforced by severe punishment. An authoritarian offers no explanation of the reasons behind the strict restraints. Such an approach produces conformity but leads to resentment, which in turn creates an unhealthy learning situation.

Permissive. A permissive teacher makes little attempt to set limits on children's behavior. An air of egocentricity and self-assertiveness prevails on the part of the teacher. Because students do not know what to do and behavior limits are not established, they often start to feel insecure. Chaos is the rule rather than the exception.

Democratic. The democratic approach to discipline is generally considered the best approach for teachers. In such an approach, children receive explanations of how they should act. Good behavior is rewarded with praise and inappropriate behavior is punished. The democratic approach creates a positive learning atmosphere based more on "do's" than "don't's."

Components of Good Discipline

Goals and objectives

Working at creating or improving classroom behavior involves some of the same ingredients and care that takes place in teaching subject matter, the most important of which is the establishment of goals and objectives. If behavioral goals and objectives are decided upon with the cooperation of the involved class, progress is likely to be measured and evaluated through group effort as well. Students must realize that the reason they need to behave is quite simply so that they can learn. After good classroom control is established, teaching can become a pleasant vocation. Once young people feel comfortable and relaxed in a classroom setting, communication can take place. Interaction between teacher and students and among students themselves begins to occur, and an extremely rewarding experience for all participants is the end result.

Developing social skills

The manner in which people treat one another is another important ingredient in creating a positive classroom climate. Unless students learn social skills along with learning the subject matter, very little of the latter will take place. Students don't necessarily need to personally like every other student in a class or ensemble, but they do need to develop a respect for one another as individuals and to work toward classroom relationships built on respect. Most young people yearn for recognition from their peers, but their peers are a very critical group, at times almost to the point of being cruel. It is the task of music teachers at all instructional levels to ask their students to perform activities they can do well so that they're able to achieve some type of group recognition. Music class offers an opportunity not normally found in other classes to improve social skills because of the close rapport that is generally present between the students and the teacher and because the subject matter appeals to the *feelings* of those students. The establishment of some form of social goals and objectives in music class is most certainly appropriate.

Physical size

A teacher's physical size has little to do with his or her success in motivating students toward a disciplined classroom atmosphere. Everyone can recall at least one educator with whom they had contact in the public schools who was a petite woman who really "ran a tight ship" in all of her classes. Even the largest young man in class could be put in his proper place by a firm comment or warning glance. At the same time, that teacher created an atmosphere of congeniality in her classroom; students felt comfortable in class and looked forward to attending. How did this teacher achieve that level of control and respect? The next section in this chapter should provide some clues.

One can also recall the big, husky, male teacher whose classrooms were in a state of constant chaos; very little learning, if any, took place. How can students who were normally well-behaved in the classes taught by the teacher in the first example suddenly become disrespectful and boisterous to the point of distraction in the classes taught by the teacher in the second example? The answer more than likely lies not in the physical size of the two teachers but in that the first teacher created a firm but caring classroom atmosphere, where behavior parameters were clearly defined and understood and where daily lessons were presented in a logical, well-prepared, creative, and exciting manner.

Primary Areas of Concern in Music-Education Discipline

There are numerous problems that can surface during a school year, but the ones that a prospective music educator must deal with from the very first day he or she walks into the classroom are extraneous talking, attendance, and students who for one reason or another are unable to participate in performance-group rehearsals on a short-term basis. Minor behavior problems, such as rehearsal posture and chewing gum, will also demand attention as well.

Talking

Young teachers must realize early on that they are wasting their time and effort teaching or giving instructions over conversations or other extraneous talking in the classroom. Complete silence in a classroom at all times is an unreasonable expectation, but students must understand that they will not talk when the teacher is teaching or providing rehearsal instructions. In a rehearsal situation, a group director is most likely to encounter talking when he or she stops the group to correct an error or offer performance advice, and when that same director is working with one section of the ensemble while the remainder of the group sits idle. If this type of behavior problem is anticipated and discussed with the students the very first day of class and they understand why a certain type of behavior is required, they are much more likely to eventually conform than if the subject is never discussed or when infractions are handled on a reactionary basis.

This writer recently had in interesting experience associated with extraneous talking during rehearsals. Within a half-day time span, an opportunity presented itself to observe two sixth-grade band rehearsals in two separate middle schools, with two different directors. This situation was made even more unique by the fact that the two directors were father and son. The young music educator was in his first year of teaching, and the father, of course, had over twenty years of teaching experience. Both instructors were highly enthusiastic in their presentations and both possessed positive motivational skills, evidenced by the fact that enrollment in each band program was extemely high when compared with total sixth-grade enrollment. It was interesting to note that the young instructor continually gave rehearsal instruction and discussed scheduling and other matters with the band without the students ever becoming completely quiet. This practice caused unnecessary repetition of instruction, which cost valuable rehearsal time. By contrast, the father was just concluding an extended rehearsal period and the students were tired and somewhat fidgety; however, when instruction were given, the students remained quiet and attentive. At the close of the rehearsal, the experienced director said, "I have something I need to tell you before you leave." There was some talking and moving about, but the teacher waited for several seconds, saying nothing. The minor noise level quickly dropped to complete silence, and the teacher then made the final announcements to a tired but attentive sixth-grade band. The difference between the two rehearsal atmospheres was dramatic. The young music educator will undoubtedly be an outstanding teacher in the near future and will come to realize that it is just as easy and more efficient to function in an environment where his students are quiet and attentive when he is talking than it is to continue working in the present atmosphere. Unfortunately, this transition could take a period of years. The points to be emphasized here are that music instruction—whether it be in the general music classroom or in a rehearsal room—need not take place over student conversation and that a patient music educator who refuses to teach like that will be successful in achieving such a goal.

Students who can't participate

Sore throats, cold sores, bad colds, and dental problems are just some of the reasons music students will legitimately offer and request that they be excused from one or several rehearsal periods. In dealing with such problems, music educators need to instill in the students the need for making the request prior to the beginning of rehearsal and that they are to sit in their regular chairs during the rehearsal and follow the activities taking place in the rehearsal. Students with excuses for not participating in a particular rehearsal should not be allowed to study (they can't practice flute in English class), or perform library or other work in the music room, and they most certainly should not be excused from the room. Students who are allowed to study during a rehearsal or who are permitted to leave the music room because of minor ailments can develop a habit of afflictions in and around test time in other academic classes. Again, a teacher's expectations regarding such occurrences must be made early in the year, and failures to meet those expectations must be dealt with in a consistent manner as situations arise.

Rehearsal and performance attendance

Rehearsal and class attendance is normally not a problem for music groups and is governed largely by the administrative policies of the school. Attendance at any extra rehearsals, and more specifically performances, is another matter. If students are notified far in advance of the event, there is absolutely no reason for an *unexcused* absence from a performance. Students who miss a performance without permission are sending a signal to the music educator concerning their feelings toward the group, and with very few exceptions they should be told to resign from the organization. To allow students with an unexcused absence from a performance to remain part of the group creates morale problems within the organization and reduces the importance of a quality music performance in the minds of all participants. It is of extreme importance that any policy with severe punishment, such as lowering grades, suspension, or dismissal, be developed with administrative approval and distributed to parents and students early in the school year. A complete calendar of all dates throughout the year should be compiled and attached to the attendance policy. Such a calendar should include all home performances, concerts, and shows, as well as contests and festivals and all-state auditions and performances. If both the students and the parents of members of performing groups are aware of and understand the attendance policy, the responsibility for students' behavior rests directly on the students themselves. Students then become more responsible for their own actions, and that's exactly the way it should be.

Another successful scheduling device for some experienced teachers is an actual calendar placed in each music folio with all performance obligations marked in suitable squares for each date. As changes or additional obligations arise, each student makes the appropriate adjustment in his or her own personal "calendar." This organizational device does not take much effort on the part of the music educator to construct and does provide a degree of involvement in the scheduling process for student participants.

Chewing gum

Some schools have a general policy against chewing gum in school. Those schools without such a policy place the music educator in a position of policing action that has no place in the music-education classroom—namely gum chewing. Music educators should simply not allow students to chew gum in any rehearsal setting, or for that matter in general music classes where some degree of singing takes place, as well as the handling of special equipment and instructional aids. A waste basket placed conveniently by the door should serve as a repository for all music students who enter the room with gum in their mouths. Once the policy prohibitng gum chewing in the music-education class is established, the teacher should not provide violators with attention by passing a waste basket around class and asking students to place their gum in it. The receptacle by the door should be sufficient. Students with repeated infractions can be scheduled for an after-school conference. This seemingly insignificnat part of classroom discipline in music is actually an important step in establishing teacher credibility. By being clear about this rule, the teacher demonstrates his or her seriousness about creating a classroom atmosphere conducive to quality education.

Posture

Student posture, whether in the general music classroom or in rehearsal rooms, is another requisite for good behavior and necessary to create an optimal physical situation for music performance. It's a known fact that students who maintain good posture in class are more alert and attentive and behave better than those students whose posture is poor. Music educators can simply not let their students slouch in their chairs or sit cross-legged during classes and rehearsals. As with the previous four areas, if students are prepared in advance for the requirement, they are more likely to respond positively. Anything less than complete compliance results in "game playing" between teacher and students; the teacher often gets placed in a "no win" situation by relaxing the policy, which signals the beginning of a potential breakdown of control in that class.

The previous five areas are offered as a total package of concerns to be anticipated, discussed, and dealt with by young music educators. What follows is additional support material, practices, and approaches that address the five areas of concern just mentioned, as well as adjunct areas.

Practical Suggestions for Discipline in the Music-Education Classroom

It is easy to understand why so many young music educators begin their teaching careers apprehensive about their ability to control a classroom environment. For the four or five years of their undergraduate work, they have lived in a very controlled and generally comfortable atmosphere, where the majority of major decisions in their lives are made for them by their college or university and their academic advisers. In three short months following graduation, the "students" must suddenly become "teachers of students." The transition from the "motivated" to the "motivator" is a difficult period in the life of many music teachers. The next several pages will deal with practical suggestions that can facilitate that transition.

Appearance

The visual impression a young music educator makes on his or her students will influence the behavior of those students before a note of music is taught or before those students can become aware of the depth of musical knowledge of their new teacher. The young teacher must *look, act,* and *talk* like the professional person he or she has elected to become. This transformation must take place rapidly, and it should begin with the student-teaching experience.

The casual look of the college and university student must be replaced with the professional look of a music educator who is proud to be a member of the teaching profession. This will involve, in many cases, an adjustment in one's wardrobe. It is interesting to note that the teacher most highly respected by students and peers alike in any school system is usually the person who daily presents a neat a well-groomed appearance.

It can be argued by some undergraduate students that how individuals feel about and treat others, their level of professional knowledge, and their genuine concern for the educational welfare of their future students transcends personal appearance. While that may be true, certain standards for personal appearance have been established in the minds of students and their parents through the years, and an overly casual approach to grooming and overall appearance sends the wrong initial message to students and colleagues alike. That message can inhibit a young educator's efforts to establish a professional relationship with students, which is necessary to the environment for learning to take place. Music educators are strongly encouraged to take advantage of the opportunity to present a positive and professional appearance to their students through their personal grooming and manner of dress. Students do notice and appreciate this concern.

Public-school students are quick to pick up on how their music teacher acts. They can respect a teacher who is *friendly* but not determined to be their *friend.* Many young music educators have failed because they attempted to establish the type of friendship with their public-school students that they themselves enjoyed with one of their favorite college instructors. Such an attempt is doomed to fail. Students have to feel the teacher is on their side, that he or she *really* wants them to succeed in their musical efforts. They can then honestly respond to leadership they respect. There is an air of dignity about all successful music educators. Such an air promotes positive responses from students and helps maintain a friendly classroom. The earlier in their careers that young music educators can develop dignified approaches to their work, the happier and more successful they are likely to be.

The strength and loudness of a music teacher's voice is important and can generally be developed with practice over a period of time. Of even greater importance, however, is *what* that teacher says and *how* he or she says it. An immediate problem for many new teachers is to replace the slang, the half-sentences and catchy phrases that might have been part of daily conversations with their peers, with clear and concise instructions delivered in professional terms to their public-school students. This can be another difficult but extremely important adjustment for prospective music educators to make. Young teachers simply cannot allow what is generally termed unacceptable language or slang phrases to become a part of the manner in which they provide instructions to their students.

Preparation

There is nothing that can build an individual's confidence as he or she approaches a particular project more than being well-prepared for the task. Teachers who prepare diligently for every class are able to anticipate and prevent potential behavior problems, prepare answers in advance for difficult questions, and, in general, provide a setting in which optimal learning can take place. Absolutely nothing breeds confidence like preparation.

Teachers who are well-prepared for their classes or rehearsals are able to "keep things moving" and to pace activities at a level that limits opportunities for misbehavior. Rehearsal or classroom pace is perhaps one of the most consistent weaknesses of young music educators. Beginning teachers need to plan every detail of a class period, including anticipating questions, and they should write in advance the definitions or explanations of terms they plan to offer during a class period.

In general music classrooms, the pace of moving from one activity to another needs to be planned and well thought out by a beginning teacher. Experienced teachers move smoothly and effortlessly from one activity to another during a class period. The ability to pace classroom or rehearsal activities takes years of experience. The novice teacher must think through the process, plan carefully, and write those plans down.

Students are uncanny in their perceptions of unprepared teachers or teachers who lack confidence in their abilities. The old saying "Those who hesitate are lost" is never more true than when discussing the need for preparation for music-education classes and rehearsals. Public-school students can be very unforgiving if they sense their time is being wasted. Readers are invited to reflect on their own high-school and college educations and recall how frustrated and perhaps cheated they felt when a teacher was not prepared and was literally wasting their time.

Veteran teachers with years of experience can, upon occasion, teach classes or rehearse performing groups with little or no advance preparation. Those teachers generally have a broad background which they can draw from that provides students with a quality educational experience. Young teachers do not possess such backgrounds and need to carefully think through all their classsroom procedures. All educators learn sooner or later that "teaching off the top of your head" is an invitation to disaster. Exacting preparation can go a long way toward creating the image of authority and confidence so necessary for successful teaching efforts.

Confidence

There are three primary ingredients in establishing confidence in a music educator's approach to instruction—knowledge, preparation, and experience. Young teachers lack experience so they must necessarily rely on knowledge and preparation. Confidence must not be confused with arrogance. There are, unfortunately, a few young music teachers who approach their first teaching positions with somewhat of an arrogant attitude. Students simply will not accept such an approach on the part of any teacher, let alone a young and inexperienced music educator. If those same teachers are unable to replace arrogance with confidence based on their training and daily preparation, they are likely to soon leave the profession, citing unruly and disinterested students as the cause for their departure.

Eye contact

An individual's inability to maintain eye contact with the people he or she is addressing can be considered a sign of insecurity. Eye contact with students in music classes is a key to preventive discipline and is also a prime ingredient in projecting an image of confidence to one's students. Even the best students are likely to misbehave or be unresponsive if the teacher continually fails to look at them. Young instrumental instructors often look at the method book during the rehearsal of even the simplest music. Choral and general music instructors often use the piano as a sanctuary shielding them from their students. Both of the above instances are perfect settings for classroom inattention and disruption

Many young teachers who begin their careers feeling insecure still fail to maintain any degree of eye contact with their students after they have become more confident in their abilities, simply because it has become a habit. Maintaining good eye contact with music students cannot be overemphasized. If it is not a natural part of the way in which individuals present themselves, they must develop that skill to be successful in motivating students and in maintaining a disciplined classroom environment for music instruction. This development can begin at the undergraduate level and can be practised in everyday situations, starting with the reader's next conversation.

An additional benefit of having good eye contact with one's students is that it allows the instructor to learn the names of students more expediently. Students appreciate the fact that a teacher cares enough about them to quickly learn their names. Name tags may also be used for young students, and a preceding year's school annual can be another source of assistance in learning students' names. A music teacher generally has many more students under his or her direction than other classroom teachers, therefore some type of organized effort must be made to memorize names. Maintaining good eye contact and knowing students' names are just two more of the ingredients that contribute to the air of dignity and confidence necessary for successful music instruction.

Sense of humor

The finest music educators are blessed with a good sense of humor. Maintaining a disciplined classroom atmosphere does most certainly not mean that the environment should be humorless. A good sense of humor also does not mean joking or telling jokes all the time, either. It does mean, however, that a good teacher can make work and learning fun for students. A sense of humor prevents walls from developing between teachers and students and places the instructor in a more humanistic light in the eyes of his or her students. A good sense of humor is a necessary ingredient in successsful teaching, and competent and confident music instructors feel comfortable with allowing a little humor now and then into their classroom or rehearsal situations.

Admit mistakes

What prevents knowledgeable adults from admitting an occasional mistake in front of a class of elementary, junior-high, or high-school students? The only logical answer, if somewhat unpleasant, is that such teachers are insecure in their abilities and feel that acknowledgement of their errors is a sign of weakness. Individuals with inflated egos are the ones who often have difficulty admitting mistakes. The fact of the matter is that almost all students are completely aware of when an instructor makes a mistake, and quite frankly so is the instructor. Ignoring the mistake is bad enough, but attempting to cover the error or explain it away results in a slight feeling of resentment on the part of the students. Confident music educators are quick to admit their mistakes and often use the occasion to exhibit an element of humor such as, "I'm sorry. I made a mistake four or five years ago, too. I hope it isn't getting to be habit forming." Students are more likely to appreciate such a humanistic acknowledgement of an error.

An egotist cannot, or at the very least has difficulty, admitting mistakes. There is no place for such an individual in a music-education classroom. Students simply will not respect, respond to, or work for a person who allows his or her ego to be the dominating classroom influence. Everyone makes mistakes. Students definitely admire teachers who acknowledge errors and have little time for those who don't.

Motivation and praise

It is a fact of human nature that individuals respond in a positive manner to praise. Praise makes students feel good, and when they feel good they work harder, perform better, and learn more. Music educators are encouraged to be generous in praising their students when praise is warranted. Students themselves are completely aware when compliments are deserved. Praise where praise is not earned, or "false praise," is worse than no praise at all and is generally not appreciated by the recipients. Too many music educators spend time telling their performing groups how wonderful they sound or what a find job they've done when the participating students know that is not the case. How much more appropriate it would be if the progress made was praised and work yet to be done was also noted. For example, following a contest or festival performance when a choir receives a Division II rating, some teachers might tell their students they did a really fine job, but the adjudicator failed to appreciate their efforts fully. How much better is would be for all involved if that same teacher provided a valid evaluation of the performance, complimenting work done well and also noting the elements of the performance that still need more effort as indicated on the adjudication form.

Heavy praise for less-than-outstanding accomplishments is simply not a good instructional and motivational policy. It is, however, extremely important to be positive about what students *have* achieved. Some educators encourage music teachers to spend more time "catching" students doing something right and praising them for it, as opposed to constantly looking for mistakes and offering criticism. Results are bound to be better when one builds a project or program from the positive side rather than the negative.

Discipline and the reprimand

When reprimanding students for some unacceptable behavior or action, extreme care must be exercised not to resort to sarcasm or to personalize the reprimand. To avoid personalizing a student reprimand, teachers must remember to criticize the action, not the person. Realistically, it is often difficult to personally like a student who is a source of class disruption, but it is not an acceptable practice to personally attack a student in order to gain a better response from that student. When reprimanding a student, comments must be direct and clear. The student must understand exactly what he or she did wrong, why such behavior is unacceptable and how that behavior negatively affects the class or group. Only the briefest criticism or reprimand should take place in front of the students' peers. Extensive and harsh reprimands should generally take place in private between the music educator and the offending student. The teacher has absolutely nothing to gain and much to lose by becoming involved in a lengthy reprimand of a student in front of that student's peers. If nothing else, such action can provoke a response from the wrongdoer, thus setting the stage for a confrontation. There are no winners in public confrontations. Avoid making threats when reprimanding a student or group of students. There is always the distinct possibility a student will accept the threat as a challenge and force the teacher into the uncomfortable position of following through on a threat, which was likely made in a time of controversy and confusion with little or no advance thought.

Finally, music educators should never be reluctant to reprimand a student because they fear that that student or other class member may not "like" them as a result. Just the opposite is quite often true. Offending students actually expect to be reprimanded and/or punished. Teachers who fail to respond quickly and efficiently in situations calling for some type of action because they consciously or subconsciously fear a loss of personal popularity are not living up to a basic educational responsibility that they have to their students.

Consistency

Students quickly come to realize whether or not a particular teacher is consistent in his or her praise and punishment of students. Both pre-teen and teenage students need to know "where they stand" with a teacher. Inconsistency is administering praise and disciplinary action can only create insecurity on the part of the students. With few exceptions, *every* time a student gets out of line he or she should be reprimanded, and *every* student should receive the same punishment. It must also be kept in mind that good behavior should be rewarded, and rewarded in proportion to the importance of the behavior to the individual or the group. A good grade on a music test received by a normally good student might receive a nod of approval or a pat on the back, while a struggling student with a good grade on the same test might deserve and receive a bit more lavish praise from the teacher. Students have a deep sense of awareness of and appreciation for music educators who are fair and consistent in their dealings with all students who are involved in the music-education program. They tend to see teacher consistency as a strength that they admire and on which they can rely.

One-on-one conference with students

When a student commits some infraction or otherwise misbehaves in some way during a class or rehearsal that can't be handled by a look of disapproval or a quick reprimand, music educators are advised to handle the matter in a teacher-student conference away from class time. As previously indicated, harsh reprimands should be handled in private. To chastise severely a student in front of his or her peers often satisfies the offender's need for recognition that caused the offense in the first place. Misbehaving students often subconsciously feel that negative recognition is better than no recognition at all. Perhaps the most difficult task confronting any music educator is the nonreinforcement of an offensive act, or, in other words, ignoring a student at the proper time.

If unacceptable behavior has been ignored by the teacher during the class period, the offender(s) can be kept briefly following class and asked to remain after school. At the after-school conference, the teacher must be friendly but firm and, as mentioned earlier, must distinguish between the person and the act. Displays of anger, ridicule, and sarcasm are generally ineffective, and unfortunately, are occasionally a part of the misbehaving student's home life. Let the student talk out his or her side of the problem. Don't force students into a defensive situation but rather attempt to arrive at a solution through mutual understanding. Such an approach may sound somewhat idealistic, but all the readers need do is reflect back as a teenager to an instance of parental or teacher beratement and recall the frustration caused by the stern "lecture" approach. Experienced music educators have found that pupils can, and will, propose satisfactory solutions to difficult situations if given the opportunity. A receptive attitude on the part of the teacher is often disarming to belligerent or misbehaving students.

It is not at all uncommon for students who have been approached in this way to talk their way through difficult situations, arrive at appropriate solutions to their problems, and subsequently become leaders in and contributing members of a particular class.

An aid in solving all but the most serious behavior problems, the personal teacher-student conference is an extremely valuable motivation and discipline technique, and it is readily available to young music educators. Inexperienced teachers are encouraged to explore it, and they will be pleasantly surprised by the results.

Classroom environment

There are two aspects to classroom environment—the mental and the physical. The mental side of classroom environment has been discussed previously, but the physical environment of school classrooms is a great contributor to successful motivation and discipline of school music students.

Students respond positively to established routines. As they enter the classroom, routine regarding chairs and other equipment needs to be established. If the class takes place in a regular music room, chairs, music stands, and other equipment should be in place prior to or as the students enter the room. If an instrumental music teacher travels from one school to another, perhaps using the school lunchroom for a rehearsal room, students can be responsible for the daily set up and replacement of chairs and stands in that room. Whether the class be general music or performance oriented, an established daily routine is important and provides an element of security for participating students.

Music classes, if at all possible, should be conducted in a neat, well-organized, and pleasant environment. A messy, disorganized, drab classroom has the potential to indicate to students a low expected achievement level. A general music classroom where equipment and music is scattered in boxes around the room provides a natural setting for conducting chaotic classes and rehearsals.

Please understand that class and rehearsal rooms need not approach an "antiseptic" state in neatness and organization, but a comfortable and pleasant room in which equipment and other physical needs of the students have been anticipated by the music teacher tends to improve student motivation and decrease discipline problems. Students actually look forward to coming to such a room.

Commercial storage racks and cabinets, built-in cabinets, display cases, bulletin boards, good audiovisual equipment, and adequate lighting and ventilation all contribute to a positive classroom environment where exciting and lasting music instruction can take place.

Out-of-Control Classrooms

Should young music educators find themselves faced with a classroom or rehearsal situation that, over a period of time, has gotten out of control, one natural tendency is to attempt to restore *complete* order. Another is basically to give up or "hang in there" until the next semester or next year and start all over again, this time with a specific set of stiff rules and regulations.

A better approach might be to schedule individual meetings with the apparent leaders in the class and involve them in establishing policies governing only *one* of several aspects of misbehavior. Say, for example, you have determined to work on unnecessary and unsolicited talking. One rule has now been established—"no talking without raising your hand." For several days this rule is strictly enforced. It is probable that not much teaching will take place, but it is likely that very little worthwhile instruction was occurring in the previous chaotic state anyway. Punishment of violators must be uniform and consistent. Other discipline problems or annoyances must not distract from the primary goal of curbing extraneous talking. *One thing at a time!*

What should the punishment be for talking without raising one's hand? That most certainly will vary from teacher to teacher, but an example might be: One violation—a reminder; second violation—fifteen minutes after school; subsequent violations—additional fifteen minutes after school and so on. This is only an example of what some teachers might do, but in the final analysis, whatever will work best for a particular teacher is the criterion for such punishment.

Young music educators who try this approach to establishing or reestablishing classroom control are likely to find that all other aspects of negative behavior become better as "talking without raising your hand" improves.

It is perhaps a good idea to establish some type of reward for the entire class for the first day that no reprimand has to be made for extraneous talking. When this is the case, students are also likely to assist in achieving the final goal. A reward in this instance could range anywhere from "treats" brought to class by the teacher to a "record day" where students can bring a recording of their choice to play for the rest of the class. (A word of caution about playing recordings brought to class by students: it is wise to screen the lyrics or establish guidelines for the "record day" to avoid any embarrassing situations.)

Rehearsal Discipline

Many thousands of words are in print in articles, books, and studies that deal with rehearsal techniques for performing groups. Unfortunately, the most efficient conducting and rehearsal techniques are of little or no value when put into practice in an undisciplined rehearsal atmosphere. A good deal of the material on classroom discipline already presented in this chapter can apply directly to performance group rehearsals. Performance group rehearsals, however, require additional consideration due to the large number of students normally involved in large ensembles. Also, most rehearsal experiences are objective as opposed to subjective, and each student has a potential source of "noise" in his or her hands during the rehearsal of instrumental ensembles. Rehearsal techniques and discipline are extremely individual matters for music educators. Two different directors using the same approach to rehearsal problems may get opposite results. With that thought in mind, several suggestions common to all music rehearsals are offered.

Rehearsal pace. Teachers need to become accustomed to conducting fast-paced rehearsals. Rehearsal pace is one of the greatest areas of deficiencies present in the work of young music educators. When a director stops a rehearsal, clear and concise, straight-to-the-point instructions for improvement must be provided, and little should be said that is unnecessary. Name the section, the error, and the prescription for improvement. Long dialogues during rehearsal stops are of little value and are appreciated even less by the performers. Talking on the part of students during rehearsal stops in unacceptable behavior; however, if the music educator is asking the students to be quiet, he or she is well advised to have something important to say.

Preparation. The earlier section on preparation as a preventive measure affecting classroom discipline has perhaps its greatest application in the rehearsal room. All ensemble directors, at all levels of performance, need to prepare carefully for rehearsals. This adage is never more true than in the case of young teachers holding their first positions. Every last detail needs to be predicted, planned, and prepared. Questions need to be anticipated and instructions to the group need to be outlined. Until nervousness and uneasiness in front of a group subsides, nothing can be left to chance.

All music educators owe it to their students and themselves to be well-prepared, if not overly prepared, prior to stepping before their performance groups. Students can quickly detect an unprepared director and respond accordingly. Music directors expect their students to practice and learn their parts. They cannot expect anything less from themselves.

Rehearsal room. If at all humanly possible, chairs should be in place and music stands, when applicable, should be in place prior to rehearsal. All equipment necessary to the rehearsal should be readily available as well. Music should be in folders, stored in cabinets with easy access near the traffic pattern to and from the room. Prior to the students entering the room, the rehearsal schedule for the day and necessary announcements should be on the chalkboard. A confused and disorderly rehearsal room atmosphere has a tremendous negative subconscious impact on young ensemble members. Students want and appreciate order in their lives.

Rehearsal rules. Rules and regulations associated with music rehearsals should be few, simple, and direct. Posture, gum chewing, talking when the director is on the podium, attendance at rehearsals and performances, grading policy, and practice expectations are several points that need to be considered. These considerations, along with others the director deems important, are best put in writing, copied, and presented to the students. Special rules governing trips and other out-of-school activities should more than likely be discussed with the school principal and included in the general rehearsal policies.

Eye contact in rehearsals. Many experienced and inexperienced musicians simply ignore the conductor. The only way this can happen is if the conductor allows it! Why should the performers watch the director if he or she never looks at them during a rehearsal or performance. Young music educators need to move their eyes away from the security of the score and *look* at their young musicians. There isn't a reader of this book who can't recall at least one instance of a band director with his head buried in the score of the "Star Spangled Banner." How ridiculous! To earn and maintain control of a performing group, the director must sustain some degree of eye contact with ensemble members. Those music educators who make it a practice to occasionally look at the members of their ensembles are likely to find some of them looking back!

Serious Discipline Problems

It would be naive to think that all discipline problems that can ever occur in a music classroom can be handled and/or solved by following the procedures presented on the preceding pages. Every day in the United States classroom teachers are threatened, assaulted, and verbally abused in some way. The likelihood that such occurrences could take place in a music classroom is not very great because for the most part students participating in those classes are there because they elect to be there. Schools that have a high incidence of violence generally have their own policies governing teacher response in threatening situations.

A music educator should never attempt to take a weapon away from a student, nor should he or she physically attempt to break up a fight in or out of the classroom. In both cases ask in a loud and authoritative voice that the weapon be dropped or the students stop fighting. A responsible student should be sent as quickly as possible to the office for assistance from school officials. It is not in the classroom teacher's domain, be they male or female, to get involved any more than verbally in such situations. The risks are too great and the benefits too small.

Sending students to the office

Some music educators go through a whole career without sending a student to the principal's office for disciplinary purposes. Other teachers initiate an almost never-ending parade from the classroom to the office. There is no doubt that school administrators admire and appreciate the teacher who can handle his or her own discipline problems, but they are also most willing to provide assistance to any teacher who experiences disruptive or otherwise unacceptable behavior by one or more students. School principals are also usually ready to help the teacher who has severe discipline problems find a different approach to classroom management.

In general, music educators should not be reluctant to send misbehaving students to the office, but they should do whatever they can to prevent it from becoming a regular practice. If the procedures presented in this chapter are observed, music educators are likely to be able to handle personally all but the most extreme disciplinary cases.

Professional in-school assistance

A student who is a serious discipline problem in a music class is very likely a problem in other classes as well. Music educators experiencing difficulty with a particular student should consult other classroom and homeroom teachers to determine if there is a behavior pattern and if a combined approach toward a solution to the student's problem might be in order. Another source of great comfort and reassurance for all classroom teachers can be the professional staff members who serve in support of their instructional efforts. School counselors, school health staff, principals, and assistant principals are all available to provide assistance to the music educator should a particular difficult or serious disciplinary situation arise. These individuals have the necessary training and are in position in the administrative structure of the school that allows them to deal effectively with serious problems. Music educators are cautioned against becoming deeply involved in counseling or advising troubled students. The school district employs other trained professionals for that purpose, and nobody will ever think less of a teacher if he or she calls on a professional colleague for assistance in difficult situations.

Detention

Most schools have some means of retaining misbehaving students after school hours for both relatively minor, as well as more serious, offenses. Most schools refer to that time as "detention," and quite often teachers can handle students they've placed in detention in their own music room, or they can be sent to a central classroom for detention. Music educators should be cautious about requiring students to do special tasks while in detention. For example, asking a misbehaving student to write a report on Bach as punishment is destructive to the goals of the English teachers, who are attempting to interest students in the joy and benefits of writing, not to mention your own ultimate goal—to excite students about music. Perhaps the greatest punishment for students in detention is to allow them to do *nothing* during that time—no studying, no writing, no talking. With nothing to occupy their time, wayward students at least have the opportunity to reflect and think about the appropriateness of the actions that brought them to detention in the first place.

As mentioned in the early part of this chapter, an entire book could be written on the subject of motivation and discipline in music education. The preceding pages include many suggestions for young music educators based on the writings and actual experiences of countless successful music educators. No two music educators are likely to respond to a given disciplinary situation in the same fashion. What has been included in this chapter are some general patterns that can be observed in dealing with minor to serious discipline problems, both preventive and reactionary.

Readers are encouraged to investigate a simulation training program in student behavior and management for use by upper-level undergraduate music-education students. This program contains a series of twelve video-taped, simulated student behavior problems, supplementary materials for use by undergraduate students, and an explanatory manual that contains additional material for the instructor. An outline is also provided to guide future teachers through the identification of specific types of problems involved in each incident and assist them in developing strategies for addressing the types of behavior problems portrayed on the videotape. It is this author's personal opinion that the Windthyme training program could be a valuable part of music-education methods classes at colleges and universities throughout the United States.[6]

Summary

The intent of this chapter has been to share with prospective music educators theories and concepts associated with motivation and discipline as they affect music-education programs in today's schools. The suggestions offered can certainly not be considered ultimate answers to any motivational problem or discipline situation. However, when applied under actual teaching conditions, the material in this chapter can greatly assist inexperienced music educators to develop in a relatively short period of time the basic expertise that can enable them to be effective forces in the musical lives of the young people with whom they come in contact.

No attempt has been made to dictate to the reader *the* discipline approach to use in specific situations involving misconduct on the part of music students. Too many variables are involved in all cases of misbehavior to enable a single mandate to be offered as the best solution. Readers are encouraged, however, to make use of the hypothetical discipline problems listed in the "Suggested Activities" section that follows and, based on the information included in this chapter, become involved in discussions regarding the *best* solution to a particular problem as they perceive it.

To close this chapter ten principles of discipline are offered that sum up the bulk of the responsibility to be borne by music educators new to the profession as they develop their relationship with students.

Ten discipline principles

1. Be sure that students understand the reasons why certain behavior is expected and what that behavior is. Involve students in determining behavior guidelines.

2. An aggressive attitude on the part of the teacher tends to develop students who adopt only an outward sense of conformity. Expect the best and look and build upon good behavior traits. Be generous with praise.

3. Rebellious or difficult students are generally troubled students. Seek help in determining the underlying cause(s).

4. Young people need to be needed. Students who don't feel needed are likely to seek recognition and self-esteem through undesirable behavior.

5. Young people who are interested and active are rarely behavior problems.

6. Keep class activities moving. Confusion and behavior problems often arise in music classes when going from one activity to another.

7. De-emphasize the importance of minor behavior problems. No one, not even the teacher, behaves perfectly all the time.

8. When involved in a difficult discipline situation with students, let them talk out their side of the problem.

9. Be firm, be fair, and "mean what you say." Students expect and need to rely on these qualities in their teachers.

10. Be consistent. Instability on the part of the teacher breeds instability in students.

Young music educators must learn from their mistakes in dealing with student motivation and discipline and build on their successes in those same areas. The result can be one of the most enjoyable and satisfying careers possible.

Suggested Activities

1. Lead a class discussion on why music classes should theoretically be less susceptible to student behavior problems.

2. Interview a junior-high-school student and a senior-high-school student regarding their favorite teacher(s) in their particular school. Compile a list of qualities that make each teacher special.

3. Prepare a five-minute report based on periodical literature concerning some element of motivating positive student behavior. Present the report to the class and have class members rate your eye contact.

4. Interview a local music educator and determine his or her most recent serious discipline problem and how it was resolved. Lead a class discussion on the topic.

5. Lead a class discussion on the importance of careful lesson planning for music-education classes and rehearsals. Support the discussion with two outside published sources.

6. Lead a class discussion on the importance of uniforms for music groups as motivational aids. Support the discussion with two outside published sources.

7. Visit a public school music class or rehearsal and (1) list what you determine to be minor discipline problems and hypothesize how they could be prevented; (2) list apparent proactive steps taken by the teacher to prevent undesirable classroom behavior; (3) list what the teacher does during class to promote a positive environment for learning; (4) list what type of behavior is reinforced and how it is reinforced.

8. As a class, develop a survey regarding what facets of music education concern prospective teachers as they approach their first teaching positions. Administer the survey to nonmusic classes and compile the results for class discussion.

9. Determine how you would respond to each of the discipline situations below and what, if anything, could be done to prevent the problem from occurring in the first place.

   a. A male student in chorus is slouching in his chair at the beginning of rehearsal. The teacher in a quiet, offhand manner says "John, please sit up." John complies but calls the teacher an unprintable name, just loud enough for the teacher and several students to hear. What would you do?

   b. The teacher catches two senior students drinking on the bus on the return trip home from the state music contest. What would you do?

   c. A male student asks to be excused from a concert performance to go deer hunting with his father. The teacher denies the request. The student goes hunting anyway. What would you do?

   d. The teacher asks a misbehaving student to stay after school for a half-hour for punishment and the student fails to appear. What would you do? What would you do if the student failed to appear the second time?

   e. A teacher observes a student reading a book at every break during a band rehearsal. What would you do?

10. Lead a class discussion on what administrative functions presented in Chapter One come into play in dealing with motivation and discipline. How? Why?

References and Suggested Reading

Benner, Charles H. *Teaching Performing Groups.* Reston, Va.: Music Educators National Conference, 1972.

Blanchard, Kenneth, and Spencer Johnson. *The One Minute Manager.* New York: Berkley Books, 1982.

Cochran, Kathy H. "Prescription for Discipline." *Music Educators Journal,* December 1983.

Documentary Report of the Ann Arbor Symposium: Applications of Psychology to the Teaching of Music. Reston, Va.: Music Educators National Conference, 1981. (Sessions I and II).

Glenn, Neil E., William B. McBride, and George H. Wilson. *Secondary School Music: Philosophy, Theory and Practice,* Englewood Cliffs, N.J.: Prentice-Hall, 1970.

Gnagey, William J. *Motivating Classroom Discipline.* New York: Macmillan Publishing Company, 1981.

Hoffer, Charles R. *Introduction to Music Education.* Belmont, Calif.: Wadsworth Publishing Company, 1983.

Kalesnik, Walter B. *Motivation.* Boston: Allyn and Bacon, 1978.

Lautzenheiser, Tim. "Action: The Key to Motivation." *The Instrumentalist,* October 1985.

———. "Motivation Attitude Concepts for Today." *The School Musician,* August/September 1985.

Motivation and Creativity: Documentary Report of the Ann Arbor Symposium on the Applications of Psychology to the Teaching and Learning of Music, Reston, Va.: Music Educators National Conference, 1983. (Session III).

Swanson, Frederick J. *Music Teaching in the Junior High School,* Englewood Cliffs, N.J.: Prentice-Hall, 1973.

Within the School Environment

Effective Music
Budget Procedures

T he financial support of music-education programs across the United States has been in a state of gradual but identifiable change since the early 1970s. There are few schools in this country that have not been touched by the trend to reduce music budgets, staff, or both. Rising school costs, combined with declining school-enrollment figures, have caused school administrators to seek ways to stretch limited tax dollars. Music programs, in many cases, have unjustifiably suffered severely from the budget-cutting process.

With declining tax-dollar support for music education across the country, concerned parents and music educators have turned to outside fund-raising to support the type of program the school and community have come to expect. This need for alternative funding has placed an additional burden on the music-education staff and often on the students participating in the program.

Seeking adequate funding to support a quality music-education program can be a complex, demanding, and at times nearly overwhelming obligation for the music educator. This is particularly true at the secondary level, where performance groups are involved. Depending on the structure of the program and how it is viewed by the local school administration, the budgeting process is often the most demanding administrative task of a music educator. For this reason, music educators need to develop basic business skills and learn budget procedures, as well as the pertinent vocabulary, and they must gain a basic understanding of the total school-budget structure. Only then can they estimate the amount of funding potentially available to the music program.

Revenue Sources

For the purpose of simplification, potential revenue sources for the music-education program are divided into five categories:

1. Taxes and state aid to education
2. Special funds collected by the music department
3. Fund-raising
4. Gifts
5. Grants

Taxes

All public school districts are supported primarily from tax moneys collected from all citizens residing within the boundaries of a particular school district. The amount of tax money allocated to each school district is generally determined by a city or county council or commission, and it is based upon the budget figures submitted by the local school board. The school board's budget is based upon a request from the school administration outlining the financial needs of the school district for the next academic year. After a school administration has considered funding requests from a variety of instructional institutions throughout the district, the music educator becomes involved in budget decisions. His or her role will be discussed later in this chapter. The entire budget process involving tax money is long and complicated and almost overburdened by checks and balances.

Another source of funds involving tax moneys is state aid to education. Money is allocated by state governments to school districts throughout the state. Funds are generally distributed based upon total enrollment figures in a particular school district. Again, this procedure is quite complicated, and the amount of money set aside for state aid to education varies widely from state to state and fluctuates on an almost annual basis.

Special funds collected by the music department

This source of funding has great potential for contributing financial support to a music-education program. For one reason or another, it also is a source that is largely ignored by music educators nationwide.

Admission charge for concerts is almost nonexistent at the public-school level. For that matter, it is not all that common in higher education. A nominal fee associated with concerts is readily accepted by the public. The fact of the matter is, they expect it! The traditional "No Admission Fee" statement accompanying concert publicity for school concerts does nothing to attract additional concertgoers.

Charging admission for concerts also aids in publicizing the event. Advanced ticket sales can be boosted through student participation in the effort. A one- or two-dollar charge for adults can bring a significant amount of money into the music budget. A reduced student fee or perhaps no student admission charge could also be considered. A "Senior Citizen's Free" policy would be an appropriate gesture, and in all likelihood it would increase the number of retirement-age people attending concerts.

Any music educator willing to change the "admission free" policy to an "admission fee" policy will be pleasantly surprised by the results. Charging a small fee for school concerts is simply a good administrative management procedure.

Rental fees for school-owned instruments and concert wear is another often-ignored source of additional funding for the music-education program. Many schools charge no "use" fee for instruments or uniforms owned by the school district and often the schools that do charge a fee receive less money from that fee than it takes annually to maintain the equipment.

Most schools have a significant investment in musical instruments to support band and orchestral programs, along with uniforms, robes, and other concert wear, which are an important part of any performing group's inventory. Again, parents and students alike do not and will not object to paying a reasonable fee for the use of school-owned equipment necessary to the music-education program. The amount of rental or use fee is difficult to determine, but a general rule of thumb is twice the amount of the annual maintenance figure divided by the number of students using the equipment. For example, forty students might be using school instruments and the annual repair, overhead, and maintenance bill is $800 for *all* school-owned instruments. Doubling $800 and dividing by forty results in a $40 instrument use fee per student, per year. The same principle applies to concert-wear maintenance and cleaning. The excess funds beyond the actual maintenance expenditures can be placed in an equipment-replacement fund. The rental or use fee may certainly be higher than described, but should never be lower.

Another legitimate benefit of charging some type of fee for the use of school-owned instruments and concert wear is that students tend to take better care of an item if they are paying for its use. Music educators have traditionally refrained from initiating rental or use fees because they feared a decrease in student participation would result. This is simply not true!

Should the situation arise in which a student's family cannot afford the most nominal use fee, some type of agreement can be worked out between the student and group director for monthly payments of the fee or a possible work/service arrangement for the student in the department. No student should be denied access to a musical instrument or ensemble participation because of inability to pay a rental or use fee.

If the music educator plans to implement an admission or rental/use fee policy, he or she would be wise to observe the "goal and objective procedures" presented in Chapter One regarding approach, information, dissemination, and follow-up.

The school *activity fund* is another special source by which the music program might benefit, if it is not already receiving such support. In many schools, each student who contributes to the school activity fund by paying an annual fee or purchasing an activity ticket benefits from all of the activities within the school system. The music department is a prolific contributor to the success of many of these activities.

If the music program is not presently receiving some financial assistance from the school activity fund, a request for some type of funding would most certainly be justified.

Fund-raising

According to a budget survey reported in a recent issue of *The Instrumentalist* magazine, total funds that support a typical music program are *increasing* at the rate of approximately 3 percent per year. It is ironic that this increase occurs at the same time that the percentage of tax dollars supporting such programs continues to *decrease* at the rate of 1.3 percent per year. Because music education has not escaped the problems associated with inflation, and because current figures indicate a trend of increased travel for performing groups, fund-raising by music students and parents has become the major source of funds to support the annual music budget increase above 3 percent.[1]

Interestingly, student participation in school music programs continues to increase at about 1 percent per year; however, average total school enrollment is increasing at 4 percent per year and the average student-to-music teacher ratio has increased from 102:1 in 1985–86 to a figure of 114:1 in 1987–88. To support increased student participation in light of decreased tax support for music programs, the level of fund-raising increased by 12 percent from 1985–86 to 1987–88.[2]

Band and choirs at the junior-high-school level are beginning to be involved in travel in unprecedented ways. A music parent proudly described to this writer the thousands of miles of travel her children had been involved in as members of their junior-high-school band. This trend is of concern to music educators across the country, especially secondary choral, orchestra, and band directors, who fear that extensive travel and performance opportunities prior to high school can cause "burnout" and reduce student participation in music ensembles at the secondary level. In addition, of course, such traveling involves a significant increase in the yearly music budget.

Fortunate is the music educator employed in a school system that accepts the administrative policy that if a program is worthy of being a part of that school, then it is worthy of being funded by that school. Of course this attitude is the exception rather than the rule, and music educators must accept fund-raising as a realistic part of the budget process if program activities are to be sustained at their current level.

Gifts

Local businesses, corporate and private foundations, as well as wealthy individuals can also be a source of additional funding for music education. Donations from performances for private organizations, parades, or similar functions cannot be ignored as a potential revenue source. Local service and music clubs are also potential sources. Outright donations often result from some special fund-raising effort in support of a particular event, cause, or trip. Music scholarships or music-camp stipends often come from community-service and music clubs. Numerous music educators have been surprised by the financial support available for their programs that is simply there for the asking.

Grants

Proposals can be written for a variety of projects to support a music-education program. Likely candidates for proposal acceptance are commissioned works, guest performances, and residency programs by regional artists. All legitimate requests will be considered by the agency awarding the grants, but a great deal of supporting material is required. The music educator should not be intimidated by the paper work involved in a grant application. There is more than likely a school official with the background and knowledge to assist in a grant proposal.

A variety of foundations, both corporate and private, support the arts through grantsmanship, as do local and state arts councils, the National Endowment for the Arts, and the Office of Economic Opportunity. A young music educator seeking a grant from one of the above agencies would be well-advised to contact the local or regional arts council chairperson for information as to the potential source of funding and the type of projects presently being funded.

The last four areas just discussed are the major non-tax sources of funding for a public-school music program. All are worthy of investigation and consideration. The need for innovative program funding will take on increased significance if tax support of public education does not stabilize in the reasonably near future.

Need for the Budget Process

Imagine the chaos that would result in even the smallest school district if an organized approach to determining annual budget needs did not exist. The system, as cumbersome as it often appears to be, is the only logical manner in which a school district can handle public moneys with a high degree of responsibility and accountability. The requesting of bids on items to be purchased, the voucher system, and the need to file purchase orders prior to buying equipment and supplies can often appear to be a needless exercise. These procedures, however, provide the type of fiscal documentation of expenditures of public moneys that the taxpayers expect and deserve.

The budget process allows the school district and the associated governmental agencies to project school program needs into the future. Based on past expenditures for particular programs, school administrators can predict programmatic needs, not only for the next budget year, but for the next several years. A music educator can positively influence this part of the budget process by submitting a multiyear budget request, a procedure that will be discussed later in this chapter.

Revenues must be estimated. The budget process also requires the estimation of anticipated revenue from the sources that financially support a school district. Local and state government agencies must be actively involved in the projection of tax revenues available for dispersal to public education.

Projected expenditures. School administrators must compile detailed and accurate estimates of all anticipated expenditures. A good school administrator will request input in this portion of the process from even the smallest program in the school district and will insist that a budget proposal be submitted for music education.

Funds to be raised. Should the anticipated expenditures considerably exceed the anticipated revenue for a school district, school administrators must raise additional funds through increased tax support and government grants or reduce the amount of expenditures for the district. This need to limit expenditures has adversely affected music education in recent years and has resulted in increased fund-raising efforts by music educators and parents who support the program.

By preparing and submitting an annual budget request, the music educator assists in the overall operation of the school. Planned spending for any program is an important demonstration of the competence of an educational administrator.

Types of Music Budgets

In 1965 Snyder described four types of school music budgets that have gained acceptance in this country: the departmental budget, the autonomous budget, the split budget, and the "no budget" budget.[3] These four plans, with slight variations, are still in use in the late 1980s. Their longevity represents both positive and negative factors when one considers the fluctuations in music-education stability in the last one-third of the twentieth century.

Departmental music budget

This plan is generally found in large school systems and is compiled by a music supervisor or music coordinator. Budget support for all music activities within the entire system, from preschool to senior high, is included in the departmental budget request. The final proposal is submitted by the music supervisor to the superintendent of schools or the business manager of the school district. The plan allows the music supervisor to ensure unity throughout the district of the entire music program, but care must be taken to coordinate budgetary planning with other department heads and building principals.

Autonomous music budget

Again this type of approach to budgeting for music programs is generally used in cities with large school districts where a music supervisor or coordinator is involved, but involved to a much lesser degree. In the autonomous budget approach, each school or unit within the district is granted funding according to the activity level of the music program in that particular school. The music educator compiles a budget document and submits it to the building principal. The principal includes the music budget in his or her total budget request and then submits the total package to the superintendent or business manager.

The danger of the autonomous-budget style is that it fragments the total music program and creates a balance problem throughout the entire district. The music supervisor has little or no control over the budget process, which results in a reduction of his or her effectiveness in administering the entire program.

The school music programs that are highly visible and active are likely to receive greater budget support, yet the total activity of a music program cannot be used as a measure of that program's success—the quality of the program's activity must be considered. It can be argued that the more active programs are justified in receiving greater budgetary support than their less active counterparts in the same district, but the primary problem with the autonomous-budget procedure is the degree of administrative control taken out of the hands of the music supervisor.

Split music budget

The split-music-budget approach allows for separate budget requests from all music units within a given school. The band, choir, orchestra, and general music sections all have to submit individual budget requests. This approach to securing funds for a music program most often takes place in smaller school districts where no single individual is charged with the responsibility of program coordination. There is often a lack of real communication between group directors and the potential for dissension and animosity is great.

The split music budget may make up part of either the departmental- or autonomous-budget plans but is not in itself a positive approach toward securing funds for music education. "No school should have a vocal music program, an instrumental music program, and a general music program. All should have a *music* program, which includes all possible avenues of activity and experience."[4]

"No budget" music budget

The "no budget" approach to funding music education exists when the school administrator allows the music educator to present expenditure requests as "the need arises" and then takes positive or negative action on each request. This practice occurs most frequently in small school systems where school officials pay "lip service" to wanting a quality music-education program in their schools and where they are dealing with an inexperienced music educator. It literally requires the music educator to beg for financial support for the program. Knowledgeable music educators and school administrators alike realize that a "no budget" approach toward program funding is a totally unacceptable and unsuccessful administrative procedure.

Although the four previously discussed approaches to the music budget are each flawed to a degree, the "no budget" approach holds absolutely no future for building a strong music program. If young music educators find themselves in such an employment situation that is without a specific music budget, they can accept the status quo for one year. During that year administrative approval must be sought for a music-budget proposal for the subsequent year. If the approval is not forthcoming, the music educator must make the decision to either accept the situation, realizing there is little chance for improvement, or seek a position in another school system. Hopefully, the material that follows will promote the acceptance of a music budget plan after that one year of effort.

Multi-Unit School District Budget Procedures

It would appear that in a school district with several junior- and senior-high schools, as well as numerous elementary schools, a combination of the first three types of budgets would be the most appropriate to fit today's needs. For example, a departmental music budget—generated by a music supervisor and based on requests by music departments throughout the district—would be a logical first step. The various units in each school would compile their own individual budget requests, and then submit them as one budget document, representative of the needs of the entire music department of that school. The music supervisor would organize all the department requests into a single document and in the end would distribute funds to the various schools within the district based on the amount of money allocated district-wide to music education.

There is no single approach that can be presented as the ultimate approach to the budget process for music education in large school systems; there are too many variables involved. One factor should remain constant, however, and that is a high level of involvement on the part of the music supervisor in the procurement and allocation of funds for music education in the entire district. This involvement is necessary to maintain the continuity of the music-education curriculum throughout the school system.

Small School District Budget Procedures

For the purpose of discussion, a small school district can be considered a "one high school" district. Small school districts can have as few as one music educator involved in the program and as many as several teachers, each with an area of speciality. The type of approach to budgeting most commonly used in small school districts is one that uses most of the elements of the split music budget combined with some elements of the autonomous music-budget plan. When no music supervisor or coordinator is involved, the teachers responsible for the band, choir, orchestra, and general music classes must develop their own budgets. The primary ingredient for success in this approach is that the several requests be submitted to the administration as a total package for the *music department*. This process requires a degree of leadership on the part of one music educator in bringing the various requests together in a single package. Separate budget proposals from the choir, band, and so on, can only provide an opportunity for hard feelings and dissension to occur.

The music educator who is completely responsible for the music program in a small school will submit a budget that combines general, vocal, and instrumental needs in a single request package. In such a situation, the music educator is solely responsible for the continuity and balance of the music-education program.

Establishing a budget plan

There are three situations in which a budget plan needs to be developed: (1) if the music educator is in a first-year teaching position and no budget plan for music education has ever existed; (2) an experienced music educator accepts a new teaching position and is dissatisfied with the budget approach in the new situation; (3) a music educator, established in his or her position, decides to seek an expanded base of funding through a different approach to budget development. All three situations can be approached in somewhat the same manner. But in the first case especially, the music educator needs to recognize the *necessity* for establishing a budget plan.

First, an effective budget plan aids the administration in determining the total fiscal needs for the school district and in planning for the future. When the music department's financial needs appear as part of the overall school budget, it lends credibility and importance to the music-education program. A budget plan allows the music educator to formulate highly organized plans for controlled growth and development. A music-education curriculum generally involves equipment of one kind or another. The music-education program cannot stay current in curriculum approaches without a budget for equipment needs to support that curriculum. For example, numerous elementary and middle-school general music programs how have access to computers for their classrooms but no budget with which to acquire software.

Finally, and perhaps most importantly, the budget plan provides the music educator with an opportunity to justify the music-education program. Without a line in the total school budget, it is difficult to justify the existence of music education on even the best of philosophical grounds. When the music educator is allowed to submit an annual budget proposal, the opportunity is also available to provide increased annual justification to the school-district administration and the members of the school board for support of the music-education program. A logical, professional approach toward an effective plan for procuring and dispersing funds is simply "good business." Far too often those music educators blessed with supportive administrations that allow them to submit annual budget requests look upon the occasion as an obligation, a task to be completed, rather than what it actually is, an opportunity to justify, build, and develop the music-education programs in their schools.

Budget approach

There are two primary ways to approach the submission of a music-budget request, the annual-budget proposal and the multi-year plan (usually three to five years), which is generally reserved for large equipment needs. Both approaches are very effective when the proper organizational groundwork has been completed in conjunction with the proposal.

The annual budget represents a year-long effort on the part of the music educator. Accurate records of expenditures and future needs should be kept on a weekly, if not almost daily, basis. Some time should also be spent investigating new products, which today are coming on the market with ever-increasing frequency. The annual budget request consists of a list of categories, or "line-items," to use a more contemporary term. Under each line-item several divisions may occur. Retail costs are included, along with approximate bid prices, and any piece of equipment to be used for a trade-in on new equipment.

The multi-year budget plan is used when a great deal of expensive equipment is needed and its cost prohibits its purchase at one time. For example, perhaps a small high-school music program has only two timpani in poor condition, no chimes, xylophone, or vibraphone, no choral risers, and the music-room piano is a 1925 upright model with a cracked soundboard. Needless to say, that music program is in trouble! If a music educator were to ask the superintendent for $15,000 to replace the old equipment and purchase additional equipment, the response undoubtedly, and perhaps justifiably, would be negative. Whereas, if a request was submitted that extended the equipment needs over a three-year period at $5,000 per year, or over a five-year period at $3,000 per year, the equipment needs would be more manageable in the eyes of the administration. The music educator has furnished the superintendent and school board with three potential solutions to a serious music-department problem.

When submitting any multiyear plan, it is always wise to indicate what effect inflation will have on the cost of the same equipment in either three or five years. In other words, a piano, if purchased today, would be $4,000, in three years, perhaps $4,500, and in five years, possibly $5,200. Any reliable music dealer would be pleased to assist a music educator in drawing up a multiyear budget proposal, complete with approximate bid prices and three- and five-year inflation projections. It is entirely possible that when the proposal gets to the school board for discussion, some board members will note that the district can save over $5,000 by purchasing all the equipment immediately rather than dividing the cost over a three- or five-year period. The school board might even approve the immediate purchase of the equipment, which happens frequently when multiyear equipment purchase plans have been allowed by the administration to get to the school board for consideration. Of course, the music educator should attend that board meeting to answer questions and provide support for the request.

Organizing the Budget Request

The level of acceptance of any budget request is directly related to the manner in which it is organized and submitted. In interviews with music educators in preparation for this book, the author asked for a copy of their most recent budget proposals. What resulted were far too many handwritten, generally sloppy, and poorly structured budget proposals. To a person, the same music educators complained about inadequate budget support, lack of adequate equipment, and a general lack of administrative interest in the music-education program. These instructors are missing a tremendous annual opportunity to justify their programs, and at the same time generate support, both moral and financial, for music education in their school systems. What follows at this point is a step-by-step plan for developing a successful budget request for music-education programs.

The cover letter

The budget request should include a concise and complete cover letter that provides a verbal explanation for the request. Because the cover letter is the first item in the budget proposal, it must be carefully structured to encourage the reader to consider thoughtfully the information that follows. General support information should not be presented at this point but should be included in the "Support Materials" section, which appears later in the request. It can certainly be mentioned in the cover letter that such material exists, and perhaps even a brief summary of the material would be in order. At any rate, this portion of the budget proposal definitely depends upon the personality of the music educator, his or her relationship with the school administration, the history of the past budget requests, and the size of the request. Bear in mind that the cover letter is an important aspect of a professional budget proposal.

Budget summary

To be administratively effective, the budget request should be divided into eleven line-item categories. Administrators and administrative boards tend to look at the "big picture" rather than all of the various elements that make up that picture. As an example, they would be less interested in the fact that the marching band needs music totaling $500, the concert band, music totaling $400, and the choir, music totaling $800 than they would be in what the total music line-item is in the budget. The separate music requests for several performing groups can be listed on a separate page as subcategories of the budget request.

Following the cover letter, the first section of the budget request is the Budget Summary. Here are listed the eleven line-item categories:

1. New equipment
2. Replacement equipment
3. Music library
4. Travel
5. Awards
6. Printing and publicity
7. Repair and maintenance
8. Contest and festival fees
9. Contractual services
10. Concert-wear maintenance
11. Contingency

Dollar amounts accompanying each line-item, anticipated nondistrict income (if any), and a total budget figure at the bottom of the page are all that is included as part of the budget summary. This page should be widely spaced and uncluttered, with the information readily available to the reader.

Budget description by line-item categories

The second section of the budget request includes a list of the eleven line-items and accompanying subcategories, complete with a list of separate needs within each subcategory.

New equipment. In this category, any equipment new to the program is listed. For example, if an additional piano is requested, or if a new bassoon is requested, and they aren't actually replacing old or obsolete instruments, the items would be listed in the budget proposal under "New Equipment." The rationale for the purchase of new equipment can be presented in the "Support Information" section of the budget request, which appears as the final section of the proposal.

Replacement equipment. If a piece of equipment is traded, sold, or retired from use, and new equipment is requested as replacement, the request appears here. Documentation for the need for equipment replacement is very important and should appear in the "Support Information" section. This might include the approximate age of the equipment, its present dollar value to the school system, its approximate trade-in value, its approximate life expectancy, and its importance and relevance to the music-education program.

　　If the replacement-equipment need can be effectively documented, school administrators are likely to support the expenditure because the case can be made that the school district is presently supporting the music program with a similar piece of equipment.

Music library. All equipment, materials, books, tapes, recordings, films, computer software, music, and other related items are requested here. Anything that can be even vaguely associated with the music library is listed as part of that line-item. Special nonmusical supplies, such as file folders, tape, labels, and similar items, are generally available from the main office of the school and need not be included as part of this line-item. The music educator can also consult the school librarian to see if school library funds can be used to purchase materials other than printed music to support the music library. School librarians often have access to government funds, part of which they are willing to release for music-related library materials. The music educator, more often than not, must take the initiative.

Travel. Included in this line-item are anticipated travel expenditures associated in any way with the music-education program. This category includes both student and educator travel expenses incurred during the year and should include transportation, meals, and lodging. School districts have a standard per diem rate established for staff travel that regulates maximum reimbursement for travel expenses. The music educator should review this policy prior to budgeting for student and personal travel. Student travel expenses, for example, can include contest and festival travel, All-State auditions and participation travel, special out-of-town concerts, and similar events. Travel expenses for the music educator to attend state and regional professional association meetings are most definitely the responsibility of the school district and should be included here.

Awards. The inclusion of an "Awards" line-item in an approach to budgeting for music education is in no way to be considered an endorsement for awards programs in music education. Awards, however, are a part of many band, choir, and orchestra programs in the public schools. If a music educator has a system for providing awards to music students, the cost of providing those awards must be included in the budget proposal. It is not uncommon for a music instructor to have some type of annual fund-raising project for the express purpose of purchasing student awards. If this is the case, "Awards" should still appear in the budget proposal and the money raised should appear elsewhere in the request as income.

Printing and publicity. Far too many school concerts are presented each year using poorly constructed, mimeographed programs for the audience. The audience and students deserve better, and the music-education program has an obligation to provide a neat and informative printed program for concertgoers and performers alike. It's a matter of image! The music educator has the responsibility to project a positive image of his or her program. A printed concert program is part of that image. A music educator should count the number of major concerts presented in a year, secure bids for a typical four-page program for each of those concerts, and include the cost as part of the budget proposal.

Promotional mailings, newspaper and radio ads, film for student-associated photos, along with any other publicity-related expense are included in this line item.

Repair and maintenance. The "Repair and Maintenance" line-item of a budget request can often be financially underestimated, particularly when extensive repair and overhaul of wind, percussion, and stringed instruments is involved. When budgeting for this type of work, the music educator should have reasonably solid bid figures from a repair shop to submit as part of the budget proposal. Repair costs and equipment overhaul rates have increased significantly in recent years, but a quality, top-line instrument that is properly overhauled can provide many years of service at a fraction of the cost of a new piece of equipment.

Also difficult to predict is the number of expensive "emergency" repairs to school-owned instruments. Perhaps the best guide is to determine the dollar figure spent on this type of maintenance in previous years and add $200 to that amount.

In addition to all planned and unplanned instrument repair and overhaul, tuning of pianos, repair of equipment other than musical instruments, and all repair supplies needed by the band and orchestra directors should be included in this line-item. Be certain to estimate adequately the number of tunings needed by the school pianos and get a performance bid from a local piano technician as part of the budget proposal.

A music educator who requests a high amount of funding for repair and maintenance will be seen by the school administration as an individual concerned with the care and preservation of school property. The case can certainly be made in the "Support Information" section of the budget document that timely equipment maintenance will in the long term benefit the school district.

Contest and festival fees. Performance is a natural result and benefit of participation in a music-education program. Contest and festival opportunities abound for all levels of solo and ensemble participants and for marching and concert bands, choirs and orchestras, as well as the more select groups that are associated with a respective large ensemble. One need only pick up a monthly music journal to see the variety of festival opportunities available throughout the year for school music organizations. These festivals are, of course, in addition to the local and regional events scheduled annually by individual schools and professional music organizations. Generally, participation fees are charged for such events.

If the contest or festival has the support of the local music-education staff and the school administration, the fee required for participation in the event should most certainly be paid by the school district and not the students involved. The students are representing the school as part of a music program supported by the school and simply cannot be asked to pay any fee associated with that representation. Music educators need to plan contest and festival appearances very carefully. Advance costs for such events are reasonably easy to determine and should pose no particular difficulty when it comes to estimating expenditures. In addition, all fees associated with All-State and any other honor group participation should be included as part of the "Contest and Festival Fee" request. Any travel expenditures for student or staff that will result from contest or festival participation can be included as part of the "Travel" line-item

Contractual services. Fees for soloists, clinicians, adjudicators, and any other outside professional who is brought into the school district to perform some type of service for the music-education program should be included here. Any compensation for work associated with the music program should also be included in this line-item. Outside-the-school accompanists, recording costs, and equipment transportation are several examples.

Most successful school music programs have guest artists and outside clinicians involved in some manner on an annual basis. The constructive criticism and positive reinforcement that evolves from student and teacher association with professional artists and music educators is a most viable and legitimate expense for any music-education program. Dedicated music educators are eager, rather than reluctant, to expose their students to musical concepts and opinions other than their own and are fully aware of the long-range benefits those outside ideas bring to the music program. Outside involvement of artists and clinicians in music-education programs should be seen as a legitimate strength of a program.

Concert-wear maintenance. The proper cleaning and storage of uniforms, choir robes, and other concert wear can add years of use to the lives of these garments and contribute significantly to their appearance during that lifetime. Annual dry cleaning of concert wear is an absolute minimum and in the case of band uniforms, which are used frequently during the fall marching season, two cleanings per year are certainly in order. Bid figures per unit to be cleaned, solicited from dry-cleaning operators serving the local area, can be used to calculate this line-item amount.

Also included in this category can be such adjunct items as good wooden hangers and proper storage racks. Preventive maintenance items, such as rain gear for marching-band uniforms, should appear as part of the "New Equipment" request.

Contingency. Every realistic budget request includes a line-item for any emergency which may arise that requires some type of expenditure. Rather than appealing to the board of education through the school administration for supplementary funding, the music educator in an administrative role should have access to contingency funding as part of the total music budget. Countless unplanned situations can annually arise that require some financial support. The marching band, for example, gets caught in a rainstorm during the first parade of the year and the uniforms *must* be cleaned immediately; two of the new choir members could be either very large or very small and additional concert wear is needed; perhaps the orchestra receives an invitation to perform at a regional conference and supplementary travel funds are needed. One thing is certain, however; emergency situations involving a certain degree of expense will occur. The most expedient and professional manner in which these situations can be handled is to have a contingency fund as part of the annual music-education budget request. By the way, this is the only budget line-item that need not be exhausted each year. An annual carryover of funds in the contingency line-item is appropriate, as well as desirable, school policy permitting.

Please bear in mind that the eleven preceding line-item categories represent a basic minimum of categories into which a music budget request may be divided. As the need arises, additional line-items or divisions can be added to support a particular program concept or philosophy.

Support information

Following the budget summary and budget description, justification for the budget request is included in section three of the proposal, "Support Information." This section includes specific reference to particular line-items, as well as comprehensive support information.

A general statement of justification for the request can open this section, followed perhaps by cost-per-pupil figures. A comparison of music budgets in area schools of similar size can also be included. Most schools belong to an athletic conference for varsity sports programs. If the music educator can gather music budget information from all the schools in the athletic conference, quite often he or she can make a case for increased budget support. A suggested way to present this material is to average all conference music budgets and also specifically point out which schools have the highest music budgets in the conference. If averaging the conference music budgets does not provide a distinct benefit to the proposal in terms of support information, then abandon the averaging concept and use as examples the conference schools with higher music budgets. School administrators are by nature somewhat competitive and proud of their schools, and very often budget comparisons lend credence to a music budget proposal if it can be demonstrated that area schools are giving their music programs better support.

School administrators and their boards of education rarely comprehend the number of school and community appearances made by the music performing groups in their own schools. Add to in-school performances all contest and festival performances, musical productions, and appearances at civic and social functions and the resulting figure generally becomes very impressive. A music educator can use the "Support Information" section of the annual budget request to demonstrate to the school administration the full extent of the music program's activities.

Cost-per-pupil figures in support of a budget request are often extremely effective. Simply take the total budget request and divide that figure by the number of students involved in all performing groups and classes that will be affected by the music budget, and the resulting amount is what it costs the school district per pupil for the music education program in that school for one year. The resulting total will be surprisingly small when compared with other programs within the school because of the large number of students touched by the music program.

Following the general statement, justification of each line-item expense takes place. For example, if a new oboe and bassoon are requested, the music educator might include under the heading "New Equipment" comments by adjudicators at past music contests indicating a need for double reeds in the band. In addition, he or she might assign a life expectancy to each new piece of equipment, with the cost of the equipment divided by that life expectancy. The resulting dollar amount is the annual cost to the school district for the life of the equipment. Such figures are generally very low. A multitude of information can and should be used in support of the line-item. New equipment is more than likely, from an administrative viewpoint, the most difficult expense to justify.

Replacement equipment is easier to justify because the school district already owns a similar piece of equipment. The support information should include the approximate age of the equipment, its present condition, why it shouldn't or can't be repaired, and the future cost per year to the school district. Given adequate support information, administrators and school boards are frequently receptive to equipment replacement requests.

The music-library line-item support information can include a statement citing increased costs of music purchase and rental in the past ten years. A performance group director need only identify a set of music purchased ten years earlier and a set of recently purchased music and compare cost figures to point out how drastically inflation has affected the music publishing industry. The number of students served by the music purchased is another valid piece of support information. In addition, one might point out that technology has increased the number of items available and necessary to a music-education program.

Travel for the purpose of student participation in contests, festivals, honor groups, auditions, and performances at athletic events is readily supported by school administrators. Personal travel by the music educator to professional conferences is another matter. The music educator needs to identify area music educators who receive per diem assistance for the purpose of attending professional conferences. He or she might also seek information within the district, particularly the degree of financial support provided for athletic coaches who attend clinics and state-level events, to support the personal portion of the budget request.

The purchase of awards is easy to justify if an awards system has previously been in place. The only reasons for an increase or decrease in funding in this category are the number of students receiving awards, a change in cost of the awards or a change in the type of awards being presented. If a music educator is initiating an awards system, then motivational support information can be included. If the awards system is maintained through a fund-raising project, the awards line-item should still appear as part of the budget request and funds raised should appear as income.

The support information for printing and publicity is primarily associated with performing groups and subsequent concert performances. This category does not require a great deal of financial support. It can be pointed out that music stores commonly offer to subsidize the printing of concert programs. While some music educators feel that program-printing is a school-associated responsibility, commercial financial assistance in the printing of concert programs is a budget-saving idea worthy of consideration.

The age, present condition, and anticipated life expectancy of equipment to be overhauled should be included as support information for the

"Repair and Maintenance" line-item. Cost of new equipment can be compared with the expense of overhauling equipment presently owned by the school district. Routine repair and maintenance of music equipment is simply a responsibility that comes with owning the equipment. This portion of the line-item can be supported by costs incurred in previous years. Administrators understand that the useful life expectancy of a piece of equipment can be extended through a regular maintenance program and are apt to enthusiastically support this portion of the budget request.

Contest and festival fees are relatively easy to justify based on the expenditures of previous years. Increased entry fees or additional participation in contests or festivals are more than likely the two principal causes of a funding increase and would require further substantiation.

Comparison with area school music programs might be useful in providing support information for contractual services. This line-item need not be an extravagant annual request but one that allows exposure of music students in a school to concepts and ideas from clinicians and music educators outide the system. The point can quite honestly be made that inviting professionals not affiliated with the school district to provide lectures, concerts, and clinics on a regular basis creates at atmosphere conducive to ongoing program evaluation. This benefit, in addition to furnishing the opportunity to remain professional and up-to-date, is an administrative tool that cannot be overlooked.

The same philosophy that justified repair of instruments explains the need for concert-wear maintenance. That is, uniforms, gowns, and other garments used in musical performances need to be routinely dry cleaned, stored, and maintained to provide optimum return to the school district on a very large investment. Several hundred dollars of annual maintenace cost to protect an investment of many thousands of dollars is a concept that should be readily acceptable to school administrators.

As previously indicated, all realistic budget requests include a contingency, or emergency, line-item. It is totally impossible to anticipate and plan for every detail that requires funding during the year. All music educators can recall numerous situations during their careers that called for some type of emergency expenditure. A contingency fund included as part of the music budget is the most expedient and administratively effective manner in which to handle unanticipated circumstances requiring financial resolution. Any moneys remaining unspent in the contingency line-item should be carried over into the budget for the following year and shown as "income," thereby reducing the contingency request from the figure represented in the previous budget period.

These methods of gathering and supplying support information for a budget request are offered only as guidelines. Support information will certainly vary and will be presented in a different style when the preceding budget model is applied to a specific school situation.

Preparation and Presentation of the Budget Proposal

The sequencing of information as it should appear in the budget request has just been presented. A final concern in preparing the budget document is the format of the separate sections of the proposal. The major format guideline is to leave a great deal of "white space" when typing each page. The budget request will read more easily and have a much better chance of being considered by the appropriate individuals if the format is clean, uncrowded, and uncluttered. Include more pages in the proposal, but make each page easily readable.

After the document is submitted to the appropriate administrative budget agent, the music educator should plan on being called upon to defend the proposal to the school administration. If properly prepared, the budget proposal will nearly speak for itself from a justification standpoint, but the music educator can humanize the proposal by personally explaining any portions of the request that relate directly to students or student ensembles. The music educator should also plan to appear at a board-of-education meeting when the music budget request is to be discussed. However, he or she should attend strictly as an interested observer and a source of additional information if needed.

At first glance, this approach to compiling a music budget request may appear both tedious and time-consuming. Yet very few worthwhile accomplishments result from minimum effort. The reader is also reminded that once the initial work is completed, a budget format can be prepared in future years by simply changing figures, descriptions, and some support information.

If a professional, businesslike approach is used to demonstrate a need for funding to support a music-education program, the chances of the proposal being carefully considered at the school administrative level are vastly improved.

Administration of the Budget

Following the budget-request approval, a systematic means of administering the budget must be implemented. A small ledger can be purchased and a section devoted to each line-item category. At all times, the music educator needs to have an approximate idea of the funds remaining in each line-item. School office personnel can be a great help in updating balances. Most schools now have computerized bookkeeping systems, that produce periodic printouts, an important aid in the accounting process.

Every attempt should be made to avoid overspending on any line-item. A certain amount of overdrawing on occasion can be expected, but habitual overspending will be looked upon as poor or sloppy management and negate positive benefits to be derived from the budget process.

Finally, a "reminder file" needs to be established for budget purposes. Music educators receive daily mailings of new equipment, concepts, materials, programs, and publications. Those that warrant further consideration can be placed in the reminder file and studied in depth during the budget process for the following year. Ideas for equipment and materials evolve throughout the year. Unless these ideas are written on a slip of paper and revived at budget time, there is a very good chance they will be forgotten and not recalled again until too late to be included in the budget request. A "reminder file" is simply another administrative tool to help keep a very busy music educator organized and efficient.

More and more music educators have computers in their offices. Available software can greatly assist in budget administration. Additionally, almost every school has at least one individual on the instructional staff who would be delighted to demonstrate his or her computer programming skills by designing a program tailored to the specific needs of the music educator.

The Role of Booster Clubs

It has become commonplace for booster organizations to be involved in some manner in the budget process. These organizations' roles in raising funds to support music education will be presented at length in Chapter Ten.

Sample Budget Request

A sample budget proposal dealing with the needs of a hypothetical music program is shown in Figures 3.1—3.4. It is an example of a proposal that might be submitted by one music educator charged with the responsibility of administering a music-education program in a small school system, grades five through twelve. It is included in order to demonstrate budget format and provide a model for its actual use. The dollar values assigned the various pieces of equipment, as well as other budget items, are given for demonstration only, not as a recommendation for actual costs.

The format presented in Figures 3.1—3.4 works equally well for large music programs with many staff members; it also applies readily to separate choral, orchestra, or band budget requests. Simple adjustment in line-items is all that might be required. The process and format remain the same.

Figure 3.1. Sample budget cover letter.

Mr. I.M. Smart, Superintendent
Bea Flat Public Schools

Dear Mr. Smart:

Enclosed please find the 1987-88 music department budget proposal. Please note that the request represents only a 3% increase over the 1986-87 budget proposal of just over $9,700.00. It also must be mentioned that of the $10,015.00 total figure, only $5,270.00 is requested in Bea Flat School District funds.

Section One of this proposal is the summary of anticipated needs and income. Section Two includes a more detailed breakdown of each budget line-item and Section Three provides support material and additional information pertaining to the budget request.

Information included in Section Three indicates low per-pupil costs for music education in the Bea Flat schools, and the level of requested school district funds remains below the average for music programs in other Southwest Conference Schools. Information also indicates that the activity level for appearances by students associated with the music education program remain high.

Finally, please note that the number of students enrolling in the music education program continues to increase. It is respectfully requested that budget support be forthcoming to sustain program quality and to maintain a systematic pattern of growth. This budget proposal reflects an honest, yet conservative representation of funding needs for music education in Bea Flat Public Schools for the 1987-88 academic year. There is no "fat" included in the request and it is hoped it will be considered in that light.

Sincerely,

John C. Kleff
Music Instructor

Upon checking school policy, the music educator might learn that it is not necessary to budget for student travel, that school bus costs are anticipated in a school transportation fund. School policy theoretically could also prohibit the carryover, from one year to another, of contingency funds. There could be a variety of school-associated provisions that would influence the "Anticipated Income" and the "Anticipated Expenses" structure; again however, it is the *format*, with its division of the proposal into three logical and comprehensible sections, that provides strength to this particular budget procedure.

The music educator should place "planning dates" on the calendar indicating when to begin the annual budget preparation process. In doing so, the chaos and panic that results when the school administrator announces

Figure 3.2. Sample budget summary.

```
                          SECTION ONE

                       MUSIC DEPARTMENT
                   BEA FLAT PUBLIC SCHOOLS
                   1987-88 MUSIC BUDGET


                       BUDGET SUMMARY


ANTICIPATED INCOME
Source                                          Amount
Student Activity Fund                      $     800.00
Music Boosters                                 1,200.00
Student Fund Raising                             145.00
1986-86 Contingency                              340.00
Concert Admission                              1,150.00
Rental/Use Fees                                  660.00
Arts Council Grant                               450.00
Bea Flat School District                       5,270.00
TOTAL                                        $10,015.00

ANTICIPATED EXPENSES
Line-Item                                       Amount
New Equipment                              $   1,720.00
Replacement Equipment                          3,960.00
Music Library                                    620.00
Travel                                           780.00
Awards                                           145.00
Printing and Publicity                           300.00
Repair and Maintenance                           770.00
Contest/Festival Fees                            350.00
Contractual Services                             450.00
Concert Wear Maintenance                         420.00
Contingency                                      500.00
TOTAL                                        $10,015.00
```

that "all budget requests are due in the office in two days" can be avoided. More importantly, a budget proposal prepared in haste, without much thought given it, is likely to be treated in a like manner.

Budget preparation and administration is an administrative obligation that simply can't be taken lightly by the music educator. However, if the

Figure 3.3. Sample budget description.

```
                         SECTION TWO

                       MUSIC DEPARTMENT
                    BEA FLAT PUBLIC SCHOOLS
                     1987-88 MUSIC BUDGET


                     BUDGET DESCRIPTION
```

NEW EQUIPMENT

Item	Retail	App. Bid	Total	
Concert Chimes	$1,800.00	$1,000.00	$1,000.00	
40 Choral Folders @	4.00	3.00	120.00	
Baritone Saxophone (used)	600.00	600.00	600.00	
TOTAL			$1,720.00	$ 1,720.00

REPLACEMENT EQUIPMENT

Item	Retail	Less Trade	Total	
French Horn	$ 800.00	$ 200.00	$ 600.00	
Oboe	460.00	100.00	360.00	
One Set Choral Risers	1,600.00	----	1,600.00	
Concert Tuba	1,800.00	400.00	1,400.00	
TOTAL			$3,960.00	$ 3,960.00

MUSIC LIBRARY

Ensemble	Retail	School Price	Total	
Marching Band	$ 120.00	$ 100.00	$ 100.00	
Concert Band	150.00	150.00	150.00	
Choir	260.00	220.00	220.00	
Small Ensemble	150.00	150.00	150.00	
TOTAL			$ 620.00	$ 620.00

music educator learns to accept the budget as a professional challenge, he or she may actually begin to enjoy the process. To be successful in their chosen career field, music educators are responsible for providing resources for the program at the maximum level the school and community can afford. This effort can be an extremely rewarding and satisfying aspect of music-education administration.

Figure 3.3. Continued.

TRAVEL

Student	Trans-portation	Meals/Lodging	Total	
Music Contest	$ 200.00	$ ----	$ 200.00	
All-State Auditions	60.00	----	60.00	
Tri-State Festival	240.00	100.00	340.00	
Instructor				
State Conference	80.00	60.00	140.00	
All-State Concert	40.00	----	40.00	
TOTAL			$ 780.00	$ 780.00

AWARDS

	Total	
Choral	$ 85.00	
Band	60.00	
TOTAL	$ 145.00	$ 145.00

PRINTING AND PUBLICITY

	Total	
Four Concert Programs @ $50.00	$ 200.00	
Four Newspaper Ads @ $25.00	100.00	
TOTAL	$ 300.00	$ 300.00

REPAIR AND MAINTENANCE

	Total	
Four Piano Tunings @ $30.00	$ 120.00	
Baritone Horn Overhaul	180.00	
Stereo System Repair	120.00	
General Instrument Repair	300.00	
Supplies	50.00	
TOTAL	$ 770.00	$ 770.00

Figure 3.3. Continued.

CONTEST/FESTIVAL FEES	Total	
Music Contest	$ 120.00	
Tri-State Festival	150.00	
All-State Auditions	80.00	
TOTAL	$ 350.00	$ 350.00

CONTRACTUAL SERVICES	Total	
Clinician's Fees	$ 300.00	
Guest Soloist	150.00	
TOTAL	$ 450.00	$ 450.00

CONCERT WEAR MAINTENANCE	Total	
Band Uniforms (two cleanings)	$ 300.00	
Choral Robes	120.00	
TOTAL	$ 420.00	$ 420.00

CONTINGENCY	Total	
Unanticipated Expenses	$ 500.00	$ 500.00

TOTAL ANTICIPATED EXPENSES		$10,015.00

Figure 3.4. Sample support information.

SECTION THREE

MUSIC DEPARTMENT
BEA FLAT PUBLIC SCHOOLS
1987-88 MUSIC BUDGET

SUPPORT INFORMATION

General Information

The music education program in the Bea Flat Public School District provides classroom and music ensemble experience for what is expected to be 220 students in 1987-88, grades five through twelve. Based on this budget request, a cost-per-pupil ratio of $23.95 in district funds results. Both the cost-per-pupil figure and the total request in district funds are well below average when compared with other schools in the Southwest Conference. The average conference school district budget for music is just over $7,200.00, and the cost-per-pupil for students in music education is approximately $38.00. Treble East Public Schools, the conference school closest in enrollment to Bea Flat, supported music education in the 1986-87 academic year with a budget of district funds totaling $8,400.00.

Students participating in music activities in the Bea Flat Public School District in 1986-87 made fifty-nine appearances at school and local functions, as well as at regional and state events. This 6% increase in the number of appearances made in the previous year can be regarded as the maximum number of appearances that should be made by students involved in the Bea Flat music education program. In addition, the total number of students involved in music education

Figure 3.4. Continued.

will increase by slightly over 10% from 1986-87 and over 50% in a three-year period.

Specific Information

NEW EQUIPMENT

Concert Chimes - Much of the concert band music available has a chimes part included. The instrument will also be used in the percussion ensemble. Life expectancy of the instrument is forty years.

Choral Folders - The choir has never had folders specifically designed for choral music, but instead has resorted to the use of manila envelopes. The new folders offer much better protection for music while it is in use.

Baritone Saxophone - A baritone saxophone is needed to complete the saxophone choir in the band and is an absolute necessity for the newly organized jazz ensemble. This saxophone is a reconditioned instrument and should provide ten years of service at a considerable savings from the $2,000 cost of a new instrument.

REPLACEMENT EQUIPMENT

French Horn - Three of the school-owned French horns are over thirty years old and are literally beyond repair. Plans are to purchase one new horn each year for the next three years. Anticipated life expectancy of the new instrument is approximately thirty years.

Oboe - The school oboe has not been used for a number of years and is badly in need of a complete overhaul. It also has a crack in the

Figure 3.4. Continued.

upper section that needs to be repaired. Rather than spend $200.00 to repair a very old instrument, it is proposed that a "student line" replacement instrument be purchased. Life expectancy of the instrument is fifteen years.

Choral Risers - The choral risers presently in use were made for the choir by the 1954 industrial arts class and are very heavy and not at all portable. They also take up a great deal of storage area. The new risers will be portable and fold into a much smaller "package" for easier storage.

Concert Tuba - Bass players in the concert band must play their parts on fiberglass sousaphones. This is not an acceptable concert instrument (see attached adjudication ballot from last year's music contest). An old brass sousaphone no longer in use by the music department will be traded in on the new concert tuba.

MUSIC LIBRARY

Marching Band - Commercially arranged music for marching band costs $25-50 per arrangement and four tunes are needed for a marching show.

Concert Band - The cost of new music for concert band has risen to between $40-100 for each composition. To cut costs in this line-item, much of the concert band music for 1987-88 will be borrowed from other schools.

Choir - Similar increases in costs have affected the purchase of choral music. Single copies of choral music average $0.85-$1.00.

Figure 3.4. Continued.

The choirs will perform nearly thirty pieces of music annually and will borrow music and rely on present library holding to hold the line on costs next year.

Small Ensemble - The basis for success in many music programs is the level of activity in small choral and instrumental ensembles. The music department must begin to build music library holdings for small ensembles.

TRAVEL

Student - Music contest and All-State related travel remains the same as previous years. The Tri-State Band and Choral Festival has been added to the 1987-88 schedule. The festival is a one day event, and expenses include transportation and a sack lunch for the return trip.

Teacher - This year Mr. Kleff is requesting travel and per diem expenses to attend the state Music Education Conference. The conference is an important source of new musical concepts to keep music educators up-to-date. Several concerts, clinic sessions and seminars will be attended. A copy of the 1986 conference brochure is attached.

AWARDS

Traditionally awards have been made annually to high school students based on total points accumulated in association with ensemble activity. The $145.00 figure is only an estimate based on awards presented the previous year. The student themselves annually

Figure 3.4. Continued.

conduct a small fund raising campaign to support the awards system, and that amount appears in Section One under "Income."

PRINTING AND PUBLICITY

Two band and two choral concerts next year will distribute commercially printed programs. Acme Printing, Inc. has submitted the lowest bid for the work. It is felt that printed programs provide an air of professionalism to the music concerts and also provide a nice souvenir for students and parents alike. Several senior citizens have called and indicated they would have attended some music events in the past, but they were unaware of when they were scheduled. A newspaper ad preceding each concert should provide ample notice to the community of each upcoming event.

REPAIR AND MAINTENANCE

The music room piano needs to be tuned at least twice a year and the two practice room pianos require a minimum of one annual tuning. The baritone horn overhaul will extend the useful life of that instrument by ten years. The overhaul includes a new case for the instrument. All components of the school stereo system need cleaning and adjusting. The left channel on the amplifier does not work and a new cartridge is needed for the record player. Other instrument repair estimates are based on actual expenses from pre-ceding years, and considering the age and condition of most school instruments, are quite conservative.

Figure 3.4. Continued.

An increase in the rental/use fee that is charged for student use of school instruments and concert wear will have to be considered in another year. It is presently falling somewhat short of providing funds to maintain equipment.

CONTEST AND FESTIVAL FEES

Music contest and All-State audition fees remain constant from year to year. The Tri-State Festival is a new expense for 1987-88. It provides non-competitive performance experience for students in both band and choir, with adjudication by highly respected judges. It is felt that the Tri-State Festival will be a valuable educational experience for music students in the Bea Flat Public Schools.

CONTRACTUAL SERVICES

Clinician Fees - Next year university staff will be retained to spend an entire day in residency providing evaluation and constructive criticism for solo, small ensemble and large music groups. This type of individual attention by several specialists will be of great personal and collective benefit to the Bea Flat music students.

Guest Soloist - An out-of-town guest soloist will perform with the choir on the concert before Easter. The soloist will also conduct a clinic session for choral students the afternoon of the performance.

Figure 3.4. Continued.

```
                                              Section Three
                                                   Page 7

        The clinician and guest soloist expenses are included in an

Arts Council Grant proposal.  Should the grant be only partially

awarded, the remaining expenses could be paid from contingency funds.

CONCERT WEAR MAINTENANCE

        Because of the amount of use during the marching season, the

band uniforms must be cleaned in November and again at the end of the

school year.  The choir robes will be used six times during the year

and must be dry cleaned at the close of school.  This type of care

should extend the life of the garments by several years and the cost

is partially defrayed through a "use" fee which appears as part of

"Income" in Section One.

CONTINGENCY

        An allowance is requested to cover any unanticipated expenses

up to $500.00.
```

Summary

Declining tax support by school districts for music education nationwide has created the need for music educators to seek additional sources of revenue and to justify funding requests to a greater degree. The school budget process is complex and the music educator must identify and accept his or her role in that process. The music educator should be constantly alert to new avenues of financial support for the music-education program.

It is important for the music educator to be aware of the various budget procedures, to be prepared to adopt a professional budgeting approach, and to accept a leadership role in the total process.

The budget process provides an annual opportunity for program evaluation and the opportunity to justify the program. Both of these opportunities can and should be looked upon with anticipation.

Suggested Activities

1. Secure a copy of a recent music budget request from
   a. the collegiate school you attend.
   b. a local public school.
   c. the public school you attended.
   Analyze each proposal and determine the following:
   a. Budget type; is it autonomous, departmental, or split?
   b. Is the information in each document easily available? Does it read well?
   c. What are the sources of funding for each budget proposal?
2. Develop a list of questions and interview a local music educator regarding his or her
   a. greatest source of frustration involving the budget process.
   b. position on school-equipment rental/use fees.
   c. thoughts regarding a concert admission fee policy.
3. Interview a school administrator and determine his or her views as to the future direction of school district funding for music education.
4. Read and summarize three recent articles dealing with the school music budget process.
5. Visit a local music store, interview its owner/manager, and summarize pricing trends in equipment associated with music education. Compare these figures with those of ten years ago, and project costs ten years into the future. Use specific equipment items as examples.

References and Suggested Reading

Bessom, Malcom E. *Supervising the Successful School Music Program*. West Nyack, N.Y.: Parker Publishing Company, 1971.

Michaels, Kenneth L. "Twelve Ways to Get the Most out of Your Budget." *Music Educators Journal*, January 1981.

Hansen, Polly. "School Instrumental Music Budgets—Our Ninth Annual Survey." *The Instrumentalist*, August 1985.

Snyder, Keith. *School Music Administration and Supervision*, Boston: Allyn and Bacon, 1965.

_____. "The 1987 School Instrumental Music Budget Survey." *The Instrumentalist*, August 1987.

Housing and Equipment in Music Education

At some point in their teaching careers, most music educators will be called on to offer suggestions and comments on a new construction or remodeling project that will affect their music-education facilities. When this opportunity occurs, teachers should be prepared to provide qualified and knowledgeable input to school administrators, construction contractors, and even project architects. Such consultation should take place early in the planning and designing stages of such a facility, with follow-up examinations and conferences occurring during the construction process. The music educator is the individual who will be using the facility and therefore has the most valuable and practical advice to offer. Everyone associated with the construction or remodeling of any music-education complex has an obligation to consider very seriously all suggestions and recommendations offered by the professional music staff.

Music instructors themselves are often unaware that they have a role to play in the building process, and they are uninformed about where to go for the information that can make them positive contributors. Three brief cases illustrate what generally results when music specialists are not involved in construction projects.

Case number one involves the construction of a band/choral room in a small, rural high school in the upper Midwest. The room was constructed using the existing outside wall of the gymnasium as an inside wall of the new room; ceiling height was just under ten feet; and all instruments were stored in cabinets at the rear of the room, creating a tremendous traffic flow problem at the opening and close of each band rehearsal period.

Case number two concerns a beautifully constructed high-school music complex, complete with an auditorium located in close proximity to the band and choral rehearsal rooms. One small problem surfaced, however, when the seven-foot grand piano from the old choral room was moved to the new building and the door to the new choral room was only a single door. The piano had to be dismantled and moved through the door on its side.

A major university is involved in case number three. A totally new fine-arts center was recently completed in which the instrumental and choral rooms shared a common wall. After the first day that the two rooms were in simultaneous use, the major contractor was called back to add an additional wall between them. The area of "dead" space created, reduced but did not eliminate the transmission of sound between rooms. This flaw occurred in a building that cost taxpayers many millions of dollars.

Similar scenarios are repeated annually across the country. Informed music educators have an obligation to become involved in construction projects that affect their programs, and as previously mentioned, school officials and others charged with the fiscal responsibility of those projects should involve music educators as a source of information and in an advisory capacity.

The first action music teachers should take when they learn that the school district is considering some type of construction project involving music education is to secure a copy of the MENC publication by Harold P. Geerdes entitled *Planning and Equipping Music Educational Facilities.* Published in 1975, this extremely valuable book contains much of the information necessary to ensure that a well-planned and acoustically sound facility will result—a facility that gets the maximum benefit from funds available and uses the space allotted for the project most efficiently. In fact, music educators would be wise to include this book in their own personal collections or as part of the library of "how to" books that can be considered valuable reference material in the offices of many music educators.

The second action the music staff should take upon learning that they will be the benefactors of newly constructed facilities is to go to school officials and encourage them, as part of the construction contract, to acquire the services of a specialist skilled in the construction of music rooms to assist in developing plans and provide on-site consultation prior to and during the construction process. While such a specialist can be an additional up-front expense, in the long term he or she can save school districts and their taxpayers substantial "remedial" expenses, such as the construction of an additional wall between rehearsal rooms previously mentioned. The national office of the Music Educators National Conference can provide names of individuals qualified to serve as professional music-building consultants.

This chapter can be considered a checklist of ways to deal with construction specifications and equipment. It should also prevent music instructors from realizing after the fact that a new facility is too "live," too "dead," or too "small" and that the new room has a poor traffic-flow pattern, restrictive sound-transfer problems, inadequate storage, or any of a number of encumbrances that could have been prevented if they had been recognized early on and brought to the attention of responsible parties.

A later chapter will be devoted to the development of a music-education philosophy. Whatever one's philosophy may be, it can and should be a major determining factor in implementing space and equipment requests that relate to the new construction of music-education facilities.

Planning for music-room construction involves a keen awareness of many factors such as room acoustics, facility layout, size, ceiling height, isolation of sound, noise control, lighting, and ventilation. The goal of any construction project involving tax dollars is generally to meet high performance standards with a limited construction budget. What follows is an attempt to aid music educators in their efforts to meet those high performance standards.

Space and Floor-Design Requirements

Rehearsal rooms

Space requirements for music rooms generally vary according to the educational level of the facility; however, a general figure of twenty square feet of floor space for each instrumentalist and fifteen square feet of floor space for each choral student can be used as minimum requirements for instrumental and choral music rehearsal rooms. This space, of course, is in addition to all space covered by cabinets, pianos, podium, and so on. Some publications recommend higher square footage requirements for music rooms than those listed above, but none list lower figures. Music teachers are strongly urged to plan for future growth. Buildings outlast students, teachers, and even theories of education.

Ceiling height should be an area of great concern when planning rehearsal rooms. The general consensus of opinion suggests a minimum height of twelve feet for music-rehearsal-room ceilings, but fourteen to sixteen feet is more desirable. A recent school of thought recommends that rooms requiring a high sound-power level have a ceiling height of twenty-four feet. A "sub ceiling" of acoustical panels "drops" the ceiling to the twelve- to sixteen-foot level. The "dropped" ceiling is suspended from the twenty-four-foot ceiling and not attached to the walls. This arrangement allows the room to comfortably accommodate a large volume of sound and still not inhibit the "hearing" requirements of the room. What is most desirable is a high *sound-power* level as opposed to a high *noise* level. Too many instrumental music rehearsal rooms in this country have too high a noise level; over a period of time music educators teaching in such rooms may suffer some degree of hearing loss. This aspect of music rooms will be discussed in greater detail in the acoustics section of this chapter.

Floor design

It is the consensus of opinion of acoustics specialists who deal with music-rehearsal-room construction that such rooms should be somewhat rectangular in shape with no parallel walls. This is a floor-plan consideration. An equally important decision must be made regarding the physical design of the floor in music rehearsal rooms. Three basic options are available to music-facility designers: (1) flat floor, (2) built-in risers, (3) excavated risers.

Most choral and instrumental rehearsal rooms constructed in the 1950s and 1960s had risers built into the floor plan. More recently, however, music rooms with flat floors have begun to appeal to music educators and administrators alike because of the obvious flexibility of the rooms. It is now quite common to see instrumental music rehearsal rooms with flat floors and portable risers.

The practicality of portable risers is quite evident. For example, an extremely high percentage of instrumental ensembles that rehearse on risers in this country perform concerts without the benefit of risers. It is somewhat of a mystery why band and orchestra directors perform in a seating configuration different from the one in which they rehearse. If a music room is constructed with a flat floor and portable risers are installed, those risers can be moved out of the rehearsal room into a performance area, allowing students to perform in an arrangement identical to the rehearsal seating arrangement. Figure 4.1 shows an example of an instrumental rehearsal room with portable risers.

More and more college and professional performing organizations have abandoned the use of risers in both rehearsal and performance settings. In this way, they can maintain their seating arrangement as they move from the rehearsal room to a single-level performance area.

Choral rehearsal rooms continue to contain some type of built-in risers. This practice is easily justified in that choral groups, almost without question, always perform on standing risers. This author would carry the design of choral rehearsal rooms one step further to include enough floor space for portable risers to be set up on a semipermanent basis; this way, a choir could move from their seated choral risers to standing risers that would more accurately simulate performance conditions.

Permanent risers can be built at the time of construction in either of two ways. The first option is to build the risers up from the existing floor line, which is the level at which students enter the room and the level at which the instructor conducts rehearsals. Such a floor plan requires percussion instruments to be moved up and down the risers before and following each performance. The piano, however, can be easily moved around the room and even moved from the room with a limited amount of effort. Ceiling height is a major consideration when planning this type of built-in riser. For proper sound control, the ceiling should be a minimum of eight feet above the heads of those students seated on the top riser. Figure 4.2 is a cutaway drawing representing built-in risers designed from existing floor level.

Figure 4.1. Rehearsal room with portable risers.

Figure 4.2. Permanent risers constructed from existing floor line.

The second option available to music educators and music-room de-signers is one in which risers are "excavated" from the level of the existing hallway and the level at which students enter the room. In other words, the director and those students who sit in the first row descend three or four steps to the "main floor" level of the room. Percussion instruments are on the top level of the rehearsal area but remain at door and hallway level, which makes it easy to transport them to and from the performance area. Figure 4.3 is a cutaway drawing of risers excavated from the level at which students enter the room.

Figure 4.4 is a photo of an instrumental music rehearsal room with excavated permanent risers. Architects often find it advantageous to use the excavation method to construct permanent risers because that method

Figure 4.3. Permanent risers excavated from existing floor line.

Figure 4.4. Rehearsal room with excavated permanent risers.

provides additional ceiling room without disrupting the outside roof line of the project.

Specifications for built-in risers vary from choral to instrumental rehearsal rooms. Risers in both instrumental and choral rooms should be six to eight inches in height. Choral risers should be a minimum of thirty inches and more ideally thirty-six inches in depth, and risers designed for instrumental groups vary from forty-eight to sixty inches deep. The top riser in both choral and instrumental rehearsal rooms should range from seventy-two to 120 inches in depth to allow for easier movement and additional equipment needs.

One last thought when determining whether or not to include risers in the new construction of music rehearsal rooms: Music educators are advised to visit schools both with and without permanent risers. Administrators and designers should use the resulting comments in making construction decisions. Also, whether permanent risers are installed or not, a set of portable risers and storage for those risers should be included as part of the cost of building and equipping the facility.

Planning a Music Department

Sound containment, traffic flow, location of rooms, access to performance area, practice rooms, auxiliary music rooms, and storage space are but a few of the considerations facing anyone involved in laying out a music facility.

The following guidelines are offered to assist music educators and building designers in this effort.

Sound containment and isolation. Music rehearsal rooms should be located in a part of the school where rehearsal sounds will not interfere with other academic classes. Rehearsal rooms should not be placed contiguous to one another. Use corridors and storage rooms as sound isolators whenever possible.

Some type of dead space between hallway doors and outside rehearsal-room doors should be planned. Figure 4.5 is a simple drawing of a sample "sound lock." An entry plan including some type of sound lock will go a long way toward reducing the amount of rehearsal sound that reaches the corridor outside a rehearsal room.

All walls, not just the major supporting walls, should extend to the roof deck. If this practice is not observed, sound can travel from room to room through the false ceilings. All joints and wall penetration by pipes, wires, and duct work require special sealant consideration. Electrical outlets should not be placed back to back from one room to another and all doors should possess acoustically treated seals that inhibit sound transfer.

Practice rooms. One of the most serious and consistent errors in music-facility design is the location of practice rooms. Practice rooms should

Figure 4.5. Sound-lock example.

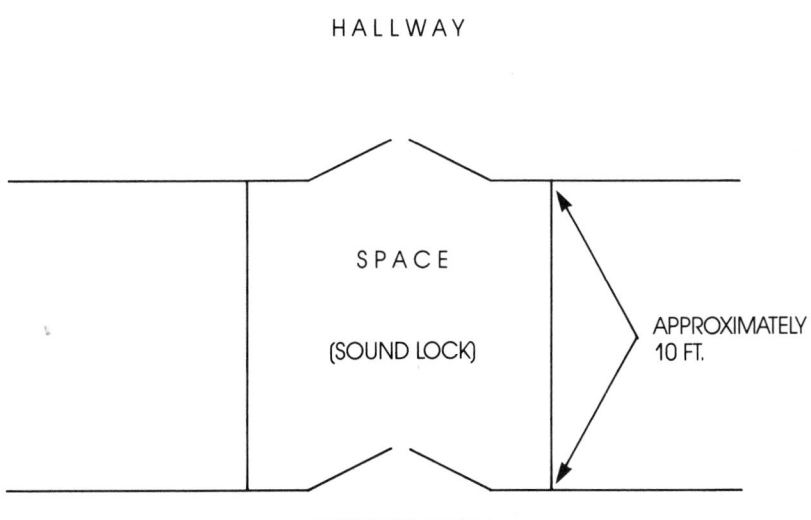

HALLWAY

SPACE

(SOUND LOCK)

APPROXIMATELY
10 FT.

REHEARSAL ROOM

simply not be placed in a location that requires students to pass through a rehearsal room to gain access to them. Such location of practice rooms limits their use in that students are unlikely to make use of those rooms when a large ensemble rehearsal is taking place, and if they do choose to use them, they will probably distract—and be distracted by—the group in the rehearsal room. Also, any time the rehearsal room is locked, student access to the practice rooms is restricted.

Another major concern in practice-room location is access to student-instrument storage. For this reason it may be best to place practice rooms on a corridor outside the rehearsal room or between rehearsal rooms with a short hallway providing access from the main corridor. In short, the two principal considerations in the location of music practice rooms is that they not be located inside the rehearsal room, but rather situated for easy student access, and that student instrument storage or lockers be accessible from the practice room area.

How many practice rooms should be included in a construction project? To determine this, one must look at the number of students who will be making use of these facilities. At the very least, there should be one practice room for every forty music students. More preferable would be one practice room for every twenty music students. Please bear in mind that these figures should be based on *projected* enrollment in the music program, not the enrollment figures at the time of construction.

The size of practice rooms should vary. Sixty square feet is sufficient for a single practice room and 140 square feet is adequate for small ensembles with a pianist. Each room should have at least two electrical outlets and a mirror. A window should be in each acoustically treated practice-room door. Some newly constructed facilities include intercom systems between the practice area and directors' offices to monitor student practice.

The use of factory-made practice rooms (Figure 4.6), while perhaps more expensive than contractor-constructed rooms, guarantees the highest degree of sound insulation and can make a "phase-in" purchase plan practical. Such units also add a degree of flexibility, since unit relocation is always possible.

The music library. If possible, the music collection should be located in a room separate from the rehearsal rooms rather than placed on shelves or filing cabinets against a rehearsal-room wall. An orchestra, a choir, and a band can all utilize a single library room within a music complex, and it is important to have the library adjacent to the rehearsal rooms. Far too often the music library is a construction afterthought, and shelves or file cabinets are placed in a practice room to house the department's music-library holdings. Such a situation prohibits the use of proper sorting, cataloging, and filing equipment and makes a newly constructed facility inadequate before a single note is sounded within its walls.

Figure 4.6. A corridor of prefabricated, factory-made practice rooms.

Space should be included in the library room for cabinets or shelving for all music, a sorting rack, work tables, a desk, and a supply cabinet. A minimum of 300 square feet should be allowed for a music library that will house combined choral/instrumental music holdings.

Uniform/concert-wear storage. Again, if at all possible, a separate room for storing uniforms and concert wear should be included in the design of a new music facility. The room should be cedar-lined for moth protection, have a door that opens to an outside corridor, and be large enough to comfortably house garments based on future enrollment figures. It is unfortunately a rare case when uniforms and other concert wear—which may cost tens of thousands of dollars—are allowed adequate storage space.

Some schools require that uniforms and concert wear be left at school. This practice requires students to change clothes prior to and following each performance. If this is the policy in a given school, dressing facilities need to be available for both sexes. It is ludicrous to think that the garments receive less wear and tear and are more secure if left at school when students are forced to change in small, general restroom areas. In such settings garments are draped over sinks and/or placed on the floor because there are no hangers. All uniforms and formal concert wear should be placed in the hands of students during the school year unless adequate dressing rooms are provided.

Another, but less attractive, storage option for uniforms and concert wear is built-in storage cabinets along one wall of the rehearsal room. This type of storage is less secure than an independent room, and, with the numerous uniform pieces generally part of today's marching-band uniforms, a large amount of cabinet space is required. Such storage could usurp valuable rehearsal floor space.

Instrument storage. The minimum space requirement for an instrument storage room is 600 square feet. This room should be located near the entrance to the instrumental-music rehearsal room and should have two sets of doors that provide good traffic flow to and from the rehearsal room. Ideally, this room should house instruments presently in the hands of students, whether they be personal or school-owned instruments.

There is a wide variety of instrumental storage options available to the music-facility designer. Commercially made wooden or metal storage cabinets are one option. Built-in open "pigeon hole" type of storage is perhaps the most economical to construct, but it could be expensive over the long term because of security problems. One good option is a commercially produced locker/cabinet with a grill front made of steel. This model allows air to circulate and provides visual access to a locked storage space. Music educators are encouraged to explore catalogs from music-storage suppliers to determine style and cost prior to meeting with school officials and/or the building designer or architect.

All school-owned instruments not checked out to students, as well as seasonal equipment, such as marching percussion, sousaphones, marching brass, and swing choir props, can be housed in a general, separate instrument-storage room. A suggested location for this room is in the back of the instrumental rehearsal room, near the area where concert percussion instruments are stationed.

Instrument repair room. To some music-room designers, an instrument repair room may appear to be an unnecessary frill. But instrumental music educators can hardly expect students to learn to keep their instruments clean and in good repair if the basic facilities to do so are not provided. A small room, adjacent to the band director's office, with emergency repair equipment, a workbench with a vice, and a large steel sink to clean and flush brass instruments is a minimum requisite. A room designated for the proper care and repair of student and school-owned instruments is simply a sound investment on the part of the school district.

Office space. Separate office space for orchestra, band, and choral instructors is highly desirable. The offices should be contiguous to the directors' respective rehearsal areas. Music office space and equipment vary depending on the size of the school and the music program. The office space need not be overly large, unless it will also serve as a teaching studio, or music library, or instrument repair room, or all of the above. A pleasant office for music educators charged with the responsibility of administering any portion of a music-education program should be a priority in the design of any music-education facility.

Other Space Considerations

The previously mentioned facilities represent what should be considered a minimum standard for any newly constructed music facility. What follows are suggestions for school-district planners who wish to provide their students with optimum music-education opportunities, particularly at the secondary level.

Recording and television capabilities. Modern rehearsal rooms should possess the capability for in-house recording and closed-circuit and cable-television hookups. At the time of construction, builders can install conduit and appropriate cables leading to a separate control room or a room adjacent to the rehearsal room, such as a music library/control room. The services of an audio engineer are mandatory in determining the proper location(s) of microphone outlets in each rehearsal room.

Piano classroom. The most modern public-school music complexes provide a room designed for class instruction in piano, complete with a minimum of eight student electronic keyboards and a teacher instruction and control station (see Figure 4.7). Numerous electrical outlets must be carefully planned as part of a class piano room. Full-size keyboard synthesizers are now moderately enough priced to make class keyboard instruction in public schools worthy of serious consideration.

Figure 4.7. The class piano room at Corona del Sol High School, Tempe, Arizona.

Auxiliary classroom. Music classrooms designed for teaching music theory and/or appreciation, as well as separate guitar classrooms, have been included in contemporary music-education facilities at both elementary, junior-high, and secondary levels. These rooms need not be overly large and may possess ceilings of normal classroom height. A music listening room can also be considered for large school districts. It is this author's belief, however, that music listening stations and appropriate recordings should be housed in the school library or resource center, where use of the equipment can be supervised on a full-time basis.

Auxiliary storage. Ideally, a separate room designed simply as "miscellaneous storage" can be a valuable asset to any music facility. Anyone visiting public-school music programs around the country is likely to find many instances of valuable practice-room space being used to store miscellaneous items. An auxiliary storage room can be a valuable buffer for future growth of a music-education program.

Orchestra rehearsal room. Funds permitting, a separate orchestra rehearsal room should be included in the design of a music complex. Recent studies indicate that orchestra rooms require less reverberation time than band rooms. The floor damage from cello pegs, the need for greater riser width, and the installation of oversized-instrument storage cabinets are just several of the special considerations that should be made when separate rehearsal areas are planned for orchestras.

Other Construction Considerations

Acoustics. Most music rehearsal rooms should have a reverberation time of between 1.50 and 2.00 seconds. Choral rooms should generally be more "live" than instrumental rooms. Multipurpose music rehearsal rooms should possess acoustical "tuning" capabilities to "deaden" or "liven" the room, depending on the type and size of the ensemble presently rehearsing. This can be accomplished in a most economical way by hanging floor-to-ceiling pull-type drapes on one or more walls.

It has become quite popular to carpet rehearsal rooms, particularly band rooms. Music educators need only ask themselves one question when determining whether or not to carpet a rehearsal area: "We don't perform on carpet, so why rehearse on carpet?" There are numerous alternative means of acoustically treating a rehearsal area other than installing permanent, inflexible acoustic material in the form of carpet. Granted, carpet is pleasing to the eye and provides a "warm" atmosphere; however, the lack of acoustical flexibility makes it a questionable design option.

Many music educators, particularly band directors, have been diagnosed as suffering from job-related hearing loss of a permanent nature. In many cases, these band directors had been rehearsing their ensembles for years in architecturally aesthetic acoustical nightmares; for example, in rooms where sound-absorbent material was covered with hard enamel paint.

Any instrumental rehearsal room should be planned to the specifications of a professional acoustician to provide a rehearsal setting in which a high sound-power level is possible without a "loud noise" level. Continuous exposure to a noise level of 85dB (decibels, the unit for measuring loudness) can cause permanent hearing loss. Many large bands produce 85dB at a piano dynamic level. Imagine the decibel level produced by a large pep or marching band. The sound-power capability of an instrumental rehearsal room should be of utmost concern to music educators, school administrators, engineers, architects, and contractors. Music educators are strongly urged to share "The Not-So-Silent Menace," an article by Ed Solomon about hearing loss, with any individual who is ultimately responsible for designing or approving new music rehearsal areas.[1]

Lighting. A combination of artificial light and natural light is most desirable for music rooms. Either an easterly or westerly exposure is considered to be the most advantageous source of natural light. Fluorescent lighting appears to be the most satisfactory for rehearsal rooms. Type A ballasts should be specified for music-room lighting fixtures because they are considerably less noisy than the less-expensive Type B ballasts.

Outside entrance doors. A music rehearsal room should have a direct exit door in order to move directly to and from the room for outside rehearsals and for the easy loading and unloading of equipment. A small loading dock with vehicle access is certainly not out of the question. An outside entrance door also makes entry for evening rehearsals and concerts more convenient.

Heating and ventilation. Air-exchange capabilities in music facilities are often inadequate, and the equipment responsible for heating and circulating room air is frequently too noisy. All ducts supplying and returning air from music rehearsal and practice rooms should be lined with fireproof, sound-absorbing material and contain baffles to prevent unwanted transmission of sound. The desirable range for humidity is between 20 and 60 percent; humidity control should be a specific requirement in building plans.

General Music Considerations

General music-education needs differ from music-education performance needs in that general music classes can be and often are taught in regular academic classrooms. By and large, the ceiling height and acoustical treatment are not as critical for the general music classroom, but room size is most certainly an important consideration. Ten square feet of floor space for each student in the room can be considered a minimum. Ample storage space for the multitude of books, recorders, ukuleles, guitars, autoharps, Orff instruments, and similar critically important general-music teaching aids should be of prime concern in designing an area specifically for general music classes.

Relatively soundproof areas for individualized instruction and computer use are certainly not to be considered a luxury in the contemporary music-education classroom.

A good stereo playback system, complete with turntable, compact-disc player, double cassette deck, high-quality speakers and remote control should be an equipment goal of every elementary and junior-high general music educator. Such a unit can perhaps be purchased with student-activity-fund assistance if the music educator is willing to allow the equipment to be used for an occasional school function.

A small room adjacent to the music-education room can serve as a storage area for project props, musical-instrument projects, and instructional materials and supplies that are used on an infrequent basis. Special cabinet space should be available for audio- and videocassette tapes, slides, filmstrips, and a record library. Because of the wide variety of activities involving movement from standing to sitting on the floor, a carpet for general-music-education rooms is preferred by many music educators.

A good quality piano with a cover, a lined chalkboard, a permanent projection screen, filmstrips, slide and overhead projectors, along with an in-residence videotape machine and monitor complete the housing and equipment needs of a modern general music classroom.

Your author admits to a degree of idealism when describing general music equipment plans, but he has seen music-education classrooms similarly equipped and the quality and variety of musical experiences available to young music students in such situations is indeed impressive.

Model Music Facilities

Three floor plans of music-education facilities follow. Figures 4.8 and 4.9 are offered not as outstanding examples of architectural design but as examples of floor-space allocations based on information included in this chapter. Figure 4.10 is included as a model of contemporary music-education facilities at the secondary level; this design is presently in use at Corona del Sol Senior High School in Tempe, Arizona. The only major shortcoming of the Corona del Sol complex is the size of the choral rehearsal room, which possesses approximately 1,000 square feet of floor space.

Suggested Activities

1. Design a music complex that can house a one-hundred piece band, an eighty-voice choir, and a sixty-piece orchestra. Incorporate the space and design requirements included in this chapter. Use graph paper and employ a scale of one inch per ten feet. Include cutaway views.
2. Design a one-rehearsal-room music complex with a rehearsal room, a music library, practice rooms, an office, an instrument storage room, and a uniform/concert-wear storage area. Incorporate the space and design requirements included in this chapter. Use graph paper and employ a scale of one inch per ten feet. Include cutaway views.
3. Invite a university physics professor to class to discuss "sound-power level" and "noise level," as well as implications of reverberation time as it relates to acoustics. Prepare a list of discussion questions in advance.
4. Interview a local music educator and report to the class on what facility and equipment strengths and weaknesses that individual sees in his or her present teaching situation.

Figure 4.8. A one- or two-teacher music facility with a single rehearsal room.

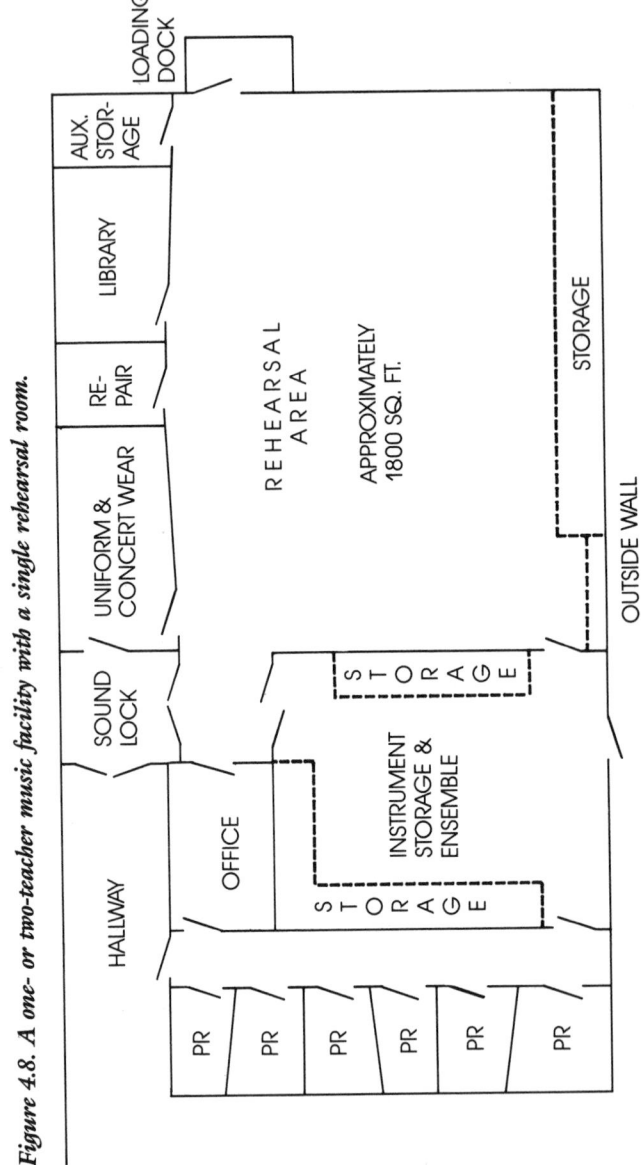

Figure 4.9. A two-room, two-teacher music-education complex.

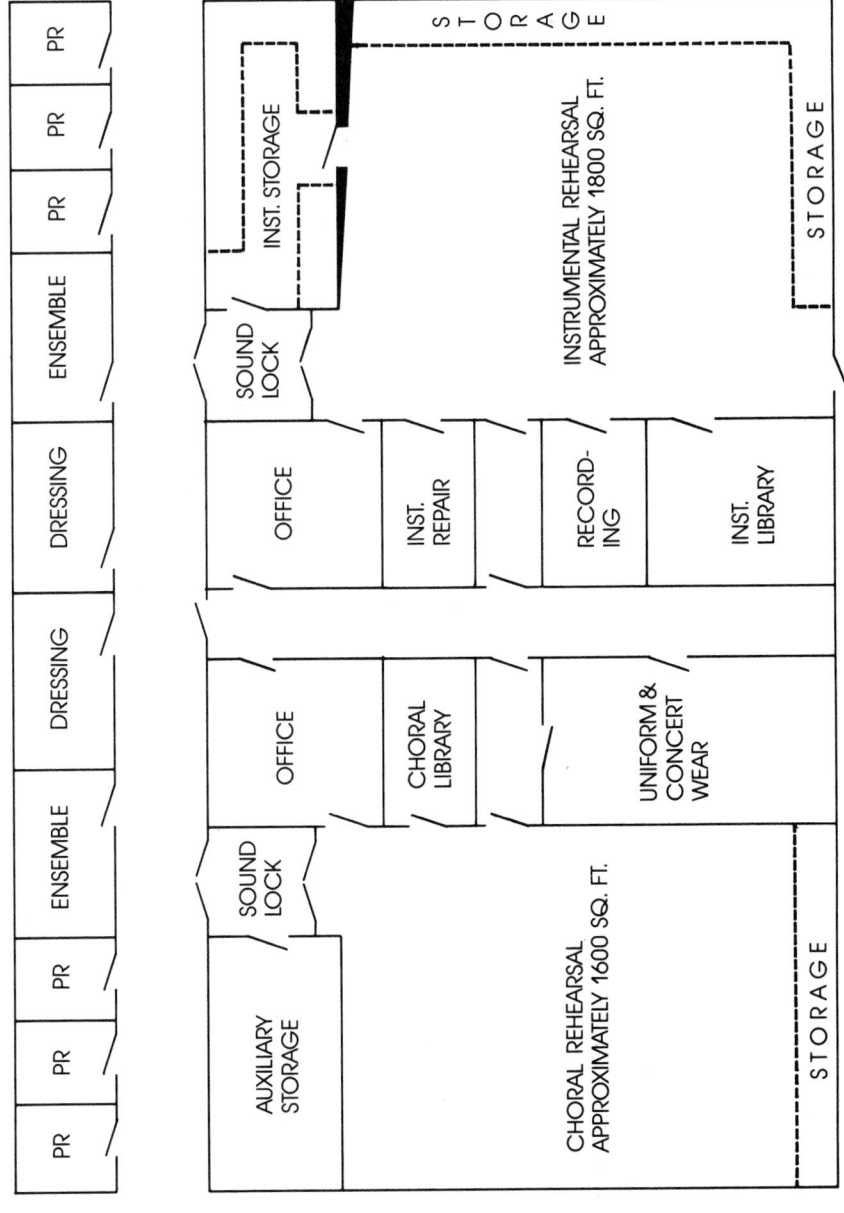

Figure 4.10. Floor plan of music complex at Corona del Sol Senior High School, Tempe, Arizona.

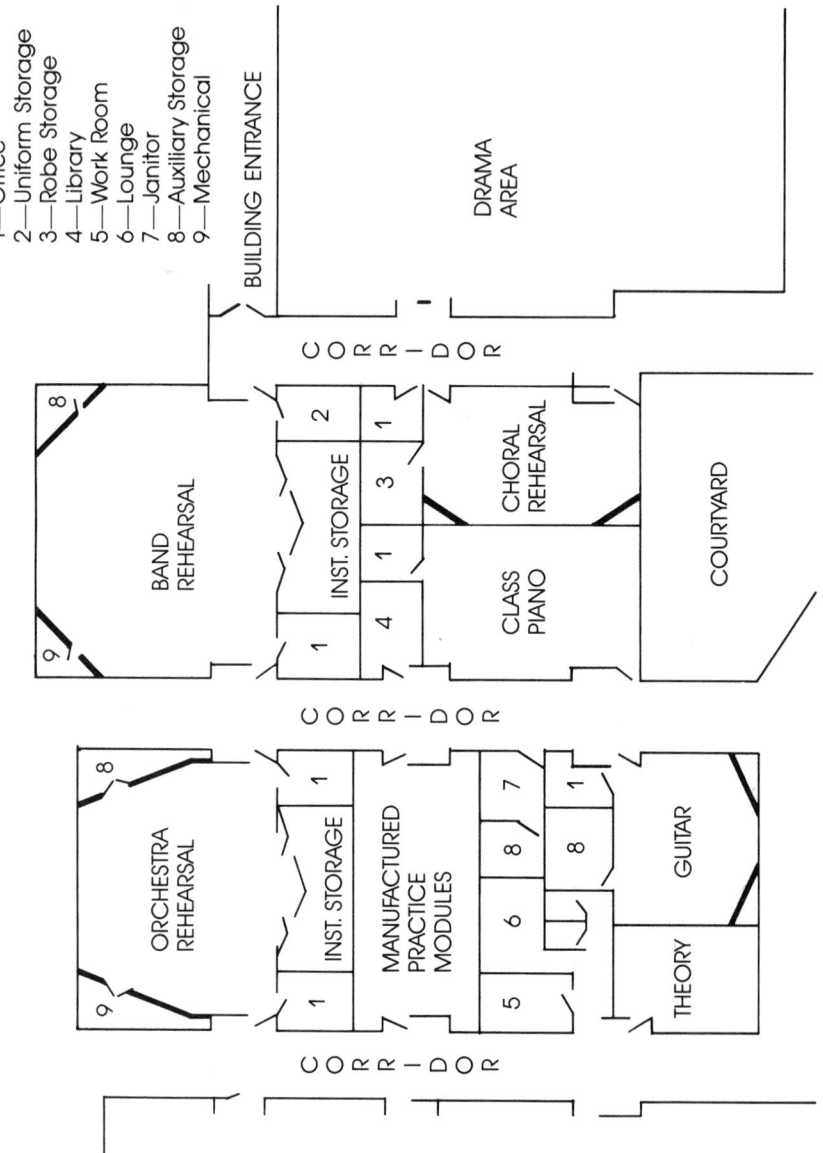

1—Office
2—Uniform Storage
3—Robe Storage
4—Library
5—Work Room
6—Lounge
7—Janitor
8—Auxiliary Storage
9—Mechanical

Summary

Across this country dedicated music educators have been "making do" for years with facilities and equipment far less adequate, on a comparative basis, than those provided for sports, drama, home economics, or science. They continue to teach instrumental lessons in broom closets, rehearse ensembles in school lunchrooms, push carts with general-music teaching aids from elementary classroom to elementary classroom, and perform concerts in dimly lit gymnasiums with risers made by the local shop class. Fortunate indeed are those music educators who teach in quality, well-equipped facilities.

The housing and equipment plans presented in this chapter can and should be the goal of every music teacher. A music-education program must prove itself, however, to be a valuable part of the total curriculum before new facilities and equipment can be justified. Once the importance of the music program is recognized and new facilities are planned, music educators must seek outside professional assistance through personal contact, seminars, and printed material so that they can give informed advice to the project designer. Music teachers are urged to encourage a visit by school administrators and board members to a nearby school with outstanding music-education facilities prior to finalizing any construction plans. School board members, a number of whom are likely to have children involved in the music program, often respond to a comparison with a neighboring school that supports its music program with high-quality equipment and well-designed facilities. Careful planning by qualified experts can avoid the "Pay me now or pay me later!" syndrome by eliminating the need to make costly remedial improvements in *new* construction.

Music educators should attempt to get as much cupboard space, audio and visual equipment, and other instruction aids "built into" the cost of any construction project. If not, they could find themselves in a new facility with old and inadequate instructional materials. A case in point here is the purchase of portable risers if permanent risers are to be built into a new rehearsal room. Music educators who are apt to benefit from new facilities are reminded that it is almost impossible to include too much storage space in the facility design.

Room acoustics and sound control can be considered the most important aspect of any remodeling or new construction. An acoustical specialist should be involved in the planning and design of any project from the outset. Continuous exposure to high noise levels can be a very exhausting experience, as well as bring about permanent hearing loss. The cost of hiring an acoustics consultant to minimize fatigue and health problems in a rehearsal setting can be considered negligible when compared with the long-term gain through increased instructor efficiency and longevity.

Please refer to the "Suggested Reading" at the close of this chapter for a current list of informational sources relating to existing music facilities and facilities that are soon to be constructed. The reader will find the MENC publications particularly helpful.

References and Suggested Reading

ASBDA. *The ASBDA Curriculum Guide*. Pittsburgh: Volkwein Brothers, 1973.

Gary, Charles, ed. *Music Buildings, Rooms and Equipment*. Reston, Va.: Music Educators National Conference, 1966.

Geerdes, Harold P. "Acoustics and the Music Director." *The School Musician*, March 1974.

———. "Adjustable Acoustics in Music Performance." *Music Educators Journal*, April 1975.

———. *Planning and Equipping Music Educational Facilities*. Reston Va.: Music Educators National Conference, 1975.

MENC. *The School Music Program: Description and Standards*. Reston, Va.: Music Educators National Conference, 1986.

Mills, Donn Lawrence. "NSOA: Rehearsal Rooms." *The Instrumentalist*, April 1979.

Snyder, Keith D. *School Music Administration and Supervision*. Boston: Allyn and Bacon, 1965.

Solomon, Ed. "The Not-So-Silent Menace." *The Instrumentalist*, October 1986.

Weerts, Richard. "Building Proper Instrumental Facilities." *Music Journal*, February 1972.

Scheduling and the Music Educator

It is not unusual for music educators to begin their teaching careers unaware of the influence that scheduling can have on the music-education program in their new schools. They also generally do not understand how the educational scheduling process works. In addition to possessing some degree of awareness of the different types of school schedules and the resulting effects on music programs, music educators must also be prepared to discuss scheduling options with administrators and be willing to make recommendations in support of those programs.

The goal of this chapter is to explain the scheduling process as it relates to music education and present methods of promoting scheduling conditions favorable to the music program. The music educator's personal schedule and the annual scheduling of events for the entire school will be discussed as well. The variety of ways in which one scheduling process or another affects a young music educator's early teaching life and the manner in which that educator reacts to those processes can serve as an indicator of his or her future success in the music-education profession.

Since the 1950s, scheduling classes in public school has become increasingly difficult, and the techniques associated with scheduling have changed frequently and dramatically, somewhat in keeping with national priorities. Increased school enrollments in the late 1950s and early 1960s created unusual demands on school administrators, which resulted in creative and innovative scheduling techniques. Other influences on academic class scheduling included an increased tendency toward emphasis on core courses for college preparation purposes, a need for school administrators to pay greater attention to staff desires, and an extension of work-related school experiences or vocational programs. The most prodigious influence, however, was the wide and rapid proliferation of course offerings. Particularly at the high-school level, students in today's schools have a vast array of academic and activity-oriented offerings from which to choose. That academic variety, along with the increased trend of youth of this country to pursue a college preparatory educational track, has forced music educators to defend the curricular importance of their programs, as well as to devise creative manners in which to ensure that those programs are included in the curriculum.

The most important influence on scheduling innovations has been the advancement in computer technology. Approaches to scheduling that had previously been too time-consuming or were considered to be impossible before the computer have become relatively simple and expedient. Any administrator failing to make use of computer technology when satisfying contemporary scheduling demands is failing to meet adequately the individual learning needs of his or her students.

Knowledge of the scheduling process is one of the most important educational tools at the disposal of administrators, as well as involved music educators. The school schedule manifests the educational philosophy of the community, the school, and its administrative staff. If a school administrator is convinced of the importance of music education in developing the lives of the children in his or her school, music will continue to remain a part of the daily school schedule. If an administrator views music education as a frill or as an extracurricular school activity, music offerings are likely to be placed before or after the school day or scheduled at a time during the day which limits participation by a large number of students. There is no school administrator in the United States who will fail to find an advantageous spot on an academic schedule for a program in which he or she strongly believes.

If the philosophy of a school is traditional, the schedule of that school will likely be conventional. Conversely, if a school's philosophy is nontraditional, its class schedule is apt to be flexible or individualized. In either case, the quality of the schedule—and the type of educational experiences provided for students—is a direct reflection of the competence and experience of the building principal, as well as the total school administration. The construction of the school schedule is considered by many educators to be the supreme test of administrative and managerial skills.[1] By the same token, what a music educator does with the amount of time provided in the academic schedule is indicative of the administrative and organizational abilities possessed by that educator. Too many teachers use lack of time as an excuse for inadequate music instruction. Much can be accomplished by a dedicated, creative and well-organized music educator in as little as one class period per week.

Understanding the Terminology

There is some disagreement among educators about the definition of a variety of terms associated with scheduling. For the purpose of clarity and consistency, an explanation of several frequently used terms follows.

Schedule. Academic scheduling may be defined as the organization of time, facilities, and personnel to meet the needs of the children for whom the school is educationally responsible. Quite simply, the schedule is a school's blueprint for present and future action, reflecting directly the educational philosophy that is promoted there. Richard A. Dempsey and Henry P. Traverso define a school's schedule as "a program and time design bringing students, teachers, curriculum, materials and space into a systematic arrangement for the purpose of creating an optimal learning climate."[2] The school schedule establishes the means through which instructional goals can be achieved and is a strong indicator of the knowledge a principal has of his or her staff. A wise administrator does not schedule beyond the educational and instructional competency limits of available staff.

Conventional/traditional schedule. These two terms are used interchangeably in referring to a scheduling style. In this chapter, a conventional or traditional schedule is one that presents classes in the same order on a daily or weekly basis. Class periods are generally of a standard length and each class likely meets for the same number of minutes, regardless of the subject matter.

Flexible schedule. The term "flexible schedule" has become widely used to suggest a departure from conventional scheduling. Numerous schools in the United States have described any change, no matter how small, from the conventional or traditional method of scheduling classes as a flexible schedule. The result has been a degree of chaos in understanding what is actually happening in a particular school.

In the truest sense, the term "flexible schedule" is based on the view that each day's class order in a school schedule need not be like any other day of the week. As originally established, flexible scheduling called for classes of varying sizes within and between courses, provided for the meeting of instructional groups at varying frequencies and for varying lengths, promoted team teaching in any content area, and required countless professional decisions by teachers about students, course content, and teaching methods.[3]

In this chapter, any schedule that has been modified in such a manner as to provide curriculum opportunities other than those normally available in a conventional schedule can be labeled "flexible."

Modular scheduling. In modular scheduling, the school day is divided into ten- to twenty-five-minute modules or "mods," and an administratively prescribed number of mods are assigned to all classes and activities within the school. Class length is thus determined by what is being taught. Students are not in formal class arrangements or study halls and an opportunity is provided for students to involve themselves in independent study. The modular schedule generally repeats itself every five or six days rather than the more structured daily pattern of the conventional schedule.

Properly constructed and implemented, a modular schedule must certainly be considered a flexible schedule; however, a flexible schedule need not be necessarily modular in construction. Readers are cautioned to make this distinction. Far too often, unknowledgeable educators fail to distinguish between flexible and modular scheduling.

Individualized instruction. Music educators have been involved in individualized instruction for many, many years through their work with students in private and group lessons, as well as small and large performance ensembles. The concept behind this type of flexible scheduling is that individual students—with their unique capabilities, interests, and backgrounds—can best develop the full measure of their talents in a program fitted to their needs. Many educators feel that individualized instruction makes a better use of students' time. Students do not study what they already know, nor do they suffer from the gaps of understanding or knowledge that may develop in a large group and can inhibit a student's educational progress.[4]

Conventional Scheduling

The basic traditional schedule remains popular and is still used in the majority of secondary schools today. The simplicity of the conventional or traditional schedule is a most attractive ingredient for school administrators, many of whom after experimenting with other models return to the traditional schedule model—both for its simplicity and uncontroversial character.

Please note in Figure 5.1 that each period and each day of the traditional schedule is exactly like the preceding one. (Letters of the alphabet that appear as part of the following schedules simply represent hypothetical academic classes.) Its basic flaw is the limitation placed on the adoption of new programs or courses into the schedule. In schools where curriculum offerings have increased dramatically and the traditional scheduling model has been retained, music offerings, particularly band, are likely to be found outside of what is considered to be the normal school day. Vocal music very likely has been or will be relegated to a schedule involving the lunch period in some way.

Figure 5.1. Traditional schedule.

Period	Monday	Tuesday	Wednesday	Thursday	Friday
1	A	A	A	A	A
2	B	B	B	B	B
3	C	C	C	C	C
4	Lunch	Lunch	Lunch	Lunch	Lunch
5	D	D	D	D	D
6	E	E	E	E	E
7	F	F	F	F	F

Of all the scheduling models available to administrators today, the traditional schedule in its truest form is the least favorable for music education because of the number of classes and activity conflicts it causes.

Mosaic method

The *mosaic method* of traditionally scheduling classes is frequently used in secondary schools of 750 students or less. Any subject may be scheduled at any time and changes from one period to another are often based on a need to resolve program conflicts. An example of how a traditional mosaic schedule might appear is indicated in Figure 5.2. This method might well be called the "experience" method because it depends on the experience and intuition of the schedule maker to place courses in such a position that a minimum of conflicts appear. The mosaic method holds some advantages for music over the strict traditional schedule as it appears in Figure 5.1 because the possibility does exist to remove or reduce schedule conflicts between music courses and other courses appearing on the schedule. Student registration cards are tallied and those courses that conflict are scheduled in different periods. The computer generally serves as a source of conflict resolution, and that in itself can be of great assistance in removing schedule conflicts with music courses. However, techniques that group students by ability are generally lacking in the mosaic scheduling method.

Block method

The *block method*, which is used less frequently by school administrators than the purely conventional and mosaic methods, is offered mostly in small

Figure 5.2. Traditional schedule involving the mosaic method.

Period	Monday	Tuesday	Wednesday	Thursday	Friday
1	A	B	A	B	A
2	B	A	B	A	B
3	C	FREE	Lunch	E	C
4	Lunch	Lunch	E	FREE	Lunch
5	D	E	D	Lunch	D
6	E	C	C	C	E
7	F	F	F	F	F

Figure 5.3. Block schedule for four periods of a traditional schedule.

PERIOD	Block 1	Block 2	Block 3	Block 4
1	Social Studies	English	Mathe-matics	General Science
2	English	Social Studies	General Science	Mathe-matics
3	Mathe-matics	General Science	Social Studies	English
4	General Science	Mathe-matics	English	Social Studies

high schools and junior-high or middle schools where large numbers of students follow the same curriculum pattern and can easily be grouped into "blocks." Any number of pupils can be divided into nonconflicting schedule blocks. For example, a hundred students could be divided into twenty-five member blocks or sections, with all students taking the same subjects, such as social studies, mathematics, English, and general science. Classes would be scheduled so that one teacher could be responsible for all four sections of English, another for all sections of social studies, and so on. See Figure 5.3.

In schools where faculty teach in more than one discipline, teachers could theoretically have the same students for both math and science for a total of two consecutive periods. They could thus retain the option of dividing the class time between the two subjects as deemed necessary.

The implications that block scheduling holds for music are quite good in that rehearsal times for music groups can be scheduled during a period when all students involved in music are free from other schedule obligations. For example, all the students participating in band could be scheduled as members of Block 1 and be free to go to rehearsal during the fifth period. A schedule employing "block" techniques is much less restrictive than other traditional methods of scheduling classes. It must be remembered, however, that it is impractical to attempt to block small-enrollment, nonrequired classes.

For a description of a block schedule, team-teaching approach to required music education at the elementary level, readers are encouraged to refer to Joseph Curatilo's article "Scheduling Sanity in the Elementary Schools," in the April 1983 issue of the *Music Educators Journal.* Curatilo offers a viable solution to what is for many elementary music educators a difficult problem.

Conventional modular schedule

A large number of secondary schools call their scheduling models "modular," but the models are actually traditional schedules in modular schedule's "clothing"! For example, with very few exceptions all classes meet the same number of "mods," and the schedule is repeated on a daily basis, removing the flexibility originally intended for modular scheduling. Figure 5.4 is an indication of a modular schedule that is actually a conventional or traditional schedule. For the purpose of examination, the sample schedule consists of fifteen twenty-five minute modules. Music classes must be scheduled against multiple sections of required classes to best avoid or reduce schedule conflicts.

Other variations of traditional or conventional scheduling offer much greater scheduling choices, and they will thus appear in the next section, under "Flexible Scheduling." While it will become evident that the greater a

Figure 5.4. Conventional modular schedule.[5]

Module	Monday	Tuesday	Wednesday	Thursday	Friday
1	Algebra	Algebra	Algebra	Algebra	Algebra
2	Algebra	Algebra	Algebra	Algebra	Algebra
3	English	English	English	English	English
4	English	English	English	English	English
5	Study	P.E.	Study	P.E.	Study
6	Study	P.E.	Study	P.E.	Study
7	Sci. Lab	P.E.	Sci. Lab	P.E.	Study
8	Sci. Lab	Science	Sci. Lab	Science	Science
9	Sci. Lab	Science	Sci. Lab	Science	Science
10	Lunch	Lunch	Lunch	Lunch	Lunch
11	German	German	German	German	German
12	German	German	German	German	German
13	Study	Study	Study	Study	Study
14	History	History	History	History	History
15	History	History	History	History	History

schedule's flexibility, the more hospitable it is to music education, in reality it is not so much the type of schedule that affects the music-education program as it is the attitude and philosophy of the music educator and the people who control the process—the school administrators.

Flexible Scheduling

Perhaps no other study in the history of American education had greater impact on public-school curriculum and scheduling than did the work of James B. Conant, which took place in the late 1950s. His recommendations to improve secondary public education resulted in expanded curriculums and experimental scheduling models intended to facilitate increased curriculum demands. He stated, "All students should be urged to include art and music in their elective programs."[6] Conant felt that talented students had previously been unable to pursue a varied academic program and at the same time elect art and music in a school with a traditional six-period schedule. His study pointed out that academically talented students who did not take two or more years of art and music in high school were enrolled in schools with a six-period schedule format.[7]

Thus the demand for scheduling flexibility was created across the United States. As the schedule process became increasingly flexible, a wide proliferation of curricular offering kept pace. What follows are descriptions of the most widely used flexible-schedule options in America today. Such schedules are designed to provide appropriate course offerings for effective instruction and the flexibility to meet the individual learning needs of the students.

One thing should be understood when scheduling large music ensembles: they must receive high priority in the total scheduling process. This is not because music educators have inflated egos but because no other high-school course offering involves students from every class in the school. In a four-year high school, bands, orchestras, and choirs are likely to have as members students from all four class levels. For this reason, those ensembles cannot be successfully scheduled against single-section classes. Computer scheduling makes it a relatively simple task to give ensembles involving such a wide cross-section of student members some type of schedule priority. The extent to which this is allowed to happen in a given school is a reflection of the role music plays in the total school program.

As previously mentioned, a schedule can be flexible but not necessary based on a modular concept. Figure 5.5 indicates what such a schedule might look like. The music staff sets the specifications for ensemble time requirements in this schedule, based on their judgment as to the most effective way to meet with their students. They may decide, for example,

Figure 5.5. Flexible schedule.

Time	Monday	Tuesday	Wednesday	Thursday	Friday
8:30	A	E	A	B	A
9:30	B		F		B
					C
10:30		A			F
11:30					
	Lunch			Lunch	
12:30	C				
		Lunch	Lunch		Lunch
1:30	F	D	C	A	
					D
2:30			F		
	D	F	R	F	F

that the traditional daily large group rehearsal is less effective than three weekly meetings of the entire group and two independent rehearsals for each section per week. Again, computer scheduling allows reasonable requests for class time to be met. This type of scheduling is flexible only to the point that succeeding daily schedules do not repeat. Changes in the total five-day format are often made at the end of quarter and/or semester grading periods. The letter "F" in Figure 5.5 represents unscheduled time for independent study or enrichment purposes.

Modular schedule

Without a doubt, modular scheduling has dominated the movement toward increased flexibility in secondary-school curriculums. When applied in its strictest sense, modular scheduling is the only true flexible schedule in that it changes schedule patterns on a weekly basis as well as daily basis. Modular scheduling generates up to 40 percent of unscheduled student time for enrichment and independent study. This advantage theoretically provides music educators with an opportunity to meet individually with students on a weekly basis. Students respond favorably to independent study time, and they like the variability of the schedule because it adds a sense of adventure and freshness to the week.

Module lengths stay the same for the entire length of the schedule, and although actual mod lengths vary from ten to thirty minutes, the tendency is to use mods twenty minutes in length. It must be noted as well that as mod length increases, schedule flexibility decreases.

Modular scheduling appears to be the most advantageous for music education because of the independent study time available and because greater flexibility is possible in scheduling rehearsal time for large ensembles. A creative music educator who understands the scheduling process and a competent, sensitive, and skillful school principal, who possesses an in-depth knowledge of computer scheduling techniques, can work together to provide sophisticated and rewarding music-education experiences for all music students in their school. Figure 5.6 represents a student modular schedule with one music class involved. This schedule involves a six-day cycle that creates both daily and weekly schedule variety. The time allotted for enrichment and independent study is just over 31 percent, somewhat less than the ideal total of 40 percent for those purposes.

Rotating-period schedule

Principals who continue to use the conventional or traditional scheduling models often introduce variety and a degree of flexibility to their students' schedules by rotating or interchanging periods to add an additional class without lengthening the school day. In essence what results is a seven-period schedule in a six-period day. By dropping one class each day, so that each class meets six times in seven days, an additional class can be accommodated. In such a system, a student taking four or five major subjects is still able to participate in music and other electives. Figure 5.7 and Figure 5.8 represent examples of this innovative approach to traditional six-period scheduling. The boxes marked with X's can be used as study or activity periods.

In his study of the American high school, James B. Conant suggested that students with the special ability and interest might be wise to take music theory in place of a foreign language. The schedule diagrammed in Figure 5.7 and Figure 5.8 provide for just such an option; however, college and university regential boards across the United States are beginning to mandate foreign language as a requirement for admission to state colleges and universities. This author predicts that such a trend will not become universally accepted and that such special courses as music theory will again be widely available for the enrichment of talented musicians.

*Figure 5.6. Modular schedule: six-day cycle. (Note: *** indicates unscheduled time. The total of time allotted for music combined with unscheduled time represents a total of 31 percent independent study and enrichment time.)*

Module	Day 1	Day 2	Day 3	Day 4	Day 5	Day 6
1	English (Lg. grp)	***	History	Biology	Spanish	***
2	↓	Geometry	↓	↓	↓	***
3			↓		***	English
4	↓	↓		↓	***	↓
5	Music	Music	Music	Music	Music	Music
6		↓	↓			
7	↓			↓	↓	↓
8	Geometry	Spanish	***	History	Biology	***
9	↓	↓	Geometry	↓		***
10	Spanish	English		***		Biology
11	↓	↓	↓	***	↓	
12	***	Lunch	Lunch	***	History	↓
13	Lunch	↓	↓	Lunch		↓
14	↓	***	English	↓	↓	***
15	***	History	***	Geometry	Lunch	Lunch
16	Biology		***	↓	↓	↓
17	↓		Spanish		***	Geometry
18	↓	↓	↓	↓	English	↓
19	P.E.	***	***	***	↓	↓
20		***	P.E.	Spanish	↓	***
21		Biology Lab.			***	Spanish
22	↓			↓	Geometry	↓
23	History	↓	↓	***	↓	***
24	↓		↓	***	↓	***

Figure 5.7. A seven-period schedule in a six-period day: vertical schedule.

Period	M	T	W	Th	F
1	A	G	E	D	B
2	B	A	F	E	C
3	C	X	G	X	D
Lunch					→
4	D	B	A	F	E
5	E	C	B	G	F
6	F	D	C	A	G

Rotating activity period

Some traditional schedules have classes that meet only four out of five days a week, but without the rotational system previously indicated in Figures 5.7 and 5.8. The fifth classroom period each week is turned into an activity period that rotates through the schedule, as indicated in Figure 5.9. Such periods can be used for music, for study purposes, or for other activities as determined by the administration and teaching staff.

The rotating-activity-period schedule holds two primary benefits for music education. The first one is, of course, that a music performance rehearsal could be rotated throughout the schedule rather than placed outside the school day. The second advantage is that private or group

Figure 5.8. A seven-period schedule in a six-period day: horizontal sequence.

Period	M	T	W	Th	F	M	T	W
1	A	B	C	X	E	F	G	A
2	B	C	D	E	F	G	A	B
3	C	X	E	F	G	A	B	C
Lunch								→
4	D	E	F	G	A	B	C	D
5	E	F	G	A	B	C	D	E
6	F	G	A	B	C	D	E	F

Figure 5.9. Rotating-activity-period schedule.

Period	Monday	Tuesday	Wednesday	Thursday	Friday
1	Activity	A	A	A	A
2	B	Activity	B	B	B
3	C	C	Activity	C	C
Lunch					→
4	D	D	D	Activity	D
5	E	E	E	E	Activity
6	F	F	X	F	F

lessons can be scheduled during the activity period when the ensemble rehearsal period is already scheduled during a regular class period. This type of schedule is less advantageous for the music program than other flexible models because pep meetings, lyceums, nonschool concerts, or other programs often usurp the activity period time. However, a cooperative effort between a music educator and an administrator who is pro-music can create a positive rotating-activity-period rehearsal schedule.

Extending the school day

Music educators across the United States are being asked with increased frequency to move their rehearsal periods away from the normal school day. This is particularly true in band and orchestra performance areas. Thirty and forty years ago it was common to find bands rehearsing prior to the beginning of the school day. In part due to Conant's recommendations and in part due to the expansion of computer technology in the area of schedule construction, music-group-rehearsal periods have been comfortably accepted into the school day. More recently, however, with the wide diversity of program offerings available at the secondary level, music groups are once again being asked to rehearse before school.

Many music educators argue against before- or after-school rehearsal scheduling, claiming that if music is to be considered a legitimate educational function, it should be scheduled accordingly. The harsh reality of the situation requires rethinking on the part of the above idealistic music educators. As more and more demands are made on an already overcrowded schedule, the likelihood of serious schedule conflicts with music education offerings increases.

In discussing this same topic, Bessom, Tatarunis, and Forcucci make the following point:

> Educators have to revise their thinking about what constitutes a school day and even what constitutes a school year. The music teacher, too, must recognize alternatives and revise his idea of what acceptable scheduling is. Why shouldn't the day be extended to earlier and later hours if it permits a more comprehensive and less conflicting curriculum?[8]

Some music educators have solved their scheduling problems by starting a rehearsal one-half hour before school and then using the first twenty to thirty minutes of the school day. The reverse situation could occur at the end of the school day by extending a rehearsal period one-half hour in that direction; however, the opportunity for conflict with athletic programs is much greater after school than before school and busing of students can create additional problems.

A visit to most secondary schools early in the morning will find many nonmusic classes and activities already taking place before the official school day begins. Expedient educators and activity advisers have found that the only way to eliminate scheduling conflicts for their courses is to move those offerings before the school day. Concerned music educators would do well to accept such scheduling options if it will remove the possibility of forcing young student musicians to make difficult participation choices. Music educators certainly have the right to seek assurance from school administrators that any music rehearsal scheduled before school will receive administrative protection from potential or already-existing scheduling conflicts.

In some schools where a six-period schedule has been put in effect, educators have added an early-morning seventh period. Those educators then recommend that the "seven-period" day be an option for those students who can benefit from the enriched learning experience of an extra class period. The typical school in such a situation runs from 8:00 A.M. until 3:30 P.M. The first period is optional and attended by students anxious for extra enrichment opportunities. A music rehearsal would certainly qualify as an "enrichment opportunity." Teachers would still teach five periods with one preparation period, and those teachers beginning work at 8:00 A.M. would complete their school days at 2:30 P.M. Through this type of school-day extension, college preparatory and honor program students can increase elective choices. This type of schedule is more expensive but makes better use of school facilities. The major determining factor in such schedule modifications is increased opportunities to meet the needs of *all* students in a school.

Rotating-Lesson Schedule

Earlier pages of this chapter dealt with rotating the periods in the master schedule of a school to provide an opportunity for increased curriculum flexibility. The use of the rotating concept to schedule private and group lessons, sectional rehearsals, and small ensembles can be one of the most important and effective tools at the disposal of the music educator as an administrator. Unfortunately, many teachers fail to avail themselves of this opportunity for increased personal contact with their students. A rotating schedule for music students works equally well at both the elementary and secondary education levels.

In Chapter One, an implementation of a rotating schedule at the junior-high-school level was used as an example of the "management of change" as part of administrative Function Number Five. Readers are encouraged to refer to Chapter One for the practical application of the material found in this section.

Gaining instructional access to students for lessons and similar activities is one of the major problems of music educators dealing with orchestra, choral, and band programs. Classroom teachers are legitimately reluctant to excuse students from academic classes for weekly music lessons. Music educators should not even consider such an alternative unless they are prepared to excuse several students from their rehearsals once a week for gymnastics, drama, or some other academic pursuit. Student lessons can be scheduled during the students' study periods, but that time can fluctuate, and such a procedure often leaves music educators with unnecessary free time when no students are available to them.

With the rotating-schedule concept, students only miss a class or a portion of a class once every several weeks. In the example provided in Figure 5.10, the rotation time is eight weeks. Each letter on the schedule represents one of eight individuals or small groups. The example represents one day of a music educator's week. Other days of the week could be similarly scheduled, creating personal contact with forty individuals or groups. From an efficiency standpoint, it is suggested that group instruction rather than private instruction be used on a rotating basis. Groups could be comprised of two or three like voices or instruments, and in this way one educator could make personal contact with 120 students during a one-week period.

Implementing a rotating-lesson schedule. Classroom teachers are likely to be opposed to any rotating-music-schedule concept because they fear the burden of getting students to their appointments or lessons will fall on them, and they are also hesitant to face the possible classroom disruption of students moving to and from their appointments. School administrators are generally in favor of any process whereby instructional efficiency is increased, but they are sensitive to the concerns of their classroom teachers as well.

Figure 5.10. Rotating-lesson schedule.

Hour	1st	2nd	3rd	4th	5th	6th	7th	8th
9:00	A	H	G	F	E	D	C	B
9:25	B	A	H	G	F	E	D	C
9:50	C	B	A	H	G	F	E	D
10:15	D	C	B	A	H	G	F	E
10:40	E	D	C	B	A	H	G	F
11:05	F	E	D	C	B	A	H	G
11:30	G	F	E	D	C	B	A	H
11:55	H	G	F	E	D	C	B	A
12:20	LUNCH							→
12:45	LUNCH							→
1:10	FREE							→
1:35	FREE							→
2:00	BAND							→
2:25	BAND							→

Parents are likely to favor a rotating-lesson-schedule proposal because it will increase student-teacher contact in music, and a portion of a class that is missed every eight or more weeks can be considered nominal. Students definitely support the idea and readily acceptt the challenge to carefully observe the variable appointment times. The classroom teacher is thus the key to the acceptance of a rotating-music schedule in a particular school.

The first step in the process involves submitting a written request to the affected administrator to implement a rotating schedule on an *experimental* basis. Highlight and underline, if necessary, the advantages such a schedule holds for both the school and the music-education program. Request a personal meeting to explain the proposal in greater detail and answer administrative questions. Also ask that a meeting of the classroom teachers be called to explain the rotating-schedule concept to the involved teachers in the presence of that administrator.

Second, meet individually with the teachers prior to the group meeting, soliciting their support for such a program. They must be assured that the responsibility for appointment punctuality and discreetness in leaving and returning to the classroom is the *total* responsibility of the music students. Be sure that they understand that the rotating schedule is an experimental project and that if teacher opinion is unfavorable at the end of the experiment, the rotating schedule will be abandoned in favor of other scheduling options for the music students involved in their classes. Rest assured that if the program is properly administered and the affected music students accept their element of responsibility, the classroom teachers will be more than willing to continue the rotating music schedule on a permanent basis.

Prepare the schedule with each group of students identified with a letter assignment, such as Group A, Group B, Group C, and so on. Group assignments appear at the top of the page followed by the rotating schedule itself, similar to the example appearing in Figure 5.10. Mail copies of the schedule to parents, along with a letter requesting their support in reminding their children about the rotating meeting times and explaining the level of student involvement and responsibility in making a worthwhile project successful.

Meet with music students and carefully explain the schedule and their role in making it effective. It is mandatory that students understand as explicitly as possible that no disruptive behavior will be tolerated when leaving or returning to their classrooms. Encourage each student to attach the schedule to his or her lesson book and make extra copies available, including posting one on the bulletin board in each room. Classroom teachers need a copy only for role-taking purposes to determine if, when roll is taken, absent students are scheduled for a lesson at that time.

Any music educator who possesses some degree of organizational and administrative skills will find a rotating music schedule a pleasant challenge to administer and an effective and efficient means of providing musical instruction to students involved in a crowded educational curriculum.

Although there are other scheduling models presently in use in the United States, those included in this chapter are by far the most common. School administrators are not uninterested in the problems of music scheduling and are often anxious to develop scheduling policies that ensure equity for all areas of the curriculum. A schedule favorable to music education depends largely upon the music educator's ability to work with school officials in a sensible and effective scheduling process. The grandest goals and objectives, along with rooms full of the finest music equipment, are all to no avail if music students cannot be scheduled for situations in which those ideas and equipment can most effectively be put into practice.

Other Schedule Considerations

Up to this point, the scheduling process has been dealt with on a daily/weekly basis. There are two other important considerations that involve scheduling knowledge and an organized approach on the part of music educators.

Yearly schedule. This schedule is most often known as the school calendar. Included on a school calendar are such things as starting and ending dates of the school year, vacation periods, drama and speech presentations, athletic contests, as well as all music events. There is literally a minimum of one event scheduled on the school calendar every night of the week in even the smallest schools. Many communities have one night, generally Wednesday, that is designated "church night," and no school activities are scheduled then.

Young music educators are urged to place their concert, contest, and festival dates on the school calendar as early as possible. In large schools, a full-time activity director is often employed to sort out the myriad activity and other schedule demands on the annual school calendar. Prior to placing music dates on the school calendar for the following year, music educators are urged to obtain a copy of the activities calendar at the state level. All-state athletic events and tournaments, drama and declamatory contests, state and regional music contests, all-state music events, professional association conferences and meetings, and similar activities need to be considered prior to placing music dates on a local school calendar. If rehearsal time is needed in a performance location, that time must be scheduled in addition to the actual performance date. Additionally, other school music events that occur at different grade levels involving music colleagues must be considered. A short meeting of the music staff prior to scheduling major events can eliminate the need for schedule changes.

Realistically, once the school calendar is established it is practically impossible to satisfactorily change calendar dates without affecting one's colleagues in a negative way. Occasional schedule conflicts are acceptable and are bound to occur, but recurring conflicts and change requests become annoying to school administrators and represent a disorganized administrative approach to event scheduling by a music educator. For that reason, extra care must be exercised when placing music dates on the annual school calendar, and those dates must be based on the music educator's cautious anticipation of potential scheduling conflicts.

Personal schedule. Music educators are encouraged to keep an accurate calendar of all school-related, professional, and personal activities. An experienced music educator will not trust his or her memory regarding activities that occur days, weeks, or months later. Every school event, along with state-level activities that could even vaguely influence a music educator's activities, should be included on a personal wall calendar. Efficient and successful educators, business leaders, and other professionals recognize the influence such an organized approach brings to their lives. They realize that meeting deadlines and avoiding schedule conflicts is an important part of being considered a professional in their chosen career field.

Summary

Music educators need to be cognizant of the problems and procedures involved in scheduling music-education offerings in the busy and crowded academic class schedule of today's schools. They additionally must possess an understanding of the different types of class schedules and the resulting effects scheduling practices can have on their music programs. Traditional or conventional school schedules were unable to accommodate the rapid increase in public-school curriculum offerings that took place in the 1950s and 1960s. Computer technology made possible opportunities for schedule flexibility and numerous schedule models were initiated on an experimental basis. Flexible, modular schedules have been instrumental in solving a wide variety of public-school scheduling problems and to this day appear to be the most favorable schedules for music education.

The rotating-lesson schedule is an ideal vehicle for increased efficiency in music educators' efforts to improve their access to public-school students for private or small-group instruction. A properly proposed and implemented rotating music schedule can benefit the teacher, student, and the entire music program. Rotating music schedules are one of music education's greatest, and generally untapped, resources in the effort to resolve schedule conflicts and to promote improved music instruction. Music educators are urged to apply their organizational skills to their own personal schedules, as well as to the annual school calendar of events. Both areas are legitimate concerns for a music educator who wishes to successfully administer a music education program.

Suggested Activities

1. Obtain a copy of your own high school's class schedule and interview your former music educators for their impressions about the effect that schedule has had on the music program. Share the results with the class.
2. Research periodical literature for three articles dealing with scheduling. Summarize the articles and report to the class.
3. Invite a middle-school, junior-high-school, or senior-high-school principal to class to discuss problems associated with the scheduling process in his or her own school. Compile in advance a list of questions based on the materials presented in this chapter to promote class discussion.
4. Work in cooperation with a local elementary, middle-school, or

junior-high-school music educator and develop a one-day, experimental rotating private or group lesson schedule for his or her school.

5. Interview a local secondary choral music educator and determine the effect, both positive and negative, that some type of rotating music schedule would have on his or her program. Report the results to the class.

6. Obtain a copy of the calendar of events for the local secondary school. Determine examples of apparent scheduling conflicts and discuss in class how such conflicts could better be anticipated in the scheduling process.

7. Recently some support has surfaced among educational leaders for year-round public school. Research this topic and lead a class discussion on the advantages and disadvantages for general education in your geographic area, as well as the implications such a schedule holds for music education

References and Suggested Reading

Bessom, Malcom E. *Supervising the Successful School Music Program.* West Nyack, N.Y.: Parker Publishing Company, 1969.

————, Alphonse M. Tatarunis, and Samuel L. Forcucci. *Teaching Music in Today's Secondary Schools.* New York: Holt, Rinehart and Winston, 1980.

Conant, James B. *The American High School Today.* New York: McGraw-Hill Book Company, 1959.

Curatilo, Joseph S. "Scheduling Sanity in the Elementary Schools." *Music Educators Journal,* April 1983.

Dempsey, Richard H., and Henry P. Traverso. *Scheduling the Secondary School.* Reston, Va.: National Association of Secondary School Principals, 1983.

Klotman, Robert H. *Scheduling Music Classes.* Washington, D.C.: Music Educators National Conference, 1968.

————. *The School Music Administrator and Supervisor.* Englewood Cliffs, N.J.: Prentice-Hall, 1973.

Lamb, Gordon H. *Choral Techniques.* Dubuque, Iowa: William C. Brown, 1974.

Manlove, Donald C., and David W. Beggs III. *Flexible Scheduling.* Bloomington: Indiana University Press, 1966.

Saville, Anthony. "Programming Advice for the School Schedule." *Clearing House,* May 1974.

Schwab, Alexander M. *School Administrator's Guide to Flexible Scheduling.* West Nyack, N.J.: Parker Publishing Company, 1974.

Smith, Charles W. "Rotation Scheduling, An Alternative." *The Instrumentalist,* January 1982.

Williams, Stanley W. *Educational Administration in the Secondary School.* New York: Holt, Rinehart and Winston, 1964.

The Music Library

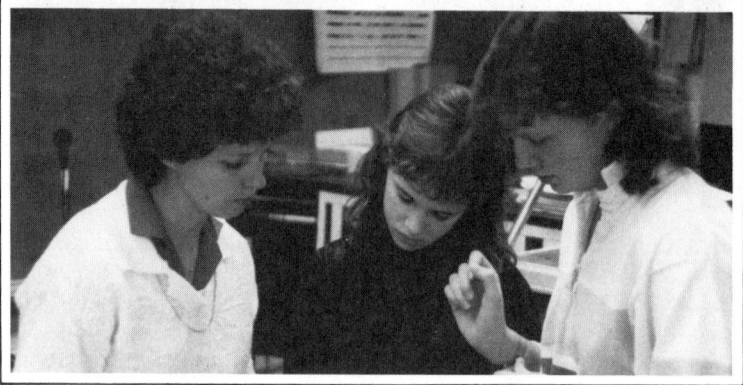

It is appropriate to begin a chapter devoted to the music library with a few words about copyright law. Over the years, music educators have perhaps been among the most flagrant violators of the copyright laws of this country, and in doing so they deprive authors, composers, and publishers of a source of income that is justifiably theirs.

Technology (the easy access to and sophistication of copy machines) is part of the problem, but ignorance of the law on the part of the music educators is not. Fast and inexpensive duplicating and copy machines have become a way of life in this country. It's too easy to break the law! Far too often a band director buys one set of a published marching band arrangement and makes sufficient copies for a 120-piece marching band. Too often a choral director, in the name of "emergency," takes one copy of a choral arrangement and makes forty or fifty complete copies for their choirs. Both of these music educators have violated the copyright law. Those copies remove a portion of the revenue due to the source that made the original copies available in the first place.

The Copyright Law

The Copyright Law, which was enacted by Congress in 1976 and put into effect in 1978, is the first new legislation affecting copyright in sixty-seven years. The purpose of the law was to encourage creative members of our society by assuring them that the results of their creativity would be fully protected within the legal limits of the law.

The 1976 law was the first attempt in history to reconcile the interests of copyright owners with the legitimate use of copyrighted material by nonprofit educational institutions and indicated that such use should be considered "fair use."

In determining fair use of material under copyright, four criteria established by previous court action were included in the 1976 law:[1]

1. The purpose and character of the use, whether such use is of a commercial nature or is for nonprofit educational purposes.
2. The nature of the copyrighted work.
3. The amount and substantiality of the portion used in relation to the work as a whole.
4. The effect of the use upon the potential market for or value of the copyrighted work.

Section 107 of the new law should help music educators clarify what can be considered fair use as it pertains to the reproduction of copyrighted material for instructional purposes. Several key concepts for determining fair use evolved from the four factors.

Spontaneity. An example of spontaneity as it relates to fair use might exist when a band director distributes a work from his or her music library and suddenly realizes that one of the second flute parts is missing. Reproducing a copy of an existing part can be considered fair use under the *spontaneity* concept provided that the director orders a replacement copy from the publisher within a reasonable time period.

Brevity. Congress, under the 1976 copyright legislation, never intended that it be legal to mass copy complete musical works. Using a brief excerpt to establish a point in an educational setting can be considered fair use, but using someone else's work to build a whole course or a major unit of that course is not permissible. As it concerns music, the key factor is the performable unit. Making multiple copies of ten percent of a performable unit is acceptable, while copying the entire movement is prohibited.[2]

Cumulative effect. The concept of *cumulative effect* is closely related to brevity. Reproducing several sections of a piece of copyrighted music cannot be considered fair use. Legislative reports clearly state that anthologies are not fair use, and in such cases permission must be secured from the copyright holder.[3]

It is permissible for a teacher to make a *single copy* of a chapter from a book, an article, a short story, an essay, a poem, and other similar copyrighted materials for that teacher's use in doing research, teaching, or preparing to teach a class. Multiple copies for classroom use can be made only if proof is provided that the copying meets the above concept of *spontaneity, brevity,* and *cumulative effect.* Also, notice of copyright must be indicated on any reproduction. Any copying to avoid purchase or to reproduce consumable materials such as workbooks or worksheets is strictly prohibited.[4]

The copyright law is also very clear on the subject of sound recordings. It states that a teacher may legally make a single copy of copyrighted recorded music if the recording is owned by the teacher or the school and when that copy is to be used for classroom use or examination. The copyright law does not deal effectively with videotaping off-the-air for educational purposes, but it is widely felt that the fair-use doctrine can be liberally applied to such activity.

Under the 1976 law, authors and composers are protected from copyright infringement for their lifetime plus fifty years. This is a considerable increase from the previous twenty-eight-year protection period, which was also renewable for an additional twenty-eight years. A copyright holder can extend a copyright in its first twenty-eight-year period for forty-seven additional years simply by applying for renewal. Thus, all copyrighted material is now protected for a minimum of seventy-five years under the 1976 Copyright Law.

Charles Gary states, "It is part of a music educator's responsibility as a professional to know about copyright and to use protected materials in the most effective, *legal* way possible to improve learning opportunities for students."[5] The fact that materials appropriate for educational use *are* copyrighted and fail to meet the previously described key concepts *does not* mean that such materials cannot be made available to music educators. What it does mean, however, is that teachers, to remain within the guidelines established by Congress, must contact publishers, producers, or other copyright holders and request permission to use such materials for educational, nonprofit purposes. Copyright owners are generally quite generous in granting reproduction permission in such cases.

Remember, Congress has been very liberal in considering the needs of all educators in allowing them the freedom necessary to do the jobs for which they receive their salary. At the same time, they are sending a message to educators that illegal reproduction of copyrighted material that deprives the copyright owners of their income is an unfair and illegal act, punishable by law.

An article in the April 1977 issue of the *Music Educators Journal* entitled "What Music Educators Should Know About the New Copyright Law" provides the "do's" and "don'ts" that music educators must become aware of in order to abide by the Copyright Act. That article should be on the "must read" list of every active and prospective music educator.

A music educator who would like to secure a personal copy of the 1976 Copyright Law may receive one free of charge simply by writing to Information and Publications Section, Copyright Office, Library of Congress, Washington, D.C. 20559.

The Need for a Music Library

A large percentage of a music educator's annual budget is spent on music or some type of instructional aids. The storage and subsequent protection of music and associated library materials is the direct responsibility of the individual who purchased the items. In schools with separate orchestra, band, or choir directors, each director is generally in charge of a specific portion of the music library. In smaller, one-teacher music departments, that music educator must accept sole responsibility for the entire vocal and instrumental library holdings.

In situations where music is poorly stored and organized, teacher efficiency is severely reduced and the possibility that music will be lost, damaged, or destroyed is increased. The prevention of music being lost or damaged is simply good management on the part of a music educator in an administrative role.

The remainder of this chapter is primarily devoted to managing the music library, how to create a maximum level of efficiency for the benefit of both student and staff. In addition to housing music for large performing groups, the music library can serve as a housing facility for scores, recordings, tapes, films, filmstrips, transparencies, videotapes, and other instructional materials.

Two Music-Library Concepts

Central music library

Large school districts with multiple junior- and senior-high schools often combine music-library resources into a single central music-library system. Choral and instrumental directors at all levels can check out materials from that one central facility. Of course, the motivation behind such a concept is one of economics. The school district will save money by avoiding duplicate purchases of music and other resource materials and, at the same time, provide a more diverse library collection from which directors representing various schools within the district may request material. The central library concept has become even more attractive in recent years with the advent of computer software that allows total library holdings to be recorded on one disc, creating easy and rapid access to items housed within the central music library.

While the central music library concept is cost effective for the school district and provides a wider diversity of materials available to music educators associated with such a library, it is certainly not time effective for teachers. They must plan far in advance for materials and music they may want to use in classes and rehearsals. To a degree, the central music library removes a certain element of instructional flexibility. Busy teachers are more likely to make use of a wider variety of materials found in a music library when the facility is located in or near their own class or rehearsal rooms. An efficient alternative to the central music-library system is to keep a master inventory of all choral and instrumental music owned by the school district in each of the schools within that district. This approach would allow all group directors to be aware of available materials within the school district and provide them with the option of borrowing music and other resources from their sister schools. Such a policy would at least deliver a degree of financial savings to the school district through a reduction in future duplicate purchases.

Single music library

The single-music-library system is nearly always found in small schools, and often in larger schools as well. In a single music library, all the instrumental and choral music and other instructional aids, such as films, tapes, slides, and recordings, are found within the walls of that particular school. The materials may be divided into such categories as band, orchestra, or choir and housed in or near the respective rehearsal rooms for those ensembles. The system can still be considered a single library system as long as the materials are kept in a single school, though placed in several rooms within the school. It is important for instrumental and choral directors to exercise a certain degree of control over materials housed in their respective libraries.

Organizing the Music Library

There are four specific reasons for music educators to create and sustain an organized music library. First of all, a well-organized library enables a teacher to determine with very little effort exactly what music is housed there. Secondly, the music educator can quickly locate a desired piece of music. Thirdly, he or she can distribute music to students in an efficient manner, thereby saving precious rehearsal time. Lastly, music and other instructional materials represents a substantial financial investment; the music library provides the teacher with the opportunity to preserve and protect this investment.

Storage of music

There are many ways in which music can be stored. Some music educators prefer file cabinets rather than open shelving; some prefer boxes rather than envelopes. Common sense dictates that, when space and funding permit, file cabinets should be used. They provide the most protection and security for both instrumental and choral music. However, open shelves are a viable and less expensive alternative and are more efficient from the standpoint of space. (See Figures 6.1 and 6.2.)

If instrumental or choral music is stored on shelves, it should be placed in storage boxes; if it is stored in file cabinets, envelopes or file folders should be used. Boxes on open shelves protect the music to a higher degree than envelopes, but more importantly, boxes give the music storage area a neat and organized appearance. When boxes are used in file cabinets, valuable storage space is lost. Music stored in envelopes consumes far less space than music stored in file boxes in those same cabinets. Boxes and envelopes designed specifically for the storage of music can be ordered through any music store. They are available in a variety of thicknesses, shapes, and sizes. (See Figures 6.3 and 6.4.)

Music stored on shelves should be placed in a vertical position rather than stacked one piece on another. The title of the music and the library number should be readily visible. Music placed in file cabinets will utilize a

Figure 6.1. Choral music storage.

filing system similar to those systems described later in this chapter. A point in favor of shelf storage is that as the library grows it is less expensive to build shelves than it is to purchase file cabinets.

A case can be made for the use of regular office-type file folders or manila envelopes, particularly when the storage of choral music is involved. However, if file folders or envelopes are used, steel file cabinets are a must. The expense of the cabinets generally negates any savings realized by obtaining folders from the school's main office.

The music educator has an obligation to his or her students to provide a positive rehearsal environment, including music stored in a neat and

Figure 6.2. Instrumental music storage.

Figure 6.3. Storage containers for instrumental music.

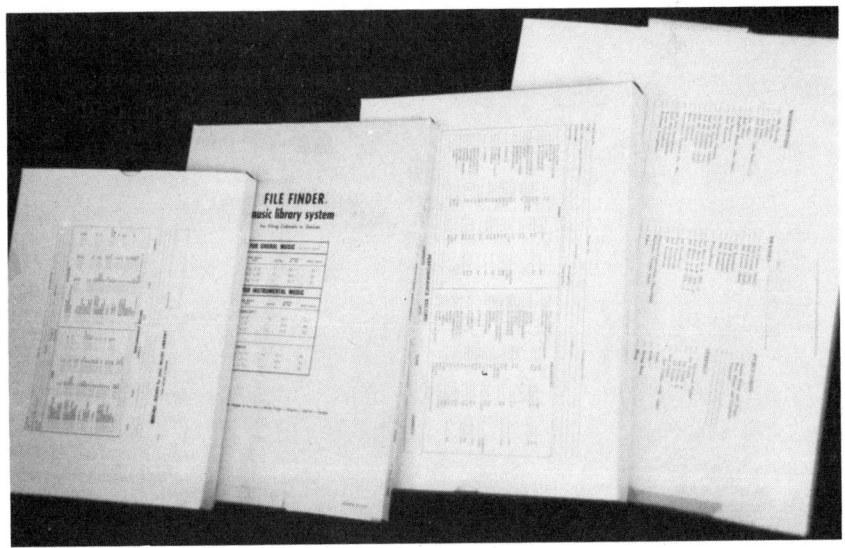

Figure 6.4. Storage containers for choral music.

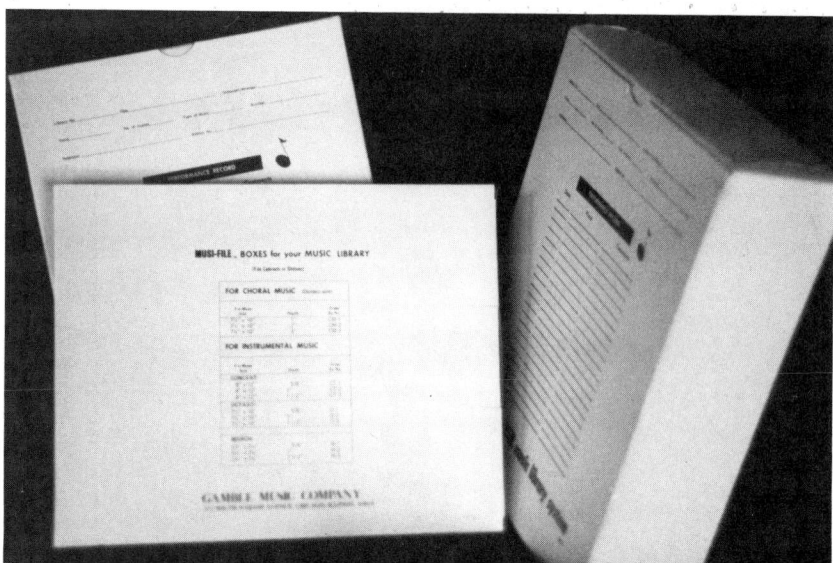

organized fashion. A music room with pieces of music stacked haphazardly about the room, with single copies of parts found on top of the piano and folio cabinet projects negative expectations from the teacher to the student.

Preferably, music should be stored in an area separate from the rehearsal room, but readily accessible from that room. In situations where music must be stored in the rehearsal room, the organization of that storage area takes on increased significance.

Music filing systems

There are four filing systems, plus variations of each, that are being used in public-school and college music libraries today. Each filing system possesses advantages or disadvantages for a given situation. The young music educator quite often inherits a filing system (or lack of system) that is a source of frustration. That teacher is encouraged to explore the four filing systems that follow and take the initiative to reorganize the music library in his or her school system. Students are eager to help in such a project, and the end result can be a source of pride for both students and teacher. Of course, separate filing systems are necessary for choral, orchestra, and band music.

Alphabetical by title. This system is perhaps the most prevalent method of filing music in the United States, particularly in smaller-school music libraries. Music is simply filed alphabetically by the title of the piece. The alphabetical-by-title system is the only music filing system where a card file is not absolutely mandatory. Still, it is a good practice to establish card files with the system, especially card files that list the pieces by composer and classification.

The principal disadvantage of the alphabetical-by-title system is that music must repeatedly be shifted. When new music is purchased, for example, there may be no space available in the file drawer or on the storage shelf for that piece of music to be filed alphabetically. If that is the case, it may be necessary to shift music down through the alphabet to create space for the new music. One solution to this problem is to allow extra space on each shelf and in each file drawer to provide for library growth, but this can also cause waste of storage space. The alphabetical-by-title system should be accompanied by the optional title card file, as well as the recommended composer and classification card files.

Alphabetical by composer. This music filing system is rarely found in the public-school band or choral programs. For that matter, it is unusual to find it in college or university band and choral departments. It is most generally used by orchestral programs with ability levels ranging from student to professional. The existence of the alphabetical-by-composer system was undoubtedly sparked by an interest on the part of orchestra conductors to keep the works of the great masters located in close proximity to one another in a music library. Orchestral works are quite often known by the composer's name rather than the title of the work. For example, when people speak of "Beethoven's Fifth" they rarely say "Symphony Number Five" by Beethoven. Band and choral literature is generally known by the title rather than the composer, and this is particularly true at the public-school level. There are, of course, exceptions, such as Handel's *Messiah,* the Hindemith Symphony, the Brahms Requiem, and Persichetti's Divertimento. The composer card file becomes optional with the alphabetical-by-composer music filing system. The title card file becomes mandatory and the classification card file is highly recommended.

Generally choral and instrumental music educators are encouraged to select a music filing system other than alphabetical by composer. The problems inherent in such a system at the school level can be avoided by selecting and implementing one of the other three filing systems described here.

Consecutive-number system. This is an accrual filing system and is simple to initiate and maintain. It has become the most widely used means in the United States, with variations at times, of filing music at all performance levels. Very simply, new music is assigned a consecutive number in the order it is purchased. For example, if the number of the most recent, previously purchased piece of choral music is #232, the next acquired piece would be assigned #233. The greatest advantage of this music filing system is that no shifting of music in drawers or on shelves is ever necessary. Another advantage, of course, is the simplicity of the system to initiate and maintain. A severe drawback is that card files are an absolute must. The title card file is mandatory, and the composer and classification card files are strongly recommended.

Inclusive numbers representing the music present in each file drawer need to be placed in the identification slot on each drawer. The same holds true for music that is stored on shelves. For example, the numbers 212–241 on a drawer or shelf would indicate that that is where to locate a piece of music that has been assigned a number that falls between those two parameters. The consecutive-number system works equally well in both choral and instrumental music libraries, particularly when a large amount of music is involved.

Letter-number system. Perhaps the most successful and popular variation of the consecutive-number system of filing music is the letter-number system which is also an accrual filing system. Upon purchase, a piece of music is assigned an identification number, such as A3-22b. The capital letter indicates the file cabinet, the first number identifies the drawer of the file cabinet, the number following the hyphen indicates placement in the drawer, and the small letter denotes classification. An identification number of A3-22b indicates that the music will be located in the "A" file cabinet, third drawer, near the back of the drawer, and the "b" suggests a previously determined classification.

This system works equally well for instrumental and choral music, and the classification code can include more than one letter. For example, perhaps a choral director determined that "a" was the letter to indicate piano accompaniment and that the letter "b" was the classification for spiritual. That particular piece of music would receive a library code number that would include the letters "ab" following the drawer position number. The same double-letter classification could hold true for band music. For example, a band director might assign the letter "e" for transcriptions and the letter "h" for multimovement works. A band transcription of six of Dvorak's "Slavonic Dances" would carry the classification "eh" following the drawer position number.

The letter-number system demands a title card file; the composer card file is strongly recommended, and the classification file is optional, but encouraged. As in the previously discussed accrual system, no shifting of music is necessary, but with the letter-number system, music is more quickly located, and classification information is provided as part of the identification code. Any music educators who find it necessary to organize a new music-library filing system or feel that a revision of an established system would be beneficial are encouraged to explore the use of the letter-number system. Filing music in this way, once the system is in place, is an enjoyable routine for both the music educator and student librarians.

Processing new music

Prior to placing new music in the hands of the students, it should be cataloged by the music librarians. This process includes a stamp of identification on each piece of music. Choral music should have an identification stamp on the cover and the first page of the music because if the cover becomes misplaced, the music still bears identification. Each piece of music should also be numbered consecutively. In choral music an assigned number can relate directly to the number on the student folder. In some choral programs, music is assigned by chair number. When the seating arrangement changes,the folder stays and people move. In band and orchestra situations, directors often ask that individual parts be consecutively numbered; in case of loss or damage, the numbering makes it easier to determine the responsible (or irresponsible) party.

File index cards must be prepared *prior* to the distribution of new music. If it is not established as a policy prior to the students receiving the music, an opportunity exists for confusion to occur when the music is retrieved, and chances increase that the music will be permanently filed without the proper file cards being completed. A file folder, envelope, or box needs to be prepared with the appropriate information, including identification number, title, and composer/arranger. Commercially produced file boxes and envelopes provide space where additional information can be included, such as the publisher and an inventory of parts or copies. (See Figures 6.3 and 6.4) For choral music, the number of copies available for a particular piece of music should already be listed on the file card, which makes it an option to include that information on the file folder or box. If a composition from the band library is being loaned to another school, it is a good practice to inventory the parts prior to mailing them to ensure the return of *all* borrowed parts. A separate instrumentation sheet with the appropriate number of each part can be included with the music when it leaves the library on a loan basis.

File-index cards

Commercially printed file cards are available for the purpose of compiling card files for either instrumental or choral music. Examples of several types of cards that are available commercially appear in Figures 6.5, 6.6, and 6.7. Depending on what type of information a music educator wants included on each card, it is certainly feasible to use standard three-by-five-inch file cards and either type the pertinent information on each card or mimeograph a set of cards designed to fit the specifications of the individual music educator.

Figure 6.5. Instrumental-music index card.

Title _____   Library
                                                  Number _____

_____   ☐ Band ☐ Orchestra ☐ Ensemble
                                                   ☐ Quickstep ☐ Octavo ☐ Concert

Composer and/or Arranger _____

Type of Number_____ (Classification Guide) _____

Publisher_____ Original Cost_____ Date Added_____

Playing Time:_____ Condensed Score _____ Full Score _____
                        (List performance dates below.)

PEPPER LIBRARY SYSTEM CARD #10-1
©1965, J. W. PEPPER & SON, INC.

J. W. PEPPER & SON, INC.
VALLEY FORGE — ATLANTA — DETROIT
TAMPA — LOS ANGELES

Figure 6.6. Choral-music index card.

TITLE _____   Library
                                                  Number _____

_____

_____   ☐ OCTAVO   CANTATA OR
                                                   ☐ EXTENDED   ☐ COLLECTION
COMPOSER AND/OR ARRANGER   WORK   (BOUND BOOK)

                                                  LIBRARY NO. _____

TYPE OF NUMBER_____ *(for Classification purposes)*

NO. OF   PERFORMANCE   INSTRUMENTAL
COPIES_____ TIME _____ SOLI _____ ACCOMPANYING PARTS _____

                                                  DATE ADDED
PUBLISHER_____ COST_____ TO LIBRARY_____

NOTES ON SPECIAL PROBLEMS_____

_____

_____

                    (List performance dates on back of this card)
PEPPER LIBRARY SYSTEM CARD #10-2
©1965, J. W. PEPPER & SON, INC.

J. W. PEPPER & SON, INC.
VALLEY FORGE — ATLANTA — DETROIT
TAMPA — LOS ANGELES

Figure 6.7. Ensemble-music index card.

```
Library Inventory        ENSEMBLE MUSIC

     Composer _____ No. _____
     Title_____ Classified_____
     Edition_____ Score _____


        List each part of ensemble              Difficulty of parts
    1  _____        _____
    2  _____        _____
    3  _____        _____
    4  _____        _____
    5  _____        _____
    6  _____        _____
    7  _____        _____
    8  _____        _____
    9  _____        _____
   10  _____        _____
   11  _____        _____

        No. 5603, Schmitt, Hall & McCreary Company   MINNEAPOLIS, MINN.
```

The three major categories of card files that support a music library are title, composer, and classification. Only one card each is necessary for the title and composer categories, but it is entirely possible that a single piece of music may be classified in two or more styles, requiring additional cards. With few exceptions, all school music libraries have a title card file, and many of those also have a composer file, but very few have a classification file. Once in place, the classification file can save a great deal of time when the music director is looking for that one special piece that will "top off" a concert program.

Choral music is usually filed by voice arrangement; thus categories include SA, SSA, SAB, TTB, TTBB, and SATB. Band music is generally divided into march size and concert size, with music matching those size requirements filed accordingly. (Pop music can be found in both sizes also, as can "concert marches." This small bit of confusion lends credence to the practicality of the classification card file.)

Both instrumental and choral music can be classified into numerous other categories as well. Instrumental categories could include marches, concert marches, Broadway show tunes, novelties, suites, solos, and ensembles with instrumental accompaniment, transcriptions, overtures, and symphonies. Choral classifications might include a cappella, piano accompaniment, instrumental accompaniment, secular, sacred, spirituals, show tunes, folk tunes, Christmas, and other seasonal music. It is easy to see how a particular piece of either band or choral music could comfortably fit into several classifications. The number and type of classifications that can be used in any music library filing system is limited only by the ingenuity and creativeness on the part of the music educator. The reader should be warned, however, that if too many classifications are used, the system loses a degree of practicality.

Mandatory information on all three types of index cards are the title, composer, publisher, and library inventory number. Optional information that can be retained includes the date of purchase, date of last performance, group performing, and the availability of a recording. Additional information pertinent to the choral library is the number of copies, voice arrangement (SSA, SATB, and so on), and the type of accompaniment necessary (piano, instrumental, a capella).

The title index cards should have the title of the music located at the top of the card, and the composer cards should have the composer or arranger (last name first) in that position, followed by the title of the piece. The classification card should state the classification of the music at the top of the card, followed by the title and composer.

Music-Library Equipment

In addition to the files, shelves, or cabinets necessary to store the music and maintain the card files, a limited amount of other equipment is needed. A typewriter, tape and a dispenser, a papercutter, labels, scissors, a work table, a sorting rack (instrumental), folio cabinets, and general storage cabinets for supplies are all pieces of equipment necessary for the efficient operation of a music library. Much of the equipment and supplies is of a nonmusical nature and available through the main office of the school. There are specific pieces of equipment, however, that deal with music and must be considered separately.

Sorting rack. No instrumental music library should be without a sorting rack that allows for orderly dispersion of music from and subsequent return to the music storage area. (Figure 6.8 is a photograph of a commercially manufactured sorting rack.) Far too many student librarians across the United States waste time trying to arrange instrumental music in score order by placing music around the rehearsal room on music stands, on the floor, or both. When placing several compositions in a band or orchestra folder at the same time, a librarian simply needs to arrange the music folders on the sorting rack in score order and place a copy of each composition on the appropriate folder. When all parts have been distributed, the librarian can place the new music inside each folder, collect them in score order, and return the folders to the folio cabinet. Music that is collected and placed in score order prior to being returned to storage is handled in the reverse

Figure 6.8. Instrumental-music sorting rack.

order. Band and orchestra directors should provide their librarians with this simple labor-saving piece of equipment. It is an element of good music administration.

Folio cabinets. Folio cabinets serve two important functions. First and most important, folio cabinets provide the most efficient means available for the daily dispersal and collection of music used in choir, orchestra, and band rehearsals. Secondly, commercially manufactured cabinets, finished in bright colors, contribute to the total positive environment of a rehearsal room. Folio cabinets should rest on wheels sufficient in size to withstand the weight generated by the large volume of music normally present in any large musical ensemble's rehearsal and performance folders. They should be located near the rehearsal room door to allow students easy access as they enter and leave the room. Music educators who settle for less than this expedient method of distributing rehearsal music overlook a basic organizational and administrative function. Figures 6.9 and 6.10 show commercially produced music folio cabinets.

Music storage. If a music educator has difficulty getting the school district to furnish steel filing cabinets, the construction of wooden shelving combined with cardboard storage boxes is a most viable, if not superior, alternative. Construction is relatively inexpensive, and the final product can create an impressive appearance when all the music is cataloged and in its proper place. The wise music educator will most certainly explore this cost-efficient manner of easily and safely storing music.

Auxiliary library storage. If recordings, reel and cassette tapes, filmstrips, movies, videotapes, photos, slides, and transparencies are to be housed in the

Figure 6.9. Instrumental-music folio cabinet.

Figure 6.10. Choral-music folio cabinet.

music library, the music educator should consult with the school librarian to locate catalogs that deal specifically with storage cabinets and other aids for audiovisual materials.

Recordings should be stored in an upright position to avoid warping. Special shelves with dividers six-to-eight inches apart can be purchased or constructed for the purpose of storing records. For ease of filing, the recordings can be divided into such classifications as classical, jazz, ethnic, folk, pop, rock, solo, musical theater, avant-garde, and so on. Card files based on the classifications selected can be completed and filed in alphabetical order for each category. Should the music educator elect to file the records by number, multiple classification cards should then be used.

All the remaining audiovisual materials mentioned above are also fragile and should be protected by cases or cabinets designed specifically for that purpose. They should be placed on file index cards and cross referenced according to author, title, subject, and media. In the case of extended-play videotapes, cue numbers should be included on the file card to expedite the search for a particular subject or program.

Administration of the Music Library

After the school music library has been organized for efficiency, it must be administered in a professional and effective manner. The most carefully structured, best-organized venture of any kind will fail unless it is accompanied by sound management practices. The music library is no exception. Music educators must keep in mind that they can set an example for students regarding the careful treatment of school-owned music.

Music librarians. The most important resource in any music library is the student librarian. Far too many music educators fail to recognize the administrative advantage in selecting students to serve as music librarians. The key word in the previous sentence is *selecting.* Good music administrators choose their librarians rather than allow them to be "elected" or to volunteer. The job should not always go to female students. Many high-school and college band and choral directors have found that male students can be superb librarians. Select at least two librarians from each class or major ensemble. If at all possible, choose librarians from different grade levels in school so that there is always a "veteran" involved in library work; this promotes continuity and avoids the need for repeated training of students by the music educator.

The duties of the music librarians include cataloging new music on file cards; distributing, collecting, and filing music; repairing music; and in general doing all the clerical work associated with the music library. If the music library is carefully organized and administered, a tremendous burden of time and responsibility will be removed from the music educator by the music librarians.

Music folders. When in the hands of either choral or instrumental students in a rehearsal setting, music needs to be adequately protected. Office file folders, envelopes, or cardboard folios available from music stores all provide a degree of music protection. The selection of music folders for performing groups is another relatively inexpensive manner in which a music educator can advance, in a small way, the image of a musical organization. Through the purchase of colorful, fiberboard music folders, personalized with the name of the school and performing organization on the outside of the folder, the music educator has added a degree of professionalism to the group and at the same time has provided maximum protection for the music while it is away from its permanent storage area. (See Figure 6.11.)

All music stores are able to secure the more permanent type of music folders. Two factors must be kept in mind when ordering such folders for both choral and instrumental ensembles: (1) The inside pockets where music is placed should be expandable, and (2) each folder should have a pencil

Figure 6.11. Personalized rehearsal folders.

"pocket" to neatly store a rehearsal pencil. After all, professional musicians use pencils in rehearsals to mark their music; music students should be allowed—and encouraged—to do the same.

Distribution and collection of music. The process of distributing and collecting music is perhaps the most important task performed by music librarians. Except in emergency situations, music should *never* be distributed or collected during the rehearsal period. The time music educators spend with their students discussing and preparing music is too precious for that type of secretarial activity. Music should always be distributed in advance of the rehearsal period by the librarians. This is a very simple task when a sorting rack and folio cabinet are available.

When music needs to be collected, the music educator should simply write the appropriate titles on the chalkboard and ask the students during rehearsal to place the music, in the order the title appears on the board, on top of their rehearsal folder prior to returning it to the folio cabinet. The music librarian can then collect the music (in score order for instrumental groups), place it on the sorting rack, and with a minimum of effort organize the music into numerical or score order and return it to the storage area.

It is also a good idea to leave the file box, folder, or envelope in its normal place in the cabinet or on the shelf while the music is out of the library. This applies, of course, to both choral and instrumental music. This policy creates an additional source for cross-referencing and ensures that the music will be returned to the correct place within the storage system.

Students appreciate such a display of efficiency and attention to detail, and the distribution of music is another factor that contributes to a positive rehearsal environment.

Filing scores. All scores from instrumental music should be stored separately in a file in the director's office. No matter which library filing system is being used, the scores should be placed in a manila office file folder and filed alphabetically by title. A typewritten label should be placed on the tab of each file folder and include the title (in capital letters), the composer/arranger, and the library identification code number. Single copies of every piece of choral music available in the music library should be placed in alphabetical order by voice arrangement in a file cabinet in the choral director's office. Each copy should also be placed in a manila file folder, with the title, composer/arranger, and library number typed on a label that is then placed on the folder tab.

The advantages of this procedure are evident. There isn't an experienced band director in the profession today who hasn't distributed a piece of music for rehearsal and then learned that the score is missing. Storing the scores in the director's office helps prevent misplacing them, particularly at the point when music has been collected and is being prepared for storage. The greatest advantage to the music educator, however, is that instrumental scores and choral music are almost at his or her fingertips when music is being considered for rehearsal and performance. Single copies of choral music used for this purpose should have "DIRECTOR'S COPY" stamped on the cover to preserve any special notations written on the music for future use of the piece. Rubber stamps are inexpensive and easy to obtain, and choral directors are urged to avail themselves of this administrative aid.

Numbering music. All choral music should be numbered consecutively. The number on the music should correspond with a similar number on the outside of the rehearsal folder. This procedure aids dispersal and collection of music as well as determining responsibility for missing or damaged choral music. Band music can also be numbered according to the suggested system that appears in Figure 6.12. Publishers of band music have not yet agreed on the total number of copies of each part to include with a publication; therefore, it becomes necessary to adopt a system similar to that appearing in Figure 6.12, which provides a degree of flexibility. A similar table could be developed for numbering orchestral publications.

The numbering of music, both choral and instrumental, enables music librarians to exercise a greater degree of inventory control over music in the folders and expedites the determination of parts or copies missing after music has been collected.

When adopting a numbering system for an instrumental ensemble, always begin an instrument or section with the same number. For example, first B-Flat clarinets always begin with number twenty-three; the first cornet part is assigned the number seventy-seven; and so on.

Loaning and borrowing music. The music publishing industry has certainly not been exempt from the devastating effects of inflation in recent years,

Figure 6.12. Suggested numbering system for band publications.

Number	Part
1-9	Flutes and piccolos
10-14	Oboes and English horns
15-19	Bassoons
20-22	E-Flat clarinets
23-43	B-Flat clarinets
44-48	Alto clarinets
49-53	Bass clarinets
54-56	Contra-bass clarinets
57-59	Soprano saxophones
60-66	Alto saxophones
67-71	Tenor saxophones
72-74	Baritone saxophones
75-76	Bass saxophones
77-87	Cornets
88-94	Trumpets
95-99	Fluegelhorns
100-110	French horns
111-121	Trombones
122-126	Baritone horns
127-137	Tubas
138-140	String basses
141-150	Percussion

and the result has been a significant and at times astronomical increase in the cost of published music. Many band publications now sell for $100 or more, and it is not uncommon to find choral music priced at $1.50–$2.00 per copy. This increase in the cost of music comes at the same time music budgets in the public schools across this country are being reduced.

The increased expense involved in the purchase of music, combined with reduced school music budgets, has resulted in less music being purchased and more being borrowed at the public-school, college, and university levels. The backlash of this entire process has been, in many cases, the collapse of small music publishing firms and the survival of restructured, larger, and more established publishing companies.

If music educators are going to loan materials from their music libraries, certain precautions must be taken to ensure the protection and subsequent return of *all* the parts and copies that have been removed from the library on a temporary basis. A supply of heavy cardboard (box weight), cut to octavo size for choral music or concert size for instrumental music, needs to be secured and stored in the music library. When mailing music, always place cardboard on both sides of the music and secure it with four rubber bands. Boxes are generally difficult to find, but padded envelopes are readily available in a variety of sizes. These envelopes provide more than adequate protection for music when enclosed by cardboard on two sides. Do not send the file box, envelope, or folder with music that is being loaned to another school. As mentioned earlier, that item should remain in its proper location in the storage system.

A music inventory sheet should be enclosed with loaned instrumental music indicating the total number of copies of each part that are being sent (see Figure 6.13). Enclose the original sheet with the loaned music and retain a copy in the local library. A notation should be made on the back of the library title file card as to whom the music was loaned, the date out, and the return date. The librarian should compare returned music with the music inventory sheet, noting any discrepancies in what was sent and what was returned. The borrower should be contacted and informed of any missing music. Missing music more than likely will be located, but if not, the borrower should be expected to purchase replacement parts.

When borrowing music, if a music inventory sheet has not been enclosed, it is a good administrative policy to have the librarian complete one prior to distributing the music. A copy can then be sent to the lending school with a short note indicating that the included sheet is an accounting of the music received. Upon collection of the music and prior to its return, the music librarian should refer to the music inventory sheet to ensure all borrowed copies are being returned. Of course, it goes without saying that borrowed music receives the same protection previously described when it is being returned to the owner.

The borrowing and lending of music can result in significant annual budget savings. However, if adequate funding is available for the purchase

Figure 6.13. Band-music inventory sheet.

```
                    Bea Flat Public School

                         Music Library

                  Band Music Inventory Sheet

   Title of piece_____

   Composer/Arranger_____

   Loaned to: _____

   Address:_____Zip_____


   Date out:_____  Date in:_____


       Number                          Number
     of copies   Part                of copies   Part

   _____   Piccolo              _____   1st Cornet
   _____   1st Flute            _____   2nd Cornet
   _____   2nd Flute            _____   3rd Cornet
   _____   1st Oboe             _____   1st Trumpet
   _____   2nd Oboe             _____   2nd Trumpet
   _____   English horn         _____   3rd Trumpet
   _____   1st Bassoon          _____   Fluegelhorn
   _____   2nd Bassoon          _____   1st French horn
   _____   E-Flat Clarinet      _____   2nd French horn
   _____   1st B-Flat Clarinet  _____   3rd French horn
   _____   2nd B-Flat Clarinet  _____   4th French horn
   _____   3rd B-Flat Clarinet  _____   1st Trombone
   _____   Alto Clarinet        _____   2nd Trombone
   _____   Bass Clarinet        _____   3rd or Bass Trombone
   _____   Contra-bass Clarinet _____   Baritone horn
   _____   Soprano Saxophone    _____   Baritone horn
   _____   1st Alto Saxophone   _____   Tuba
   _____   2nd Alto Saxophone   _____   String bass
   _____   Tenor Saxophone      _____   Timpani
   _____   Baritone Saxophone   _____   Mallets
   _____   Bass Saxophone       _____   Other percussion
```

of music, music educators are most certainly encouraged to buy rather than borrow. The purchase of music supports an extremely important chain in music education—that is, the publishing companies and the composers whose music they publish.

Computers in the music library. Now appearing on the software market are computer programs specifically designed to accommodate the indexing and record-keeping needs of a music library. Suffice it to say that presently available software does not adapt well to all music filing systems, and, at least for the time being, card files need to be maintained as a backup in case of program loss or damage. Also, unless a music educator has a computer in his or her office, the computerizing of the music library lacks practicality.

Summary

This chapter has been devoted to an in-depth examination of the organizational and administrative concerns associated with an effective public-school music-library. As with numerous aspects of any program administration, the extent to which a project is organized relates directly to the ease with which that project is administered. In other words, the more effort and careful attention devoted to the organizational aspects of a music library, the less time the music educator must spend in dealing with the daily work involved in its administration. What at first glance may seem like an overwhelming organizational web can become a clearly accessible and functional library if the procedures presented in this chapter are followed.

Music educators are strongly encouraged to make use of student assistance, both in organizing and operating a music library. Students are eager to help, possess the ability to make positive contributions, and have the youthful patience necessary to see a project through to completion. The music educator, in turn, will be providing those students with a positive, supervised work experience. The music library is the heart of the music department, and those students who collaborate with a dedicated music teacher in organizing it will likely gain a great sense of accomplishment and increased self-worth.

References and Suggested Reading

Bessom, Malcom E., Alphonse M. Tatarunis, and Samuel L. Forcucci. *Teaching Music in Today's Secondary Schools.* New York: Holt, Rinehart and Winston, 1980.

Brown, Andrew F. "Organizing Your Music Library." *The School Musician,* January 1973.

Garretson, Robert L. *Conducting Choral Music.* Boston: Allyn and Bacon, 1970.

Gary, Charles. "What Music Educators Should Know about the New Copyright Law." *Music Educators Journal,* April 1977.

Intravaia, Lawrence J. *Building a Superior School Library.* West Nyack, N.Y.: Parker Publishing Company, 1972.

Jipson, Wayne R. *The High School Vocal Music Program.* West Nyack, N.Y.: Parker Publishing Company, 1972.

Lamb, Gordon H. *Choral Techniques.* Dubuque, Iowa: William C. Brown, 1974.

Snyder Keith. *School Music Administration and Supervision.* Boston: Allyn and Bacon, 1965.

Aptitude Tests in Music Education

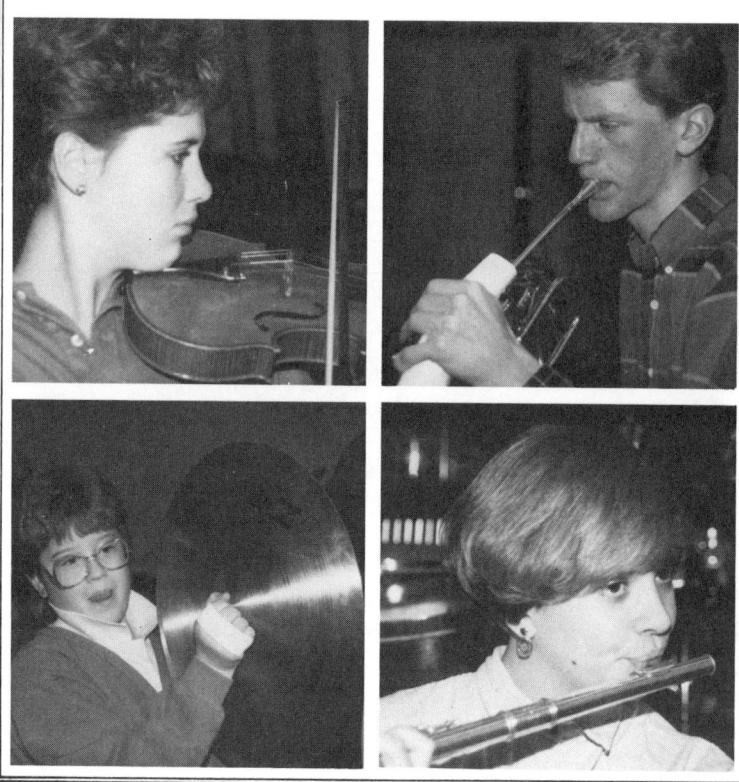

T he study of the psychology of music and tests and measurements in music is unfortunately another of the topics in music education that has been traditionally reserved for graduate school. Rarely is a course involving tests and measurements in music offered to undergraduate students in this country. If the subject is presented at all at that level, a brief reference is made to the fact that published tests *are* available to measure aptitude and musical achievement. Leaders in schools of education on the campuses of colleges and universities across this country feel that their own educational-measurement classes provide prospective music educators with all the knowledge in that field they will ever need to be successful public-school teachers. This position regarding tests and measurements cannot be professionally justified.

Music educators need to possess sufficient knowledge of tests and measurements in music to enable them to select measures that can best serve their purposes in differing situations. This author's experience has shown that many music educators are not so equipped.[1]

It is the obligation of every music educator to identify and nurture musical talent. Frequently even the most experienced teacher will fail to recognize the presence of outstanding musical ability in some shy or stubborn child. If such talent can be discovered through the use of a good test, it may be the basis of helping a child to a better life by capitalizing on abilities previously unrecognized.[2]

Brief History

Measurement of traits and abilities began to appear in American society during the latter part of the nineteenth century. There was increased social concern about the welfare and care of the mentally retarded. This concern resulted in the establishment of many special institutions to provide for their care and thereby created a need for some type of uniform means of identifying and classifying such cases. Early work on the part of physicians and physiologists associated with the classification and treatment of the mentally retarded gave rise to the school of experimental psychology. Early scientists were at first interested in measurements such as sensitivity to visual and auditory stimuli and simple reaction time. Their attention gradually turned to measurement of the rate of learning, perceptual span, and timing of various mental tasks, all of which were matters that can be characterized as psychological.[3]

The 1920s saw increased interest in the measurement of specific aptitudes. Psychologists and educators both focused their efforts on the measurement of the potential for an individual's accomplishments in a wide variety of fields. Early studies listed the traits that the authors considered to be important elements in musical talent. Most of these studies involved analysis of the abilities and personalities of individuals known to be gifted musicians.[4]

The earliest and best known test of musical talent was Carl E. Seashore's *Measures of Musical Talent,* published in 1919. No test in the history of music has been examined with more careful, and often biased, scrutiny than was the Seashore battery. *Measures of Musical Talent* will be examined in more detail later in this chapter.

The period of greatest growth in the testing movement took place during the 1920s—not only in the number of tests produced, but also in the wide extent to which they were administered. Unfortunately early results of tests, including Seashore's, were often accepted uncritically and were applied universally. Persons using the tests lost sight of the fact that the measures were very crude and that care in interpreting the results was necessary.

After the 1939 revision of the Seashore test, other musical-aptitude tests began to appear. As each test came along, it was accompanied by numerous studies relating to the use and potential of the instrument. There was little activity in the designing of new measures during the 1950s, but in 1965 Edwin Gordon released his *Musical Aptitude Profile,* and Bentley published his *Measures of Musical Ability* in 1966. These two batteries touched off an unprecedented flurry of scholarly activity associated with musical-aptitude testing. Over a ten year period, the measurement studies involving musical aptitude became an extremely popular topic of doctoral dissertations in this country. One need only to look at copies of the *Journal of Research in Music Education* during that period to get a sense of the activity level in the area of musical aptitude. Few issues were published in the late 1960s and early 1970s that didn't include a new study dealing with some aspect of musical-aptitude testing.

By the late 1970s and early 1980s, the amount of research associated with musical aptitude drastically subsided and was replaced with research in computer-assisted instruction, music needs in special education, musical achievement, comparison of instructional methods, musical perceptions in early childhood, and, in general, the "effects of something on something else."

Understanding the Terminology

Prior to investigating uses, purposes, and examples of musical-aptitude tests, it should prove helpful to the reader to have a better understanding of the definitions of various terms associated with measurement methods in general and, more specifically, musical-aptitude tests.

Standardized tests. Tests with fixed content that are devised so that they can be administered to different groups of people at different times are called standardized tests. The method and details of administering standardized tests must be thoughtfully and carefully described so that the test will be given in an identical manner upon different occasions. Scoring procedures for standardized tests also must be given close attention. William E. Why- brew defines standardized tests as "those tests which have been so devised and set up that they can be administered and scored in a uniform way upon different occasions by different persons."[5]

Norms. Test norms can be defined as scores that have been established as typical for a population—that is, typical for all persons grouped according to common characteristics and/or criteria. Standardized tests can exist without norms, but a very important value of standardization is eliminated if norm scores are not present. After all, comparison of the test group with scores of previously tested subjects is one of the most attractive ingredients in standardized testing. Norm scores are often presented in terms of percentile ranking. For example, if a subject's raw score on a standardized test is 122, and if that test score is found to rank in the 80th percentile, it means that 80 percent of the test scores for that group are found to be below 122. Test norms in the form of percentile ranking allow one to make a group comparison when using a standardized test. For example, when comparing two raw test scores of 35 and 45, it's impossible to tell how much better the 45 score is than the raw score of 35. But if the score of 45 ranks in the 90th percentile and the score of 35 ranks in the 30th percentile, it can then be said that the raw score of 45 is three times better than the raw score of 35.

Musical aptitude. Musical aptitude may be defined as a predictor of abil- ity to retain, recognize, and reproduce a short musical phrase, and it is an indicator of the potential of capacity for musical achievement.[6] Those qual- ities are likely to develop over a long period of time, resulting in higher aptitude scores, although they may then cease to improve beyond a certain level in spite of additional training. Music scientists and psychologists feel that musical aptitude is a product of innate potential and early environmen- tal influences.[7] When all the above qualities are taken into consideration, it's easy to understand why musical aptitude is so difficult to determine accurately.

Musical achievement. Musical achievement can most readily be defined as a measurement of "what has been learned." An achievement test attempts to measure facts, skills, appreciations, or other aspects of learning.[8] Yet achievement tests necessarily reflect the initial aptitude that individuals bring to the learning situation. To some extent aptitude tests may indicate level of achievement, but music educators are strongly encouraged to refrain from using them for this purpose.

Reliability. Test reliability refers to the consistency with which a test measures. Reliability is reasonably easy to determine by using the test-retest method, through administration of a test on two separate occasions to the same group under identical conditions. If two sets of scores from the same test were to match exactly, the reliability score, or coefficient, would be a perfect 1.00. An acceptable indication of score similarity is a reliability coefficient of 0.85.

What makes a test reliable? First of all, a test that is too easy for the level of the group will yield a high reliability score. A test that is too difficult will involve an abnormal amount of guessing, which creates poor reliability. Care must be exercised on the part of the music educator to select an aptitude test that is suited for the grade level to which it will be applied, which should ensure optimum reliability for the instrument. The length of a musical-aptitude test affects reliability. The longer the test, the higher its reliability. Again, a test that is lengthy with high-reliability scores when applied to ninth-grade students could lose a great deal of reliability when the same test is administered to fourth-grade students, because of the fatigue factor. A test's objectivity influences its reliability. The musical-aptitude test with the highest reliability coefficients have eliminated any possibility of student interpretations or viewpoints.

The clarity of the exam and its instructions affects reliability, as do the conditions of administration. Test scores are more reliable when the test is administered in familiar surroundings. Test items also need to be independent of one another so students can't determine answers to some questions from information contained in other questions. The arrangement of test items in order of difficulty can also positively affect musical-aptitude-test reliability. Finally, the scope of the test must be considered, in that the more limited the aptitude field to be covered, the smaller the range of item difficulty. Questions too easy or too difficult are of no help in determining potential knowledge or skill.[9]

Validity. When determining the validity of an aptitude test, one should ask, "Does it measure what it's supposed to measure?" If it can be said that an aptitude test measures an individual's potential for some type of musical achievement, then validity may be determined as the truthfulness of that test. Though a good test must be valid, measurement of that validity is complex. There's no minimum acceptable validity coefficient score. Coefficient scores relating to validity are generally lower than those for reliability and are determined through a less objective type of research. A test can be reliable, yet not valid for the use for which it's being considered, but a test cannot be valid without also being reliable. A music educator is encouraged to base the decision of which aptitude test to use upon reliability scores and personal examination of the test for apparent validity. For example, if the main use of the test will be to predict future success of beginning instrumental students, the content of the test must accurately measure aptitude in the areas of pitch and rhythm discrimination, sense of time, and musical sensitivity. If the test is to predict success in sight singing, different criteria will assume increased significance. Any musical aptitude test must be judged in the light of its specific purpose.[10]

Purposes of Musical-Aptitude Tests

An examination of doctoral dissertations and other studies made in conjunction with musical-aptitude tests indicates that far and away the most popular use of aptitude tests has been to predict the success of students enrolling in instrumental-music programs. As previously mentioned, the most recent research took place in the 1960s and early 1970s and involved Gordon's *Musical Aptitude Profile* and Bentley's *Measures of Musical Ability*. The bulk of the research indicates that musical aptitude tests have a reasonably high level of success in predicting future musical achievement of students involved in instrumental music. The accuracy of predictability increases significantly when aptitude-test scores are combined with intelligence scores and classroom achievement.[11] Thus, the principal use of musical-aptitude tests in this country has been associated with instrumental music at the elementary level.

Additional purposes for the use of musical aptitude tests include the opportunity to encourage musically talented students to participate in some way in the music program. Musical-aptitude tests increase the music educator's ability to adapt classroom music-instruction methods to meet the ability levels and individual needs of the students. Musical-aptitude determination assists music educators in formulating educational plans and allows them the opportunity to provde parents with objective information regarding their children's potential for future achievement in music. When used correctly and on a regular basis, musical-aptitude tests become a music educator's most valuable, practical, and objective diagnostic tool for adapting instructional methods to meet the individual musical needs and abilities of elementary music students.[12]

Criteria for a Good Test

There are widely recognized criteria established to determine the necessary ingredients of a good test, be it purely academic, achievement, or aptitude. Two important elements in a good test are the ease with which it can be administered and scored. Time efficiency for the busy music educator becomes a central concern. The objectivity of a test is another important concern in determining test quality. As previously indicated, test subjects' personal opinion and individual interpretations have no place in a quality instrument attempting to measure achievement or potential. Economy of both time and money is another important consideration; however, music educators are cautioned against sacrificing test validity and reliability for economy. A good test must be standardized and should include norms to compare students' test performances with other students who are the same age and in the same grade in school. This comparison can often prove enlightening to a struggling young music educator who is inadvertently attempting to overteach a particular grade level. Good tests are well-organized with clear and concise instructions, both printed and oral; they have an easy-to-read format, and the items should be arranged in progressive order of difficulty. Some students tend to become frustrated and perhaps even resigned to a degree of failure if items that are overly difficult for them appear early in the test.

Musical-aptitude tests should not be designed totally as timed speed tests, that is, tests that are planned so that the speed with which a subject responds holds great importance in determining the score. When speed is not a necessary examination ingredient, the potential for maximum test performance is present.

There is no "ideal" or perfect musical-aptitude test. Music educators must examine carefully the available tests, weighing their relative merits, and make their selection based on their specific requirements.[13]

Published Musical-Aptitude Tests

There are a number of excellent published, standardized musical-aptitude tests available for use by music educators, but by and large music educators don't employ them to any great extent. If the reason for that lack of use lies in the fact that music educators don't understand aptitude tests and the purpose of their use, perhaps the preceding pages can help to change their attitude. If the reason for not using musical aptitude tests is a basic lack of knowledge regarding the tests available, their sources and costs, as well as pertinent information regarding each test, the next few pages will prove beneficial.

What follows is an examination of six published musical-aptitude tests. Essential information about each test—author; dates of publication and revisions; address of the publisher; age, or grade levels; and time required—has been included. The tests appear in alphabetical order. The information provided has been summarized from the publications of Paul R. Lehman, William E. Whybrew, Paul R. Farnsworth and J. David Boyle.

Arnold Bentley—Measures of Musical Ability

Publication date: 1966
Administration time: 25 minutes
Age level: Elementary grades, ages 7–14
Publisher and distributor:
  George G. Harrop and Company, Ltd.
  Educational Department
  Box 70, 182-184 High Holburn
  Holburn, London, England WC1V 7BR
Includes: Record, instructions, manual, twenty-five answer sheets and key

Measures of Musical Ability is presented in four separate tests: Pitch Discrimination, Tonal Memory, Chord Analysis, and Rhythm Memory. Sounds produced on the 33⅓ rpm recording involve an oscillator and electronic organ. The record presents thorough instructions with numerous examples offered throughout the test. The pitch discrimination test asks the student to determine if the second of two successive pitches moves up or down. The tonal memory test asks, "Which tone in the second playing of a melody is changed?" Students are asked to determine the number of tones in a chord as part of the chord analysis test, and the rhythm memory test involves determining in which of four beats in the second playing of a pattern is the rhythm altered. One reviewer indicated that the British accent of the narrator might prove to be distracting for elementary-age children.

The answer sheets provided for use with the test are easy to read, uncluttered, and provide ample space for responses. The answer sheets must be hand-scored with a master key provided with the test set. Evaluation of the test scores is accomplished through the use of a five-place system of norms that is provided with the test. A separate scale is provided for each age group from age seven to fourteen.

The author boasts of high validity (0.94) and reliability (0.84) coefficients. The MMA is one of only three musical aptitude tests designed specifically for the elementary grades. Due to the technical level of the battery, Bentley's test is a valuable aid in fulfilling a need felt by many elementary teachers.

Raleigh M. Drake—Drake Musical Aptitude Test

Publication date: 1954, revised in 1957
Administration time: 80 minutes (both test forms)
Age level: Age 8 through adult
Publisher and distributor
  Raleigh M. Drake
  711 Beach Road
  Sarasota, Florida 33581
Includes: Cassette tape, manual, and 100 answer sheets.

Two test forms of equal difficulty are provided, with each form including twelve items. The two forms (Form A and Form B) of the musical memory test are equivalent, and with test subjects who have five or more years of musical experience, Form B may be omitted. However, in the rhythm test, Form B is more difficult, and it alone is recommended for use with persons possessing five or more years of musical experience. When testing unselected subjects, both forms of both tests are recommended. The musical memory portion of the Drake Musical Aptitude Test involves determining whether or not the key, time, or notes are changed in a subsequent playing of a melody. As part of the rhythm test subjects are asked to listen to an established tempo and then count silently after the metronome halts until they are asked to stop counting. The number a subject is counting at the moment the voice says "stop" is his or her answer.

The answer sheets are scored by hand, a process that is somewhat complicated by the lack of scoring stencils. For the rhythm test, norms are provided for both musical and nonmusical subjects for each test form and the combined forms. Norms are provided for the musical memory test by two-year steps for ages 7-8 to 19-20.

The reliability of both forms for students without musical training is positive, with a coefficient of 0.85 for both test forms. Reliability scores were somewhat higher for those students indicating past musical experience. Validity scores, on the other hand, are somewhat problematic. Validity coefficients are based on teacher ratings, with median scores of 0.55 for the musical memory test and 0.58 for the rhythm test. Nonetheless, Drake's test battery is well-prepared, well-standardized, and can be regarded historically as an important and positive step in the movement toward identifying musical talent.

E. Thayer Gaston—Test of Musicality

Publication date: 1942, with revisions in 1950, 1956, and 1957
Administration time: 30–40 minutes
Age level: Grades 4–12

Distributor:
  Bob Duffer or Victor Sisk
  Lawrence High School
  Lawrence, Kansas 66044
Includes: Record and manual. User may freely copy answer sheets.

The first seventeen items on Gaston's test consist of a personal-interest inventory with self-rating questions concerning the use of music in the home, attitude of the subject's other family members toward music, and so on. Item eighteen asks the student to list in order the instruments he or she would like to play. All musical test items on the recording were produced by a piano and consist of chord, aural-visual melody completion, and tonal memory tests. Subjects are asked to determine whether or not a given tone is in a following chord, whether a notated melody differs from a melody heard, if the final note of a melody is higher or lower than the last tone heard, and if notes or rhythms are altered in a subsequent playing of a melody.

At this printing, the answer sheets are scored by hand with a scoring stencil provided. Percentile norms are included, and the manual provides explicit instructions for their use. Separate norms are included for the interest-inventory section of the test and for the recorded portion of the test. Also, norms are divided into categories by sex and grade levels—grades four through eight and grades nine through twelve.

Reliability coefficients are provided at three levels: grades four through six (0.88), grades seven through nine (0.88), and grades ten through twelve (0.90). Gaston used unusual and difficult-to-understand statistical techniques to determine the validity of the battery. The author of the test states emphatically that the test does measure what it's supposed to measure. Some investigators have questioned the accuracy of coefficients associated with the test because of its brevity and believe that more validity data should be provided. As it is carefully constructed and reasonably standardized, some music psychologists feel this test deserves wider use.

Edwin Gordon—Musical Aptitude Profile

Publication date: 1965
Administration time: 3 Sessions of 50 minutes each
Age level: Grades 4–12
Publisher and distributor:
  Houghton Mifflin Company
  One Beacon Street
  Boston, Massachusetts, 02107
Includes: Three tapes, manual, scoring masks, 100 answer sheets, record-keeping files

Gordon's Musical Aptitude Profile contains three separate tests: Tonal Imagery (Melody and Harmony), Rhythm Imagery (Tempo and Meter), and Musical Sensitivity (Phrasing and Balance). The melody and harmony tests involve determining if the embellished playing of a recorded melody would be the same as the first if the added notes were removed. In the tempo test, students are asked to indicate if the tempo of the answer to a previous statement is the same or different, and the meter test requires students to determine if the "accents" in a recorded melody are the same or different from the first. The Musical Sensitivity subtests ask subjects which of two performances of the same musical excerpt "sounds better," which of two endings to a melody "sounds better," and which of two performances of a melody "sounds better."

Reliability coefficients are provided separately for each of the nine grade levels, for each of the three tests (0.80–0.92), for the subtest (0.66–0.85), and for the composite score (0.90–0.92), all of which are unusually high. Validity coefficients for homogenous groups for the three tests, seven subtests, and composite scores range from 0.19 to 0.97, with the composite scores and main-test scores lying generally between 0.60 and 0.70. Percentile norms are provided for all standard scores at the nine grade levels (4–12).

The test can be scored manually with the provided scoring masks or sent to Houghton Mifflin for machine scoring. The test manual is the most complete and helpful manual published with any musical-aptitude test. There is, for example, a useful section on the interpretation of test results. The MAP is noted for its thoroughness and care and has become one of the important contributions to the field.

Edwin Gordon—Primary Measures of Music Audiation

Publication date: 1979
Administration time: 20 minutes for each of two parts
Age level: Grades K–3
Publisher and distributor:
  G.I.A. Publications, Inc.
  7404 South Mason Avenue
  Chicago, Illinois 60638
Includes: Two tapes, 100 tonal and 100 rhythm answer sheets, manual, scoring mask.

The Primary Measures of Music Audiation is intended to help teachers and parents evaluate tonal and rhythmic aptitudes of young children. Audiation is a term coined by Gordon and refers to sound recalled or imagined without the source of the sound's being physically present except when one is performing. It is similar to the phenomenon referred to as imagery by other test makers and music psychologists.[14]

The PMMA consists of two parts, Tonal and Rhythm, and is administered through the use of two 7½ ips tape recordings.

As with tests designed for older children, the subjects need to determine if two phrases for each of forty items are the same or different. Because each child responds by drawing circles around pictures on the answer sheet, it is not necessary for them to be able to read language, music, or numbers. This test can be administered by a music specialist, classroom teacher, or interested parent. A profile card is provided for each child as well as a class record sheet for each group of children.

Composite scores, in addition to Tonal and Rhythm scores, are presented through percentile norms for each of the four grade levels for which the test was designed.

Reliability scores are quite good, especially when considering the difficulty in distinguishing between aptitude and achievement at such a young age. Validity scores for younger test subjects are understandably difficult to determine, but the composite scores of the PMMA and Gordon's Musical Aptitude Profile correlate at the 0.61 level.

Directions in the test manual and the explanations included in the verbal commentary to the children are very clear and easy to understand. Test reviewers find the PMMA test to be an interesting and meaningful experience for young children and feel it will probably serve an important need for that particular age level.

In 1983 Gordon released an advanced version of the PMMA titled Intermediate Measures of Music Audiation, intended for grades 1-4. The test is similar in every way to the PMMA except the difficulty level of the test items. The IMMA test is also available from G.I.A. Publications, Inc.

Carl E. Seashore—Seashore Measures of Musical Talent

Publication date: 1919, with revisions in 1939, 1956, and 1960
Administration time: 60 minutes
Age level: Grades 4-16 and adult
Publisher and distributor:
  The Psychological Corporation
  757 Third Avenue
  New York, New York 10017
Includes: Recording, manual, scoring key, and 50 answer sheets

Today, the Seashore test is valued more for its historical significance than for assessing musical aptitude; but it is the test that set the standard by which all other musical-aptitude tests have been measured. Its construction and thoroughness of testing procedures have been recognized, even by critics, to be of the highest quality. This recognition is certainly well-founded when one considers that Seashore had no established format or precedent to follow.

Seashore's battery contains six separate subtests measuring pitch discrimination, loudness, rhythm, time, memory, and timbre. In the pitch tests, the subject must determine if the second of two tones is higher than the first, and in the loudness test if the second of the two tones is stronger than the first tone. The rhythm test asks if the second of two rhythm patterns differs from the first. As part of the time test, a subject identifies if the second of two tones is longer or shorter than the first, and in the timbre test if the timbre of a recorded tone differs from the first. In the memory test, subjects respond to the question "Which tone in the second playing of a melody is changed?"

Percentile norms are available for three grade levels: 4-5, 6-8, and 9-16. Reliability coefficients are provided for the three levels and range from 0.62 to 0.88. Difficulty in sustaining the attention of the test subjects is thought to negatively influence reliability coefficients. In the manual, Seashore discusses the validity of the battery exclusively in terms of logical or content validity. Much research associated with determining accurate validity coefficients of the Seashore test has taken place over the years, and the resulting figures have been quite low. An enormous body of literature exists dealing with the use of the test in studies concerned with faulty speech, hearing, foreign-language accents, and other selected fields. During World War II, candidates for training in submarine detection were tested with the pitch and intensity subtests.

The test manual provides clear and concise instructions for administering the test, and the answer sheets can be either machine or hand scored. For each subject taking the test, a profile sheet can be made which shows a person's standing in each of the subtests. History indicates that when it is properly administered and when the results are properly interpreted the battery is a useful tool in determining musical aptitude.

Industry Promotional Tests

Through the years several instrument manufacturers have designed their own "measures of musical aptitude" that measure with some degree of accuracy potential skills in rhythm, pitch, melody, and chordal recognition. Such tests are in no sense serious evaluative devices, but they do determine a degree of relative ability and can often be what an instrumental music educator needs under certain circumstances.

Promotional tests can create a sense of identification of the student with the instrumental music program, and they are short, easy to take, and very inexpensive. The principal motivation for a music educator to use promotional tests is to create interest in the program. Such tests are designed for administration in grades four through eight.

Few promotional tests are standardized, and they are offered without norms or validity and reliability information. The following is a list of available industry promotional tests. In general, such tests can be obtained through the music dealers with whom a music educator does business or by contacting one of the companies whose addresses follow:

Music Aptitude Test
   Conn Corporation
   Box 727
   Elkhart, Indiana 46515
Cost: Manual $1.50, answer cards $3.00 per 100, grading masks free.

Instrumental Appraisal Test
   King Musical Instrument Company
Available from:
   Continental Music
   150 Aldredge Boulevard
   Atlanta, Georgia 30336
Cost: $8.00 per 100 student answer forms, LP record $5.00, cassette tape
   $6.00.

Talent Quiz
   G. LeBlanc Corporation
   7019 30th Avenue
   Kenosha, Wisconsin 53141
Cost: $14.00 per 100 student questionnaire/answer forms; test booklet and
   score card free.

Music Guidance Survey
   The Selmer Company
   Box 310
   Elkhart, IN 46515
Cost: $5.00 per 100 student answer forms, $.25 for score card, $.25 for
   instruction form, $5.00 for record or cassette.

Summary

The study of the use and benefits associated with musical-aptitude testing
has been an area sadly neglected in the training of music educators by
colleges and universities across the United States. Evaluative technology for
predicting musical success presently exists, but it's not being used in this
country because music educators are not aware of the measuring devices,
let alone where to obtain them. The pioneering work by Seashore and his
associates has contributed in a most significant way to the steady advances
in accuracy of devices designed specifically to measure musical aptitude.
Aptitude tests of any nature are of little use to educators unless the tests
are standardized with acceptable validity and reliability coefficients, and
unless percentile norms are included for the grade levels for which the

test is designed. Once music educators become aware of the purposes of music-aptitude tests, they are very likely to use them as a valuable teaching tool, no matter the level of instruction.

Many published and unpublished musical-aptitude tests exist today. Music educators must choose which test to use based on the requirements or circumstances associated with their particular situation. For further insight into musical-aptitude testing and available tests, readers are encouraged to make use of the reference materials that follow.

Suggested Activities

1. Secure one of the previously presented musical-aptitude tests and administer it to a group of children in your local public school on a test-retest basis. Determine its reliability and compare it with that of the coefficients found in the test manual. Compare the scores of the local subjects with national norms found in the test manual.
2. Compile a list of factors that can affect how musical aptitude correlates to music-history, applied-music, and music-appreciation grades. Lead a class discussion on the topic.
3. As a class project, develop a music-aptitude test with ten items in each of the following: pitch discrimination, rhythm, melody, and tempo. Administer the test in the test-retest manner and compose reliability coefficients for the instrument.
4. Compile a list of considerations that serve as restrictions for the author of a group test that do not necessarily inhibit the author of a test for an academic class. Lead a class discussion on the topic.
5. Summarize three studies presented in the *Journal of Research in Music Education* that are indicative of three different uses of musical-aptitude tests in research in music education.
6. Compile a list of principal differences between and similarities of the six musical aptitude tests presented in this chapter. Lead a class discussion on the topic.

References and Suggested Reading

Boyle, J. David. "Selecting Music Tests for Use in Schools." *Psychology of Music Education Bulletin,* Fall 1981.

———— , and Rudolf E. Radocy. *Measurement and Evaluation of Musical Experiences.* New York: Schirmer Books, 1987.

Deutch, Diana, ed. *The Psychology of Music.* New York: Academic Press, 1982.

Farnsworth, Paul R. *The Social Psychology of Music.* Ames: Iowa State University Press, 1969.

Froseth, James O. "Using MAP Scores in the Instruction of Beginning Students in Instrumental Music." *Journal of Research in Music Education,* Spring 1971.

Gordon, Edwin. *The Psychology of Music Teaching.* Englewood Cliffs, N.J.: Prentice-Hall, 1971.

Harrington, Charles J. "An Investigation of the Primary Level Musical Aptitude Profile for Use with Second and Third Grade Students." *Journal of Research in Music Education,* Winter 1969.

Helwig, Carl, and Michael S. Thomas. "Predicting Choral Achievement through Use of Musicality and Achievement Tests." *Journal of Research in Music Education,* Fall 1973.

Lehman, Paul R. "Review of Primary Measures of Music Audiation." In *Mental Measurements Yearbook,* edited by James V. Mitchell. Lincoln: University of Nebraska Press, 1985.

_____. *Tests and Measurements in Music.* Englewood Cliffs, N.J.: Prentice-Hall, 1968.

Mitchell, James V., ed., *Mental Measurements Yearbook* (2 vol.). Lincoln: University of Nebraska Press, 1985.

_____. *Tests in Print III.* Lincoln: University of Nebraska Press, 1983.

Mursell, James L., and Mabelle Glenn. *The Psychology of School Music Teaching.* New York: Silver Burdett, 1931.

Shuter-Dyson, Rosamund, and Clive Gabriel. *The Psychology of Musical Ability.* New York: Methuen, 1981.

Whybrew, William E. *Measurement and Evaluation in Music Education.* Dubuque, Iowa: William C. Brown, 1972.

Young, William T. "The Role of Musical Aptitude Intelligence and Academic Achievement in Predicting the Musical Attainment of Elementary Instrumental Music Students." *Journal of Research in Music Education,* Fall 1971.

Outside the School Environment

Contests and Festivals: Friend or Foe!

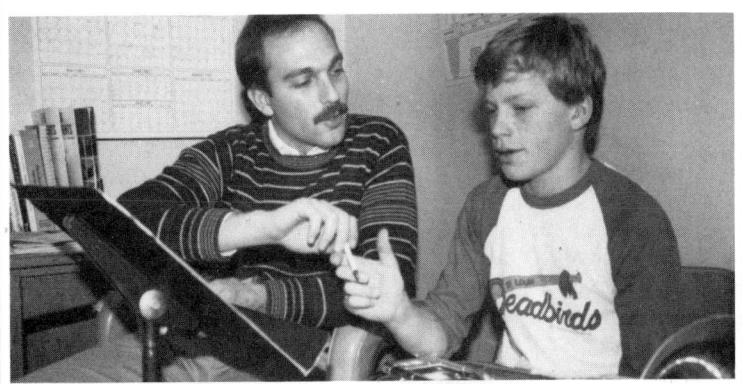

A s will be noted in Chapter Eleven, the music-contest movement, and more specifically the National Music Contest, profoundly influenced the acceptance of music education as a legitimate offering in public-school curriculums. Indeed, large-group contests were organized prior to music education acquiring any degree of curriculum status. During the past thirty years controversy has intermittently surfaced regarding the relative value that music contests hold for music education. The purpose of this chapter is to provide prospective music educators with the strengths and weaknesses, the advantages and disadvantages, the administrative concerns, and, in general, an understanding of the role of music contests and festivals as they relate to contemporary music education.

Understanding the Terminology

Prior to proceeding any further, it is necessary to become acquainted with the terms associated with the topic and the definitions those terms assume in this chapter. An event that is called a contest in one section of the country will be called a festival in another geographical area. Events that are called festivals could be highly competitive in one state and be noncompetitive in the next state. To avoid confusion, the following definitions are supplied.

Competitive music contests. When the word *competitive* is used in conjunction with the term *music contest* it may be assumed that individual or group participants will be ranked. In other words, a winner will be determined. Nonwinners are often ranked from second place to last place based on scores they receive from a panel of adjudicators. Some competitive music contests simply determine the first place entry and do not attempt to rank the remaining entries.

Noncompetitive music contests. Music events that provide constructive criticism as well as unranked ratings can be considered noncompetitive contests. In such events contestants are awarded a number, a grade, or some similar rating, and several contestants can receive a top rating. In such situations entries are awarded ratings based on the subjective opinion of an individual judge or panel of judges. When several contestants receive a "Division I" rating, for example, no winners of the contest are established—hence the term noncompetitive music contest.

Music festivals. In this chapter, the term *music festival* may be defined as an event that includes one school or several schools and involves some type of performance activity that is nonrated and nonranked. Such events may involve performance critiques without ratings for participants, or they can simply consist of a performance by a group made up of music students from several schools.

The Controversy

Early music contests that determined winning entries in a variety of categories at the local level, with subsequent winners progressing on to regional, state, and national competitions, provided student music ensembles with a high degree of personal and community motivation, as well as notoriety, which positively influenced the progress of the total music-education movement. Solo, small-ensemble, and large-group competitive contests were the rationale for the existence of many music-education programs. As music began to be accepted as a curricular program in the 1950s, many music educators began to question the validity of competitive music contests as educational functions. Competitive music contests involving choirs, orchestras, and bands were gradually replaced by noncompetitive events that provided an opportunity for several groups to be judged "superior," several more to be judged "excellent," and so on. Such a move by interested music educators seemed reasonable and in keeping with established educational goals and objectives. These events continue to this day on an annual basis throughout the country.

A degree of controversy still exists that is associated with the noncompetitive music contest (rated, but not ranked)—that is, some educators question whether even these events are in the best interest of music education. By and large, however, music teachers have embraced a noncompetitive contest structure for orchestras, bands, and choirs, as well as associated solo and small ensemble participants, and feel that such events support their music programs.

Contest strengths. There is no reason why music educators cannot take a straightforward and honest look at the results of their instructional efforts, whether they be good, bad, or mediocre. Moreover, participating in an event that enables student musicians to perform for the purpose of comparison, evaluation, and constructive criticism can have a positive influence. Many music educators are clearly aware of the strengths and weaknesses of their programs, but they feel that an important part of contest participation is that resulting ratings are made public. In addition to serving as the culminating activity in a series of musical learning experiences, noncompetitive music contests can provide the incentive to work on the most minute musical details with the utmost care.

Few subject areas other than music provide any real moment of completion. Noncompetitive music contests provide music students with an opportunity for just such an experience. Contest performances give music educators and their students an opportunity to look back and see how far they have progressed, to have that progress evaluated, and their accomplishments measured.

Contest weaknesses. Some music educators feel that music contests, competitive or noncompetitive, cannot provide them with an accurate measurement of their instructional efforts. They feel that ten to twenty minutes of exposure to a judge or panel of judges is insufficient time to evaluate the results of several months of work. They also feel that participation in music contests puts the curricular work of music education on a level with extracurricular activities, such as intercollegiate sports. Contest critics argue that emphasis on the extrinsic values of the music-education profession to gain exposure for music-education programs cannot be allowed to become the primary justification for the existence of such programs. They feel that continued emphasis on competitive and noncompetitive music activities could destroy the gains made in placing the study of music solidly in the total educational curriculum.

Like it or not, in reality music contests are here to stay, and the number of student participants continues to grow. The level at which a music-education program becomes involved in such activities is governed entirely by the music educator charged with administering the program.

Music-Contest Abuse

There is probably no area in all of music education where a greater potential exists for abuse of sound music-education principles than in marching- and jazz-band competitive contests. Contest participation for public-school concert organizations has generally become noncompetitive (rated, but not ranked). It took years of program examination and evaluation to reach that stage. There presently exists in the United Stated a near mania on the part of many marching- and jazz-band directors to win competitive contests. Whether the events are competitive or noncompetitive, more than three appearances at such contests on an annual basis approaches abuse of the program. It is not uncommon for student musicians to spend countless hours, both in and out of school, and travel thousands of miles to perform in a series of marching-band contests. Many music educators in this country have become legitimately concerned with this overemphasis on marching- and jazz-band contests and the out-of-balance participation level of student musicians.

Limited music-contest participation can be a stimulating and effective means of sustaining student and community interest and, as mentioned earlier, does provide a certain degree of program evaluation. But a problem exists when young music teachers get caught up in the contest race before they have the teaching experience to develop a philosophy or establish the goals of the music program. It takes a truly mature and experienced teacher to approach music contests in such a way that the participation becomes an *educational* experience. Unfortunately, many young instrumental-music educators "burn out" without even knowing the rewards and joy of teaching music to young people and of providing those students with quality educational experiences.

How sad it is that bright young student musicians are placed in a situation by their band directors where they view their counterparts in neighboring schools as "the enemy." Contests with such titles as "Battle of the Bands" and the "Tournament of Champions" help promote that type of approach to an event. Those same events, if addressed in a professional manner, could provide student participants with an enjoyable educational experience. Disturbing as it may seem, the directors who create a "fever" to win are themselves the ones who are reluctant to face the reality of losing. How much better it would be if those same directors taught their students to be the best they can be, rather than stressing the importance of "beating" the students in a neighboring school.

With few exceptions in the swing-choir and jazz-choir areas, choral-music educators have generally avoided being absorbed by the competitive-contest movement. Public-school jazz-band directors are not as likely to be guilty of abusing contest opportunities as their marching-band colleagues. It should be realized that competitive opportunities are generally fewer in number for jazz bands and that, more than likely, the marching band director in a school is also responsible for the jazz band. Any band director who overemphasizes one aspect of his or her program is not likely to have the time or energy to carry to extremes any other portion of that same program.

Industrial motivation. Promoters of the marching band "movement" have followed very closely the pattern established by organizers of early contest and concert organizations. The number of competing marching bands, as well as the number of students participating in those bands, has increased significantly since the early 1970s. This growth pattern coincides exactly with the direct involvement of marching-band-equipment manufacturers and distributors in promoting competitive contests. Such contests are imitations of drum and bugle competitions that have been in vogue for many years. Some branches of the industry have realized substantial sales gains for their companies by promoting and sponsoring competitive contests for high-school marching bands, which culminate in a national finals competition each year.

The relationship between band directors and the marching-equipment suppliers has been a mutually beneficial and satisfying one for both parties. Companies have gained new markets and increased sales, and many band directors, eager to build support for threatened music programs, have been quick to take advantage of any concept that provides opportunities for increased exposure and public awareness. What does happen, however, is that those same directors who previously worked so hard to justify music education's existence can now upon occasion allow themselves to get caught up in a process that contradicts basic educational goals.

Competitive marching contests can and do provide a variety of benefits for student participants, but many music educators consider marching contests to be extracurricular activities in a curricular music-education program. Moderate involvement in such activities *can* be beneficial to a music-education program, but caution must be exercised to avoid overemphasizing one portion of a music program at the expense of another. Generally, music-education programs and associated art forms should not be based on or supported by nonmusical reasons such as "competitive spirit" or a director's ego.

Toward noncompetitive contests. Contest events for solo, ensemble, and large-group concert participants moved toward noncompetitive formats years ago. The concept prevails today that more than one invididual or concert group can be judged outstanding or superior. That philosophy is slowly beginning to appear in jazz and marching-band contests as well. Generally, competitions sponsored by state activity associations or professional music-education organizations provide for rated but not ranked adjudication for participants. Competitions sponsored by industry-influenced organizations, travel agencies, or even many colleges and universities, are likely to have a rated and ranked adjudication format.

Leading jazz educators feel that a contest or festival structured in such a way that clinicians' comments replace adjudicators' scores holds the most value for young jazz musicians. They also feel that it is justifiable, and perhaps even important, to recognize outstanding soloists (not *the* outstanding soloist) at such as event through some type of award. (It should be noted here that many jazz contests and festivals are becoming large and impersonal. Music educators are encouraged to carefully select a smaller event, with practical limits on applications, which enables their ensembles to spend more time with guest clinicians.)

Music educators who have established an atmosphere within their performing groups that winning is an all-important aspect of the group's existence often discover that they have created a monster. Many such teachers eventually find it difficult, if not impossible, to maintain the level of instructional intensity, an they either leave the profession entirely or move on to a different music-education position that involves little or no performance pressures. This outcome is most certainly an indictment of a process that, when correctly applied, can be a strong component of music education.

Program Balance

It is possible to maintain balance within a music-education program as it relates to contest participation. Music educators need to be constantly aware of their own motivation for contest participation. *Why* are they participating in a music contest? *Who* benefits the most from that participation? Does the effort required for contest participation balance with the benefits to be derived by student members? Is the event or the music educator the catalyst? These and many other questions need to be answered on a continuing basis for adequate balance within music-education programs.

Marching-band contests. Three competitions in any one school year can be considered a maximum number for any public-school marching band. Whether competitive or noncompetitive, such events can benefit a band program and its student participants in several ways. This depends largely on the philosophy and experience of the director, and on whether that director has established viable goals and objectives.

Large-ensemble contests. One annual contest appearance by choral or instrumental concert organizations is strongly recommended and is sufficient to maintain program balance and instructional feedback. On an infrequent basis, a trip to some distant contest or festival is acceptable for school concert organizations. Student musicians can benefit from listening to and comparing their performances with other musical groups away from their own geographical area.

Jazz ensembles. Two contest appearances during an academic year by school jazz bands or swing and jazz choirs can serve as adequate evaluative opportunities for those groups. Colleges and universities sponsor such contests and festivals at a variety of times during the school year. This allows a director to enter his or her ensemble at the most opportune and beneficial time of year for that particular group.

Solo and small ensembles. One or two actual contest opportunities per year are all that are available to solo and small-ensemble musicians. Because solo and small-ensemble participation can be considered an extremely important component of any quality music-education program, as many school-level performance experiences as possible are recommended.

Advantages and Disadvantages of Music-Contest Participation

Through the years, music educators have come to accept a rather specific list of advantages and disadvantages of music-contest participation. Those educators who advocate music contests tend to de-emphasize weaknesses in the process, while those educators opposed to music contests are prone to overlook potential benefits.

Advantages of contests. Contest proponents maintain that such participation promotes a feeling of cohesiveness within the group and that through that closeness goals are more easily established and are worked toward with enthusiasm. Musical groups participating in music contests are likely to establish and attain higher musical standards, and through that attainment a long-term interest in good music is developed and strengthened. Music contests provide an opportunity to perform outstanding music. Students participating in music contests are evaluated by someone other than their own instructors, and through constructive comments they are helped in the preparation of future performances. Parents and school administrators alike become more aware of the value and quality of the music program. In other words, contest participation can hold positive public-relations value for the music-education program. Finally, those educators who support music contests feel that students who attend such events have the opportunity to hear their peers in performances, both good and bad, and can view the musical life in other schools. This final advantage to contest participation, which the music educator can help promote, is an often overlooked benefit of attending music contests.

Disadvantages of contests. Opponents of competitions claim that music contests can bring about ill feelings and that contest pressures often keep excellent musicians from participating because they fear failure or criticism by their peers. They believe that too much time is devoted to preparing music for contests at the expense of learning a greater variety and quantity of music. Stressing competition only causes learning to center on using music to "win," and music educators frequently compete for the trophy or award rather than using the musical value of the event as the incentive for performance quality. Too few constructive criticisms are provided by the adjudicators and too little opportunity is available for hearing the performances of other individuals or groups. Ratings are based on subjective judgments, which makes the idea of determining a "winner" questionable. Students who feel that they are "the best" often have those feelings replaced with the desire to beat someone. Music educators opposed to competitions also feel that the expense involved in contest participation cannot be justified and that, finally, the standing of the music educator in a community can be jeopardized if local contestants do not receive high ratings.

The list of advantages and disadvantages of music contests are numerous and vociferously defended by both sides. Yet it is a fact that music contests are increasing rather than decreasing in popularity. Prospective music educators are urged to develop an approach to music-contest participation that is compatible with positive music-education goals and objectives and is in keeping with their evolving philosophies of music education.

Music contests and motivation. Proponents of music competitions suggest that such events motivate students to performance and achievement levels much higher than would be reached without contest participation. If students are motivated toward greater achievement, what does contest participation do for the music educator? Exactly the same thing! Granted, many music educators do not need such motivation to provide their students with high-quality music-education programs. Such teachers approach every performance with the same meticulous care, whether is be a home concert or a state or regional music contest. There are also, unfortunately, a number of music educators who cannot be motivated to excellence regardless of the stimulus. They are the ones who take their groups to music contests year after year, receive the same poor ratings, return home, and place the blame on their failure everywhere except where it properly belongs.

Many other competent music educators fall somewhere in between the two previously described classifications. They are the teachers who are motivated toward higher levels of excellence through music-contest participation. They are also dedicated and talented enough to take suggestions resulting from contest performances and use such constructive criticism as a basis for personal and collective musical improvement. Music-contest involvement can certainly be a successful, positive, and motivated educational experience for students and teachers alike. The level of that success, as is so many other aspects of administering a music-education program, is related directly to the manner in which music educators philosophically approach the event itself.

Objectives of Music-Contest Participation

Music educators must provide personal leadership in establishing objectives for participation in music contests. Chapter One dealt with the process of establishing and monitoring the progress of objectives. Objective-setting must be, by necessity, a personal activity for individual music educators, but it is also a mandatory aspect of entering competitions if the experience is to be considered educationally sound.

A few general objectives of music-contest participation are offered as examples that a music educator might offer prior to beginning preparation for a competition.

1. Establish a positive attitude toward learning and music competitions through reducing emphasis placed on the contest results.
2. Promote a musical learning experience by providing as much appropriate information as possible concerning the literature to be performed.
3. Provide an opportunity for students to apply previously learned material.
4. Provide students with the opportunity to experience a rise in personal performance standards.
5. Create a greater community awareness of student efforts and their resulting musical performances.

At first glance, these objectives may appear to be somewhat lofty in nature, but through closer examination, each one can easily be supported by specific procedures designed to aid in objective achievement. Music educators are urged to carefully consider establishing goals and objectives in conjunction with music-contest participation and are encouraged to share such aims with their students during the preparation process.

Contest Rating Systems

The most prevalent system for rating music-contest participants in the United States is to award a Roman-numeral rating that is intended to signify the following:

I - Superior
II - Excellent
III - Good
IV - Fair
V - Poor

This system, if used properly, provides for the range of diversity necessary to reflect fairly and adequately an individual or group musical performance. What has transpired throughout the years, however, is an almost total elimination of the two lower ratings by individuals adjudicating school music contests. Donald Ivey, in a MENC source-book publication, more accurately describes today's music-contest-rating system as interpreted by student and music-educator participants.

I - Wonderful job, glowing success.
II - Not so hot, maybe a mistake to try.
III - Ugh! Total failure; give up.
IV - Suicide!
V - Never heard of it![1]

Students, teachers, and the public need to realize that the five-place rating system used in music contests is synonymous with the A, B, C, D, F system used in most typical grading systems. What in effect is presently taking place is an inflated impression of the performance quality of student musicians at music contests. In all honesty, the manner in which the present system is used is likely to continue and will tend to vary in application from one section of the country to another. Our Canadian friends have taken a more honest look at contest-rating systems and have established a three-tier process involving quite simply the letters A, B, and C.

Another approach to contest ratings has been adopted by several state activity associations for use in school music contests under their jurisdiction. It is called the "Star System." In such a rating system, contestants receive constructive criticism from an adjudicator based on their performances. If a performance reaches a level of excellence determined by the adjudicator, a STAR is awarded to that individual or group. Those entries earning star ratings at the district level are then allowed to perform at the state music contest. At both levels, adjudicators are encouraged to limit their star ratings to approximately 30 percent of the entries in each performance area. Extra star ratings may be awarded above the specific number if an adjudicator is willing to complete a form stating the reasons supporting such a request. Students not receiving star ratings will only receive comments concerning their performance.

Favorable reaction by music educators to the star system of contest ratings has been quite widespread. Positive comments are made in reference to the star system because the negative stigma attached to not earning the top award in a particular category is not as great as it is in the I, II, III, IV, V or A, B, C rating systems. Quite honestly, there is no perfect system, but the star system appears to align itself more closely with the educational principles expressed most often by music educators in conjunction with noncompetitive music contests.

Aiding the Adjudication Process

Music educators have an obligation to their students, themselves, and the individuals charged with the responsibility of evaluating the performance of those students to prepare contest music as carefully and thoroughly as possible. They can aid in the adjudication process by numbering the measures of all music submitted for adjudication—choral as well as instrumental. Measure numbers allow adjudicators to pinpoint problem areas more quickly, as well as those passages deserving praise during a performance. Adjudicators are always pleased and impressed by the concern of music educators whose students submit contest solo music with the measures numbered. They also appreciate receiving large-ensemble scores with numbered measures. Such consideration is one indication to an adjudicator that a music educator is serious about the adjudication process.

All contests have specific rules governing the operation of the event. Music educators can aid adjudicators by carefully following the classification and timing rules of the contest. To comply with the copyright law, most contests also stipulate that music used at contest and submitted to a judge be an original, not a copy.

Select and prepare quality music for a music contest. There is a wealth of performance material available to all music educators. They don't need to rely on the latest "hot" number on a recent promotional recording. Many contests now have required, graded music lists. This is a positive step to exposing young musicians, as well as young teachers, to what is considered by experienced music educators to be quality musical literature.

Finally, some additional measurement of musicality on the part of student participants has been attempted from time to time, such as sight reading by large ensembles. While it would appear that this requirement would hold some value as an aid to the adjudication process, it has not met with a great deal of favorable reaction from affected music educators. Some music educators have gone so far as to suggest that a musicianship test be administered to individual students following a contest performance. Such a test would include listening items, would cover a variety of music, some literature, and theory items, and would not exceed fifty minutes in length. It is felt that such a test would recognize and reward *musicians* instead of performers. The complexities of implementing such a test and a degree of disagreement as to the needs for objective measurement of musicianship has prevented the test concept from becoming anything more than experimental.

All music educators are aware that music contests produce "winners" and "losers." The biggest "winners" come away from music contests with a greater depth of musical understanding, accelerated musical growth, a personal sense of accomplishment, and an awareness of the uniqueness of concentrated effort toward a specific set of goals.

Music Festivals

Through the years, noncompetitive music festivals have filled an extrinsic performance void for those music educators who made the determination that music contests were not in the best interests of their music-education programs or the students involved in those programs. Other music educators who felt that music contests played and important role in the success of their programs recognized the importance of music-festival participation for enrichment purposes.

Music festivals, as described in this chapter, consist of nonrated, non-ranked performance experiences, combining two or more schools, and culminating in some type of final performance. Many schools have their own "festival" and bring in an outside conductor to work with music students throughout the day, but such a format is more appropriately referred to as a clinic than as a festival.

Types of festivals

Three basic types of festivals will be discussed. Of course, variations on each festival format are possible and quite common. Each festival type is somewhat unique, but each one brings together young musicians from a variety of educational settings under the leadership of an outstanding guest conductor in a day-long schedule of rehearsals and performances.

Massed festival. A massed festival exists when several schools, generally three or four, bring the entire band, choir, or orchestra to one of the involved schools and combine into one large, "massed" group. Music has been prepared in advance by each performing group, the guest conductor rehearses the group several hours in the morning and afternoon, and a concert is presented in the evening.

While the intent of music educators involved in such festivals is honorable, all too often the benefits to students are somewhat suspect. Two realistic reasons for this exist: (1) *The music is too difficult.* Music educators select music for the festival that their own individual groups would have difficulty performing alone. (2) *The groups are ill-prepared.* Though much of the selected repertoire is quite difficult, each participating school fails to prepare properly the music in advance of the festival. It is not uncommon for students to appear at the first rehearsal of such a festival having never seen the music prior to that day. If even one participating school fails to adequately prepare for the festival, the resulting potential for a learning experience for all other students has been severely reduced. When all festival schools fail to prepare music in advance of the festival, the potential for any musical benefit to the students has been totally eliminated. In such situations, the festival is reduced to a simple social experience, and for most of those involved an unpleasant social experience.

Many fine guest conductors and music educators no longer agree to take part in such events becaue of the two serious flaws mentioned above. A massed festival can be a quality and enjoyable learning experience if involved music educators make a serious commitment to themselves, their students, and the festival concept by establishing educational objectives and preparing festival music as carefully as time allows. Then, and only then, will students receive musical benefits in proportion to the time spent on the project.

Honor festivals. Festivals involving the best student musicians from each participating school have remained quite popular through the years. Such a select group provides the opportunity to experience a higher performance quality than does the massed festival. Students in a select festival are also generally able to perform more difficult music.

Honor festivals are often citywide in membership, involving schools in a particular organized athletic conference, or schools from such a specific geographic area as those of the Northwest Iowa Music Festival. For some honor festivals, students are selected through a strict audition process, but for most such festivals students are recommended and selected by local directors. The number of students allowed to participate is more than likely to be based on the size of the school and the number of schools involved in the festival. An honor group with membership between one hundred and two hundred students is recommended, although select groups of under one hundred members and over three hundred members have proven to be successful as well.

Again, the main ingredient in festival success is preparation. One or two schools whose musicians arrive at an honor festival totally unprepared for rehearsal are going to limit considerably the potential learning experience of the other participants. As with the massed festival, the honor festival culminates in an evening performance of music prepared during the day. Due to its select nature, the prospect for performance excellence is considerably greater for an honor festival than it is for a massed festival. The exclusivity of the honor festival is questioned by some music educators, but supporters of the honor concept contend that the musical enrichment that takes place for the more interested and talented musicians outweighs the fact that not all musicians from each school are able to participate in such a festival.

Clinic festivals. What appears to be the most educationally sound type of music festival exists when several schools combine a clinic-type experience with the massed festival concept. Clinic festivals are limited to three or four participating schools.

In a clinic festival, a performing group from each school performs fifteen to twenty minutes of music for the guest clinician/conductor at some time during the morning schedule. The guest writes constructive comments, much the same as would an adjudicator at a music contest. During the remaining fifty-minute-to-one-hour time allotted for that group, the clinician/conductor verbally critiques the music performed and works with the ensemble on the musical aspects that need attention. A competent and experienced clinician/conductor can have a dramatic influence on the musical performance potential of a student goup during a one-hour period.

A sensitive guest is also quick to point out the many excellent musical aspects of the performance as well.

The morning hours of a clinic-festival day are consumed by clinic sessions with each participating group. Ideally, if travel conditions permit, each performing group has the opportunity to listen to the other performances and clinics. This type of observation is highly recommended and can be an important attribute of the clinic festival.

During the afternoon, all participating groups are combined into a massed ensemble and the clinician/conductor rehearses no more than a total of twenty minutes of music that will be presented as part of an evening concert. During the afternoon rehearsal period, the guest is provided the opportunity to demonstrate rehearsal techniques and convert into action the concepts discussed as part of the morning clinic sessions.

At the evening concert, each school ensemble performs five to seven minutes of music from the morning clinic session, followed by a massed ensemble performance. The evening concert, including set changes, is less than one hour in length, and participating music educators, their students, and the guest clinician/conductor all go home with a feeling of confidence that through the day's activities the best interests of music education have been served. Of course, as with the other two festivals, preparation for the festival by local directors is the key to success for the event.

Selecting festival music

There are three ways in which repertoire for a music festival is selected:

1. *The guest conductor makes the selection.* This can result in under-programming or over-programming, but most experienced conductors are able to make a proper selection of literature with which they are familiar. The festival committee (involved directors) most certainly has the right and obligation to reject any suggested festival music that they feel is inappropriate in any way for the festival ensemble.

2. *The committee decides.* Involved music directors are in a position to know the type and level of music most suitable for their festival groups. The disadvantage in total committee control of festival music selection is that it is possible that some music might be selected that is unfamiliar to the guest conductor. It is understandable that guest conductors are more apt to provide all participants with a quality learning experience when they use music with which they are familiar and music they know to be successful learning and performance vehicles in a festival setting.

3. *A combined decision.* Perhaps the selection of festival music can best be accomplished when the committee and the guest conductor make a joint decision. Such a decision is likely to produce a repertoire that is familiar to the guest conductor and is within the musical grasp of the massed ensemble.

As previously mentioned, the major flaw in selecting repertoire for a music festival is selecting music that is too difficult for the ensemble. Such a situation is sure to result in an uncomfortable and frustrating experience for all parties concerned. Music educators must bear in mind that "challenging" does not equate with "frustrating." There is a much better opportunity for musical learning experiences to occur when festival music is too easy than when it is too difficult.

Music-festival objectives

As with music contests and almost every other aspect of music education, the best learning experiences result from established, achievable, and monitored goals and objectives. Music festival objectives should be established for the event by the participating music educators. Objectives for a music festival might include: (1) Broaden student musical growth through the experience of rehearsing and performing with fellow student musicians under an outstanding guest conductor. (2) Introduce participating teachers to rehearsal techniques that offer long-term musical benefits. (3) Acquaint students with challenging, developmental, and interesting musical literature. Objectives such as "Give the kids a treat," or "Provide an opportunity to meet others with like interests," or "Have a pleasant time in a musical atmosphere" are not educational objectives. Making music in a festival setting implies learning. Social interaction must be considered a worthwhile by-product of that learning experience.

Music educators who participate in music festivals and who have established objectives for those festivals should meet within several weeks following the event to review the success in terms of meeting objectives and to make preliminary plans for the next festival. All too often, music educators wait for nearly a year to pass before they think about the festival, and in that period of time memories tend to dim; a valuable opportunity to upgrade the festival and improve the learning experience for their students has been partially lost.

Organizing a music festival

Because music contests are generally sponsored by state activity associations, professional music organizations, or colleges and universities, no contest management concerns are offered as part of this chapter. However, since music festivals are very often locally sponsored and organized by one or more music educators to meet their specific program needs, it is appropriate that some general organizational considerations for music festivals be presented. Because music festivals are often personal undertakings, some of the organizational and management suggestions may not be appropriate for every situation, but young music educators should find them to be of some assistance in planning that first festival.

Committee meeting. Teachers from participating schools should meet several months prior to the event and determine the following:

1. Festival objectives.
2. Date, place, format, and festival title. Titles are important to provide a sense of identity for the event, both for present and future use. "Festival for Young Voices," "Tri-State Band Festival," and "Quad-City Chorale" are typical festival titles.
3. Festival budget.
4. Clinicians and/or conductor. Recommend several in order of preference in case of date conflict.
5. Repertoire. The final determination will likely be a combined decision of the conductor and committee.

Contact clinician/conductor. Several months in advance, telephone the conductor who is the first choice of the committee. Highly respected clinicians and conductors are in demand and need to be contacted several months to a year in advance of the festival. If the clinician is available, briefly outline pertinent information in addition to the date, such as festival format, hours involved, and the honorarium the committee will pay for the event. Follow the contact with a letter. *Never* trust anything to memory. The purpose of the letter is to confirm the telephone conversation and reiterate the date, time, hours, fee, and place. Also, request input for festival music literature and ask that a photo and a brief biographical sketch for publicity purposes be sent within a reasonable period of time.

Festival preparation. Eight weeks prior to the festival, send registration materials to participating schools requesting information pertinent to the particular type of festival that is being organized, including fees (if any).

Submit festival poster to the printer five weeks before the event. Include the name of the clinician/conductor, time and place of the festival concert, a list of participating schools, and where to secure tickets, if applicable.

Three weeks prior to the event, send the following information to participating schools:

1. Festival schedule.
2. Sketch of school with bus parking, unloading area, warm-up, and performance areas clearly marked.
3. Name of the group's host. It's a nice touch to have a local student serve as host and guide for each school group as it arrives at the festival site.
4. Home room or storage area as applicable.
5. Equipment that the host school will furnish.
6. Indicate concert attire.
7. Meal locations and costs.

8. Reminder to have school identification on all instruments and equipment.
9. Festival posters should be included.

Two weeks prior to the festival, press releases should be mailed or delivered to appropriate media sources. Include specific festival information, such as clinician/conductor, participating schools, concert program, and other suitable information as outlined in Chapter Nine.

Two weeks prior to the festival, copy for the festival program should be submitted to the printer. Include a picture and appropriate information (one or two short paragraphs) about the clinician/conductor, the program, program notes (optional), participating schools and their directors, and acknowledgements of any other nonparticipating individuals who made some type of contribution to the success of the festival, such as any local school officials or music parents.

One week in advance of the festival, personally invite the local newspaper to send a photographer to the festival for some "action shots." Such events are definitely newsworthy, and editors are interested in events that affect large numbers of readers.

If at all possible, have a check ready immediately for the clinician/conductor(s). Meet with the school business manager or other school official at least two weeks in advance of the festival to see what steps need to be taken to expedite the process. Guests appreciate and deserve to receive payment at the close of the event for services rendered.

One final thought. A complete notebook or file needs to be compiled with copies of all correspondence and paperwork associated with the festival. Such files become extremely valuable when planning subsequent events, particularly if the festival is rotated among participating schools.

No more than eight weeks after the festival, the participating music directors should schedule a follow-up meeting to discuss festival-objective achievement, determine quality and success levels of the festival, and make preliminary plans for the next year's festival.

Undoubtedly numerous small details and organizational concerns will arise that weren't mentioned in the previous section, but information has been provided that should allow even the most inexperienced music educator to organize and manage a successful music festival. The establishment of planning dates and anticipatory planning are two major ingredients for the success of any music festival.

Music educators who elect to participate in music contests can enrich that experience through festival participation. Other music educators, who for one reason or another do not participate in large-group music contests, find that music festivals can provide a valuable opportunity for an enhanced music-education learning experience if a majority of the practices presented in the preceding pages are observed. This author recommends, economic and geographical conditions permitting, that all junior- and senior-high-school performing groups participate in at least one music festival on an annual basis. When properly organized and administered, such events are avenues for excellence in music education, as well as an element of good public relations for the total music program.

Summary

Music contests have been on the music education scene since the latter part of the nineteenth century, although the scope and format of music contests has changed considerably through the years. Perhaps no other entity has sparked more controversy than has the value, or lack of value, that music-contest participation holds for specific music programs and music education in general. The consensus of music-educator opinion is that moderate competitive or noncompetitive music-contest participation is of some benefit to music-education programs, and that of the two types of contests, the noncompetitive contest is more in line with the general philosophy of music education. In recent years, overemphasis on marching-band field competitions, with a corresponding decrease in quality of other facets of the instrumental-music program, has been a source of concern for many music educators in this country. There has been a recent trend toward noncompetitive contests in both the jazz and marching-band areas, and such a move has met with favorable reaction from the music-education community. Noncompetitive music-contest rating systems tend to project an inflated image of performance quality because only the first three ratings are generally used in a five-tier system. This is a subject that needs to be realistically dealt with at both the state and national levels of music-education professional organizations.

Music festivals have provided an alternative for performance experiences outside the school for those teachers electing not to participate in music contests. It appears that a music-festival format that provides both clinic and performance experiences for participants is the most acceptable to music educators, although honor-type music festivals provide quality music performance opportunities for talented and interested student musicians. No matter the format, the key to success of any music festival is found in the establishment of worthwhile festival objectives and the organization and management practices enacted by participating music educators. Music-festival participation should be an annual event on the calendar of all junior- and senior-high-school performing groups.

Suggested Activities

1. Secure a copy of the rules or bylaws relating to music contests in your state from the governing agency, whether it be a state activities associa-

tion or professional music educator's organization. Discuss in class the implications such policies hold for music education in your geographical area.

2. Secure a set of adjudication forms that are available from MENC and discuss in class such terms as "artistry," "fluency," "instrumentation," "appearance," "stage presence," and "choice of music" as they apply to the contest-adjudication process.

3. Invite one or more experienced contest adjudicators from your own campus to discuss their impressions of what is positive and what is negative about the music-contest adjudication process.

4. Invite an experienced music-festival conductor from your own campus to class to discuss the positive and negative implications to music-festival participation.

5. Research periodical literature and determine advantages or disadvantages of solo and ensemble music-contest participation for elementary- and junior-high-school students. Discuss findings in class.

6. Classes for contest-participating organizations (Class A, Class B, and so on) are generally determined by high-school enrollment or the size of the participating ensemble. Discuss advantages and/or disadvantages of those two classification systems.

7. Discuss in class what effect the elimination of jazz contests or festivals would have on jazz-ensemble programs in the public schools.

8. As a total class project, assume responsibility for planning, organizing, and managing a music festival on campus or in the community.

References and Suggested Readings

Barresi, Anthony L. "Music Objectives for Choral Festivals." *Music Educators Journal,* March 1979.

Corcoran, Gary. "Adjudication/Director Relationship." *The School Musician,* March 1983.

Gagliardi, Frank. "Do We Really Need Competitive Jazz Festivals?" *The Instrumentalist,* April 1983.

Hoffer, Charles R. "The Music Contest Steps Off in a New Direction." *Music Educators Journal,* January 1976.

Ivey, Donald. "Can We Afford to Deceive Ourselves?" *Perspectives in Music Education,* 1966.

Jipson, Wayne R. *The High School Vocal Program.* West Nyack, N.Y.: Parker Publishing Company, 1972.

Leeder, Joseph A., and William S. Haynie. *Music Education in the High School.* Englewood Cliffs, N.J.: Prentice-Hall, 1959.

Moody, William J. "Education and Contests." *The Instrumentalist,* August 1983.

"Point of View on Competition." *Music Educators Journal,* October 1983.

Raessler, Kenneth R. "Warning! The Comprehensive Music Festival." *The Instrumentalist,* December 1983.

Public Relations and
the Music Educator

The reader may recall the short discussion presented in Chapter One relating the association of the music educator as an administrator to the thirteenth administrative function, COMMUNICATION. It was pointed out that communication can influence in a positive or negative manner nearly all of the remaining fifteen administrative functions.

Actions that keep the parents and community informed of the purpose, usefulness, conditions, and needs of the music program come under the domain of public relations. Public relations, a two-way system of communicating between the community and the music educator, can promote the public's good will and assure future indispensability of the music-education program. If the public-relations approach is well planned, it will reflect the positive qualities of both the school and the music-education program and result in favorable public opinion and, therefore, acceptance of that program.

It is of the utmost importance that music educators in today's schools "sell" their programs and themselves to the broadest constituency possible. The creation of a broad base of support for music education in the community can be of great value, whether for seeking increased budget support or simply greater program support through concert attendance. Two-way communication between the music educator, administrators, parents, and the entire community is a natural part of that "sales" effort. Far too often public relations is thought of only as a one-way communications channel, creating a degree of isolation that is nearly as fatal to the music-education program as no communication whatsoever.

For some young music educators, the necessity of having to promote their programs to both the school and community is somewhat distasteful. They feel that music education is a wonderful experience for young people and should stand on its own merits. Such a philosophical approach to developing support for a music-education program in today's schools is at best impractical. Of course, it's ideally desirable to touch every public-school student in some manner with the music-education program. However, the reality is that those students will *never* be touched unless the need has been created, demonstrated, and communicated to school officials and the community alike. This can best be done by a logical and practical course of action involving public relations.

Broad-based parental and community support can significantly contribute to reducing or preventing program cutbacks, if and when they should occur. Parental advocacy is a natural and important part of the total broad base of support; if community representatives other than parents endorse the music-education program, it has an even greater impact on any individual or group considering program reductions in music. This broad base of support is most effectively achieved through an active and positive public-relations effort. It is not enough to have a good orchestra, choir, or band at either the elementary or high-school level. People have to know about it! They must be informed, and in turn must provide feedback to the music educator as well as to students involved in the program. The music educator must be prepared to take action on the feedback offered. Hence, communication results.

The music educator should evaluate the music program in terms of community needs. How strong is the economy of the community? Is it a suburban, urban, or rural community? What is the principal occupation of its residents? How strong is the tax base and level of support for the school? The social structure of the community should be considered. How are the arts accepted in the community? Is there a community concert series or a community chorus, band, or orchestra? Are there music stores in the community? Is there a newspaper and are there radio and television stations? Answers to all the above questions can assist the music educator in determining the depth, focus, and activity level for a public-relations program associated with music education. Community attitude toward music should be considered in conjunction with the scope and direction of the music-education program as one forms the associated communication efforts in support of that program.

Concerts presented by the school's various ensembles are a tremendously important community public-relations vehicle. Generating and sustaining strong concert attendance is an administrative responsibility of the music educator. Getting an audience to a concert involves the element of public relations known as publicity. How the audience is treated, both aesthetically and musically, after arriving at the concert also involves public relations. For example, a two-and-one-half-hour concert is generally not positive public relations. When a great deal of time spent at a concert is consumed by set changes or a seemingly endless parading of personnel to and from the stage, it is not positive public relations. No matter how well-rehearsed and musical the performances are, if they appear between long periods of time required for scene changes, the resulting public-relations benefit is severely diminished. Parents will tolerate overly long programs and programs that are not expedient from an organizational standpoint. They have no choice! The general public, however, is a different story. If a music educator really wants to use attendance at concerts as a means of communicating music-program quality to parents and the public, then the concert programs should be short (rarely over one hour) and organized with the audience in mind. This is public relations!

If a music educator continually finds program length to be between two and three hours, too many people are involved in the production. For example, if the annual band and choir Christmas concert falls into the lengthy category, two choices exist: (1) Present separate concerts, either on the same or different evenings, and (2) have each group perform less, but better prepared, music. Continuing "as is" is not a viable alternative.

Across the country, school music concerts that are consistently well-attended by parents and the general public, have several similar characteristics. First, they are well-publicized and well-promoted; secondly, they are prepared musically to the best ability of the participants, and thirdly, the concert itself is a production that makes the most efficient use of audience time and student effort.

The all-school extravaganza is a possible exception to the previously described approach. It must be kept in mind, however, that the immensity of a major project in no way precludes an efficient and organized approach to the production. Students, parents, and the public alike greatly appreciate this demonstration of efficiency on the part of the music educator.

Promotion can be defined as advertising for a single event, such as "selling" a concert. In order for any promotional campaign to be successful, the foundation for such an effort must be laid through an ongoing program of public relations. An atmosphere is created by an active public-relations plan that allows promotion to succeed. For example, a music educator has an excellent chance to receive positive media coverage for a particular event if the media has been informed on a continuing basis of past successes and previous community activities, and if other prior newsworthy features have been submitted in a professional and informative format. Public support for a major fund-raising effort is likely to be promising when the music-education program is considered to be an important part of school and community life. This type of support is generated through a systematic approach to public relations on the part of the music educator. Also, as will be discussed later in this book, should some type of fiscal difficulties arise, a solid public-relations base will be invaluable.

Goal-Setting in Public Relations

When working to strengthen a music program's public relations with the school and community, the music educator needs to determine both long-range goals and short-term objectives. Long-range goals will be few and quite broad. An example of one such goal would simply be to "Establish a strong relationship between the music program and the community." Short-term objectives to support that long-range goal could be to increase the visibility of music groups in the community, better inform the community of music events and achievements, and become personally involved to a greater extent in the community. The general goal and objective process of setting, verifying, and monitoring goals and objectives was discussed in greater detail in Chapter One. Bear in mind that the goals and objectives must be achievable and should be monitored and verified.

Young teachers often have difficulty establishing goals and objectives because they fail to see themselves teaching in a given situation for more than one or two years. Music educators new to the profession should try to approach their work with a sense of permanency, with the idea that they will be teaching in this new position for a number of years. The sense of commitment to that permanent role needs to be great. If a music educator can assume such an approach to a new teaching position, enlightened and practical goal and objective setting in public relations, as well as throughout the entire music-education program, will be less difficult. In the final analysis, it will be more beneficial to the school, the community, and to the music educator.

Short-term objectives should be designed to be achievable in the time span of one school year. Using such parameters provides ample opportunity to measure progress of any public-relations effort. Objectives can most certainly be renewed, adjusted, and revised each year, but thinking in terms of achieving objectives in one year will help motivate the music educator.

Several short-term objectives were just mentioned in conjunction with the long-term public relations goal to "Establish a strong relationship between the music program and the community." Another short-term objective vaguely associated with the ongoing long-term goals could be to "Improve communication with parents concerning: (1) performance and special rehearsal dates, (2) student responsibilities, and (3) the total scope of the music-education program." Note that short-term objectives tend to be more specific than long-range goals. The level of specificity increases when listing "ways and means" toward objective achievement. For example, in support of the above short-term objectives, several techniques or strategies could be listed.

1. Send to parents a calendar of events and a list of student responsibilities associated with those events.
2. Establish a schedule and encourage parent visitation to classes and/or rehearsals.
3. Initiate an annual "Parents Night" where they assume students' roles in class and rehearsals.

These three techniques are very specific, and the success of each, along with program benefits noted, can be easily verified and measured at the close of the school year. The strategies that seem to work and to increase communication could certainly be continued, while any techniques deemed nonbeneficial to the short-term objective could be discarded and replaced with other techniques the following year. Achievement of objectives similar to the above is certain to result in greater constituency support. The music educator needs to become involved in providing a quality "final product" to the school and community and must assume the responsibility for making them both aware that the "product" exists. Setting long-term goals and short-range objectives can certainly be a means to that end.

Public Relations through Programming

How the music educator prepares and presents concert programs to the public can be a most effective tool in the total public-relations plan. Group directors, caught up in tradition, often ignore the potential to enhance the image of the music-education program and to increase concert attendance through a creative approach to concert programming. The level of the musical experience achieved by student participants is closely associated with the manner in which the music was taught and not so much as to the format or environment in which it was performed. Music educators with successful programs are those who are receptive to the needs, wishes, and enjoyment level of their audiences, as well as those of their students.

Dedicated teachers are constantly alert for new concepts and proce-dures that promote innovative approaches to performance programming. The number of new ideas potentially available to a music educator is propor-tionately related to the educator's dedication to developing new performance avenues, as well as his or her willingness to experiment with contemporary performance concepts.

A year-long program built around the music of a particular ethnic group has potential for an increased level of community interest. For ex-ample, music from a certain national tradition could be included as part of every concert presented by all performing groups during the year. "A Salute to Scandinavia," involving citizens from the community in authentic costume, could provide an opportunity for a more historical approach to the preparation and presentation of the music and heighten interest on the part of the media. Such an effort would increase student awareness of music from another part of the world and make it possible to involve other depart-ments within the school system, such as social studies, speech, and drama. This same approach to promoting music from another country could be de-veloped for a single concert featuring only music from that country. Either option would be effective, but the most important aspect is the ethnic-music concept.

During a recent visit to Illinois, this author learned of an innovative way to handle the rush of events requiring attendance that transpire shortly before the school Christmas vacation. Because of a crowded school calendar and the multitude of parental obligations during that time of year, a creative middle school teacher in Champaign scheduled a "Continental Breakfast" concert hour. It was scheduled early in the morning, before school, allowing parents to stop by the school for breakfast and a little music on their way to work. Each group was scheduled to perform two or three selections, which allowed the parents to coordinate their "breakfast" schedules with their children's performance schedules. Coffee, juice, and rolls were available at a nominal fee, and parents were urged to come and go as their personal commitments permitted. The parents gave rave reviews to the experiment, and it provided an opportunity for students to participate in an exciting and memorable performance setting. An experimental project born somewhat out of necessity will in all likelihood become an annual, noteworthy, *and* newsworthy affair.

Some music educators schedule "pops" concerts or programs of lighter music in conjunction with an "Ice Cream Social" concert theme. This type of concert is presented with tables and chairs, complete with checkered tablecloths, and refreshments served by music students costumed in vests and straw hats. School jazz ensembles have been known to perform their concerts in "night club" settings, with punch and cookies on the menu. Both settings provide a different and attention-getting concert experience for students and audiences alike.

Madrigal dinners have become popular with school choral groups. Musically demanding and expensive to produce, this type of musical production requires a great deal of expertise and organizational and promotional skill on the part of the music educator. After gaining community acceptance and support, an annual madrigal dinner can become a potent fund-raising vehicle, as well as providing a distinctively special performance for students participating in the choral program.

Another means of attracting attention to a concert program is to change the location of a performance to another site within the community. Local churches and auditoriums can certainly be considered. A concert in a shopping mall is another option. If a group isn't already performing in a school gym, a performance could be scheduled there and perhaps involve gymnastics in some manner. Outdoor concerts hold some potential, but the possibility of inclement weather must be considered. Performances scheduled inside or outside any public building are sure to include a percentage of those in the audience who have never before been exposed to a school music performance.

The use of local dignitaries and officials as guest conductors, narrators, and even "soloists" can provide an enjoyable concert experience for the audience, performers, and guests. School administrators and community officials are often honored to be asked to participate in a school music program, and such an event once again provides a newsworthy public-relations opportunity. State and regional political figures, as well as other noteworthy individuals, are other possible concert program guests.

Another way to increase the number of people exposed to performances of school music is to schedule an evening "Arts Festival." A possible structure for a program of this nature could include an "open house" format for all school concert groups. In different areas within the school building, various groups could perform at fifteen to twenty minute intervals during a two-hour period. At the same time, work by students involved in art classes could be on display, a fashion show of garments recently completed in a home-economics class could be scheduled, and perhaps projects completed in an industrial arts or woodworking class could be placed on display. By using the "open house" format, parents and other interested parties can come and go as they wish and see and hear exactly what they'd like to see and hear.

Such an effort can generate greater exposure for school performing groups. It also provides an opportunity for public display of student projects normally relegated to a classroom showing prior to the projects being taken home. Perhaps more important, it creates, by necessity, an opportunity for a wide range of school instructional staff and their respective students to work together toward a common goal—that of displaying their individual and collective talents.

"Side-by-side" concerts—in which two or more groups perform a portion of a single concert—hold numerous benefits for all participants. The groups traditionally would not have been involved together in a concert setting. For example, a high-school choir concert could include a performance by the sixth-grade choir; the high-school band could share a concert with a touring college or university group; a school orchestra could appear as part of a program presented by a community symphony. The public-relations benefits are obvious: increased publicity opportunities, both preceding and following the event; increased audience size; and performance exposure to individuals who normally would attend only the concert of one group or the other. Of equal or greater importance are the personal and musical benefits gained by the participants through the opportunity to hear one another perform. Side-by-side concerts involving a creative combination of performing groups can be one of the easiest and innovative concert proposals to implement and can produce unusual and interesting audience composites.

Any individual bright and creative enough to graduate from college with a degree in music education has, without a doubt, the ability to develop innovative ways in which to occasionally present his or her students in performance situations. The resulting value in improved image and public relations is well worth the effort and extra energy it takes to prepare and present such a concert program.

Concert Promotion

In addition to the usual information about promoting a concert, such as who, what, when, where, the exact time, and the admission cost (if any), a music educator needs to answer one more question: "Why would people want to attend this concert?" If realistic answers can be provided, then the first major obstacle to concert promotion has been overcome. Without answering this question, the music educator cannot enthusiastically and effectively promote the event. If the "why" is difficult to ascertain, then perhaps the program, from a conceptual as well as musical standpoint, needs to be reexamined.

Concert publicity efforts can be developed into a routine. The writing of press releases, taking pictures, and the submission of promotional material to the proper news media need not be a difficult and time-consuming task once the routine is established. Determining what the media is interested in and what type of material is likely to be used is the first and perhaps the most important aspect of concert publicity. The type of articles that are of interest to the local newspaper may surprise that music educator. Determine what kind of material is appropriate and use it as a guide to submitting additional information.

It is wise to make media contacts in person, especially when making such contacts for the first time. Media representatives view personal contacts as an indication of the promoter's concern for detail, and they appreciate the personal attention. An opportunity is also provided for them to know the music educator as a real person, not simply a name on a page, and they're also able to ask pertinent questions regarding the event.

Even the smallest communities are served by a daily and weekly newspaper. Though the daily paper is perhaps published in a larger nearby town, the publishers of such newspapers are very concerned with providing local news coverage to smaller neighboring communities, and they are aware of the potential for advertising dollars in such coverage. For this reason, news articles and accompanying photographs about an upcoming school concert are generally welcomed by the arts editor or other individual on the newspaper staff charged with providing that type of coverage. In larger metropolitan areas, it can be more difficult to receive newspaper coverage for a school concert because of the multitude of professional events that compete for attention with amateur performances. That doesn't mean that a music educator should necessarily resign himself or herself to no media interest. News releases and photographs should still be submitted, and on occasion they may be used.

A weekly newspaper in a small community is certain to publish anything available regarding school concerts because every item in the newspaper is of a local nature. Music educators should not fail to explore the use of this very valuable public-relations tool in promoting all events.

One or two days before a concert, it's a good idea to purchase a small ad in the newspaper(s) serving a community, simply to remind the public about the event. The chances of the ad being read are greater if its background is black, with simple artwork and type copy "dropped out" of the background. A small ad constructed in this manner will compete nicely with larger, more expensive advertising. A newspaper advertising representative will be happy to provide assistance designing the ad.

Radio stations serving a community are another medium for concert publicity. Again, the smallest communities may have only two nearby radio stations vying for listening attention and advertising dollars. Press releases sent to these stations are likely to be covered as news items, as well as part of their public-service announcements, particularly if the music educator has made the effort to deliver the material personally to the station. Also, radio advertising is not expensive. A series of ads one or two days prior to a concert could cost as little as fifty dollars and greatly increase public awareness of the event. Free coverage from both radio and newspapers is more likely to be forthcoming if concert advertising is purchased.

Area television stations can also be informed about future music programs via a press release. All radio and television stations are required by the Federal Communications Commission to devote a percentage of their air time to public-service announcements, free of charge to the public. School music productions definitely fall into the public-service category. Everyone who listens to radio or watches television will be exposed to numerous daily public-service announcements. If the music educator is already using newspaper advertising, it takes no greater effort, and almost no time whatsoever, to submit a copy of the press release to radio and television stations, along with a short, handwritten note requesting the use of the material as part of the station's public service announcements.

The school newspaper is another source of free advertising for concert productions. Every ensemble in both junior and senior high school is likely to have a member of the school newspaper staff enrolled. A "choir reporter" or "band reporter" can be the correspondent between the ensemble and the school paper. Students can generally devise unusually creative means of presenting concert publicity in the school paper. It must be kept in mind as well that school newspapers are read by many more people than just the students in that school.

Bulletin boards, both in and out of school, can be another avenue for concert advertising. Neat and attractive posters inviting attendance to a particular event can be assembled and distributed by music students under the supervision of the music teacher. In-school bulletin boards can be decorated, again by a student committee with teacher input. Many students relish and excel at this type of responsibility. The busy and wise music educator would do well to explore this relatively effortless means of concert publicity. One very important detail must be kept in mind, however. Nobody has ever been attracted to a concert by sloppy, careless, haphazard, and generally slipshod poster invitations. If a music concert is going to be publicized through the use of posters, information on the poster must be presented in a concise manner in a neat, well-designed format. Anything less reflects directly on the likely quality of the concert to be presented. Again, "image" is of great importance in public relations.

Another very positive and effective approach to concert publicity is the compilation and use of a mailing list to personally invite members of the community. Mass mailing is not expensive, and, once again, a good deal of the effort involved in a mass mailing is "secretarial" and can be completed by students participating in the music program. The letter of invitation to attend the concert should be printed on letterhead stationery. In addition to the usual information concerning time and place, other data regarding the music to be performed, length of the program, special features, and other similar material can be included. The mailing list can be compiled by asking students to submit the names of families and neighborhood friends who do not have students participating in the music program. Additional names of community businesses and political leaders should be included. The list can be revised annually, and although it is not necessary from an information standpoint to include music parents on the mailing list, parents do appreciate the reminder. Those parents, of course, remain on the list after their students graduate from high school.

Administration of such a mailing list is not necessarily a simple task. Through the use of computer software designed for just such a project, the work involved becomes manageable. People come to school music concerts if they're made aware of the occasion through the use of effective promotional methods.

It is not necessary to "pull out all the stops" in publicizing or advertising every school concert, but once or twice a year, perhaps in combination with some special event, the music educator should accept the challenge of creating the broadest possible publicity base for a concert performance. The results could be pleasantly surprising.

Music educators should be constantly alert to what their professional peers are doing regarding concert publicity. Many creative teachers in charge of quality music-education programs in this country use successful approaches to concert publicity. The young music educator is encouraged to observe and ask questions of "veteran" teachers regarding this very important aspect of music-education administration. It is wise to remember that good public relations *starts* with good teaching. Good teaching can often advertise itself with organized assistance from the music educator.

Planning dates. Dates placed on a music educator's calendar indicating certain tasks to be accomplished in conjunction with concert promotion can be very beneficial. Without a reminder, publicity efforts are likely to be haphazard or left undone unless scheduled and planned in advance. For example, three weeks prior to the event pictures must be taken, developed, selected, enlarged, and copied. This process could more than likely take two weeks. Two weeks before the concert, envelopes need to be labeled for the mass mailing and the letters to be enclosed must be written, typed, and printed. Posters must be designed and prepared, press releases must be written, and ad copy for the media must be readied. A week preceding the concert, letters should be in the mail and ads and press releases should be in the hands of the appropriate parties. Adjunct publicity efforts need to be accomplished as well, but whatever the promotional strategy, the entire effort will come together with greater efficiency and a higher level of success if work begins well in advance of the concert. Successful promotion involves planning dates.

Press releases. When writing a press release a few fundamental guidelines must be kept in mind. As mentioned earlier, the basic information to consider is *who* needs to know about the event, *what* is the event, *when* is it scheduled, *where* is it to take place, and *what time* will it take place. Special features can be mentioned, the concert theme, if any, and the concert type ("pops," serious, and so on) can be included. Above all, *why* would people want to attend must be clear. Concert admission, if any, should be mentioned as well. The above information is assembled in sentence form and presented in a double-spaced, typewritten format. Copies can and should be sent to anyone even vaguely in a position to assist in the promotion of the event.

Use 8 1/2-X-11-inch white paper. Odd sizes make an editor's job difficult. Never use onion skin, tissue weight, or paper that will not take the pencil marks an editor may want to insert. Never send carbon copies. Carbons smear easily, causing possible errors in the spelling of names or in dates and hours. Copies should be mimeographed or xeroxed. Leave wide margins, approximately 1 1/2 inches on each side of the paper.

Give full reference data in the upper left corner of the first page of the release. This information can be single spaced. List the name of the organization and the name, address, and phone number of the individual submitting the release. Type the release date in the upper right corner of the first page. If at all possible, stipulate FOR IMMEDIATE RELEASE, which means that the editor or broadcaster can use it at once. If you ask for a specific publication date, it should read: RELEASE TUESDAY, APRIL 10.

Four spaces below the reference material, a few words of explanation should appear. This group of words identifies the story and is called the "slug line."

Start the copy of the release a third of the entire page length below the slug line. The editor needs this space to use for a headline or other instructions to his staff. If your story must run more than one page, write "More" at the bottom of each page except the last page. Always end each page with a complete sentence or paragraph.

When the release runs more than one page, type the organization's name, the slug line, and the number of the page in the upper-right-hand corner of each succeeding page. The story then continues one inch below the three single-spaced identification lines.

Do not hyphenate words at the end of a line. A ragged right margin is acceptable. Type "END" two spaces under the final paragraph (see Figure 9.1.) The release should be checked for absolute accuracy in typing and the pages should never be stapled together. Press releases are not difficult or time-consuming to formulate and are an often-ignored public-relations tool.

Other public-relations opportunities. Contest and festival participation and/or results can be presented in both the local and school newspapers.

Figure 9.1. Sample press release.

```
BEA FLAT HIGH SCHOOL CHOIR                    FOR IMMEDIATE RELEASE
John C. Kleff
Bea Flat Public Schools
873-2888


(BEA FLAT HIGH SCHOOL CHOIR TO PRESENT SPRING CONCERT)




        BEA FLAT, MN -- The Bea Flat High School Choir will
present its annual spring concert in the school auditorium on
Thursday, April 20.
        The concert is scheduled for 8:00 p.m. and will feature
music from the Broadway musicals "Oklahoma," "West Side Story"
and "The Music Man." Mary Simmons, an alumnus of Bea Flat High
School returns to her alma mater to perform solos selected from
each of the three featured productions.
        According to music instructor John C. Kleff, the concert
will last approximately one hour and will be followed by a
reception for Ms. Simmons in the school cafeteria. Kleff
indicated that the public is invited to the reception after the
program.
        "The students have worked very hard on this program,"
Kleff said, "and everyone is excited about the opportunity to
perform selections from three of the all-time great musical
productions."
        Tickets may be purchased from any high school choir
member and at the First State Bank. Tickets will also be
available at the door ($2.00 for adults, $1.00 for students).
        For more information concerning this performance or for
special seating requests, contact John C. Kleff at the Bea Flat
Public Schools, 873-2888.

                            - END -
```

Such events can provide interview opportunities for the music educator. If the participation is a major event, media coverage is likely to increase. News releases on students receiving scholarship assistance or planning careers in music can be offered to the media. Community appearances by soloists and ensembles at hospitals, nursing homes, churches, service clubs, and similar locales are also newsworthy. Ensemble tours and student participation in music camps can also be publicity opportunities. In short, *anything* music students do, perform, or accomplish can be brought to the attention of some segment of the media. This effort certainly falls within the realm of the music educator as an administrator.

Visual images. The use of photography is a valuable tool for promotion, publicity, and public relations in general. Music-room bulletin boards, scrapbooks and collages, as well as school display cases offer broad opportunities for the use of photographs. Quite simply, students like to see themselves and other students. Parents like to see photographs of their children, and the public enjoys the opportunity to see its youth involved in worthwhile activities. Good-quality photographs that accompany press releases are likely to be published. Candidates for publication are pictures taken in a rehearsal setting in preparation for an event, a teacher assisting a student in preparing for a concert, or a director talking with several students about the future event.

Color slides of specific events can always be shared with parents organizations, music clubs, or community-service clubs. Black and white enlargements can be produced from color slides for publicity purposes. The image quality is not quite as good as if black and white film had originally been used, but it is an acceptable alternative if no black and white prints exist.

Often there are students with good equipment who can assist in photography. In all certainty, there is at least one parent of an ensemble member with a whole room full of photographic equipment who would be willing, if not anxious, to serve as a photographer for the ensemble. Black and white film is not expensive and print choices can be determined from "contact" sheets, which provide a developed positive image in negative size, thus permitting an entire roll of film to be previewed on an 8 1/2-×-11-inch sheet of paper. Funds for photography are a legitimate part of the printing and publicity line-item in any music-education budget.

Most schools in the United States are likely to possess a video camera and playback equipment. Music educators are somewhat casual in their approach to their work if they fail to use this "state of the art" equipment, not only for analysis for performance purposes, but as a means of communicating music-program activities to their constituencies as well. Numerous parents now own quality video camera, and they could be called on for assistance in videotaping rehearsals or performances should similar school-owned equipment not be available to the music educator. Long-range music-education budget plans should include a video camera and playback equipment simply to be up-to-date in the increased use of audiovisual materials and equipment in the music classroom.

Community Involvement

The level of community involvement attained by a music educator can have a direct effect on how the music program is viewed by the public and can provide a substantial base for public-relations success. First of all, the music educator, with very few exceptions, should live in the community in which he or she works. It is difficult to become involved in community activities unless one resides in that community. The public does notice! Exceptions, of course, are the densely populated urban areas and the sparsely populated rural areas. In either of those cases, the music educator could have difficulty finding housing.

Community involvement can include such activities as forming a parents group, organizing community activities, creating a community musical performing group, directing or participating in a church choir, and teaching adult music classes, such as appreciation, musical theater, piano, guitar, or ukelele. The development of music programs for older and retired adults can be an extremely worthwhile and personally satisfying community activity. There are many opportunities for the music educator to perform some type of community service. It does take a bit of courage on the part of the music educator to leave the security of the school environment and venture out into the unknown realms of public service. Those that do will generally find an amenable and genuinely enthusiastic reception from the community.

Music educators should join a service club and perhaps even a social club. Many service club's activities involve support of youth work in some manner. The young teacher is encouraged to locate such an organization and become a member. Social and fraternal groups provide the music educator with an opportunity to meet and become acquainted with countless numbers of community members in a relaxed, social environment.

Activities such as bowling and golf hold a tremendous potential for the music educator to become known to community members other than those associated with the local school. Even if the bowling, golf, or similar activity is done with teachers, it is taking place *in* a community environment. This is positive!

Music In Our Schools Month

No discussion on the need for and value of public relations in support of music education would be complete without at least a brief reference to the annual Music In Our Schools Month, sponsored by the Music Educators National Conference. This month-long event provides an imaginative opportunity to expose both school and community to the importance of school music programs and associated activities on a national level. During the month of March each year, special concerts, adult involvement, mayoral proclamations, and a general "spreading of the gospel" of the importance of music education in today's schools occurs all across the United States.

Numerous promotional items such as posters, banners, buttons, lapel stickers, transfers, bumper stickers, pencils, mobiles, memo pads, balloons, certificates, and program covers are available at a reasonable fee for use in any promotional effort during the important month. Many of the items can be used all year long. Remember to order extra memo pads to give to all school administrators.

For more information regarding Music In Our Schools Month and suggested activities, simply contact MENC, 1902 Association Drive, Reston, Virginia 22091. Please inquire far in advance and order promotional items at least two months prior to anticipated use. This is a superb manner in which a young music educator can become involved in public relations on a grand scale.

Membership in MENC and other professional organizations provides an opportunity for music educators to keep abreast of current trends in their chosen field. Most of the professional organizations include in the annual dues paid to the national office a subscription to a monthly periodical. Music educators have an obligation to their profession, not only to become members of such a group, but to become actively involved in the organization at the state and regional levels. In doing so, a career can become a profession, not simply a job.

Summary

Public relations is primarily a means of communication between the community and the music educator. A music-education program cannot generally be considered successful unless it is also looked upon as such by its constituency. Promoting an image of success is accomplished through public relations and a certain level of "selling" on the part of the music educator. Active and ongoing public-relations efforts provide an atmosphere that allows promotion to succeed. Goal-setting is an extremely important part of any public relations process and is as important an aspect of public relations as it is of any other non-instructional element in music education.

Musical performances can have a positive effect, no effect, or a negative effect on the total image of a music-education program. Concerts that have been carefully prepared and thoughtfully constructed will undoubtedly convey a positive image to the public if general public-relations strategies are employed. The music educator must be constantly alert to new and interesting approaches to concert performance.

Concert promotion can evolve into a routine, but in the early stages, it requires in-depth planning and extra effort on the part of the music educator. Any publicity in conjunction with musical performances that appears before the public eye is in itself a form of public relations, and the quality must be carefully considered. A variety of ways to promote and publicize a musical performance is available to music educators. They must choose the publicity method or approach that best suits their individual needs. The mailing list concept is perhaps the most effective means of communicating concert information to the potentially interested public.

The use of photography and video technology in music education as a means of performance evaluation has been on the scene for several years; however, the use of these media as instruments of public relations has yet to gain widespread use.

The music educator should make it a point to become involved in the community. Music educators possess special skills that can make them valued assets in community activities, and such participation often leads to a greater depth of understanding and support for the total music-education program.

Suggested Activities

1. Visit a local radio station and determine its policy on public-service announcements and the advertising rates for a school-concert promotional effort.

2. Design and put into effect a promotional campaign for a future concert to be presented by one of the major performing ensembles on your campus. Under the supervision of the group director, write the press release, design and distribute posters, write the letter for mass mailing, and so on.

3. Locate and evaluate promotional efforts associated with at least ten events that appear in the next Sunday edition of the newspaper serving your area.

4. Devise a hypothetical long-range goal in public relations and the accompanying short-term objectives used to support the long-range goal. Include support techniques for implementation of the short-term objectives.

5. Invite a local or regional corporate public-relations specialist to visit class and discuss the corporate importance of public relations and image "polishing."

6. Evaluate the local community in terms of its needs for music and music education. Then present public relations activities suggested by the evaluation.

7. Invite a local music educator to class and discuss his or her associated public relations and promotional policies, restrictions, and handicaps.

8. Design a hypothetical series of five side-by-side concerts involving public-school ensembles and evaluate the public-relations benefit and promotional potential of each.

References and Suggested Reading

Bessom, Malcom E., Alphonse M. Tatarunis, and Samuel L. Forcucci. *Teaching Music in Today's Secondary Schools*. New York: Holt, Rinehart and Winston, 1980.

Brand, Manny. "Putting Our 'PR' Techniques to Use." *The School Musician*, January 1980.

Brian, Keith. "How to Build an Audience." *The Instrumentalist*, March 1979.

MENC, *Promoting School Music*. Reston, Va.: Music Educators National Conference, 1984.

Snyder, Keith. *School Music Administration and Supervision*. Boston: Allyn and Bacon, 1965.

Parents
Organizations and
Fund-Raising

The two topics included in this chapter were combined because it is difficult to talk about one without involving, in some way, the other. For example, a widely accepted function of parent support groups is to provide a degree of financial assistance to a performing organization. When discussing fund-raising, booster organizations are frequently involved in an advisory capacity and are also a source of willing volunteers for fund-raising projects.

The percentage of American tax dollars going to public-school education from state and federal governments decreased significantly in the last ten years, while inflation pushed the cost-per-pupil figures in public education higher and higher. The result has been a series of legislative propositions and resolutions placing the burden of financially supporting public-school education on local governments. Many city and county commissions were already at or near the maximum allowable mil levy for education. School administrators were forced to reduce or eliminate program offerings and postpone plans to enlarge or remodel the physical plants of their school systems. In certain elementary schools in Nevada and California, principals hold annual fund-raising programs involving the students and parents of the district. The money raised from these major efforts provides funds for such projects as reroofing a building, replacing old windows with more energy-efficient models, and replacing a ventilation/air-conditioning system.

Arts and vocational programs have been caught in the budget crunch at the public-school level in many parts of the country. Parents groups that were already in place were called upon for moral and financial support when music budgets were reduced. In many instances parents organizations were hastily organized to perform that same function and then became a permanent part of the music-education program.

The purpose of this chapter is to acquaint prospective music educators with one of the most important administrative responsibilities that they may face in the early years of their career. Horror stories have been told about parents groups that have "attempted to take over the band program" or have "tried to get the choir director fired" or some similar scenario. Such cases are extremely isolated and can most certainly be prevented by appropriate anticipation, organization, and action on the part of the music educator. The following material is intended to aid music educators in developing the expertise to carry out with confidence this significant administrative responsibility.

Parents Organizations

Parents organizations, or booster clubs, as they are often known, can serve as a strong support group in the advancement and better understanding of the music program, and they can also provide increased visibility and an improved image to that program. A booster organization's main goal should be to promote the education of students in the field of music. An active organization will include not only parents of students presently involved in music but can also include other individuals within the community who support the work of the music department.

Benefits of a parents organization

Through participation in a booster organization, parents gain a better understanding of music education. They learn the purpose of the music program and become involved to a degree in their children's education. Through their participation, parents can develop a sense of appreciation for the work that both the students and their director contribute to the music program. The line of communication between staff and parents is a most positive benefit of an active music parents organization. This important link between the school and community can provide an element of strength to the music-education program that is simply not available in other academic programs.

Through energetic involvement with a parents organization, a music educator has the opportunity to get to know the parents of his or her students to a greater degree, and the parents, in turn, appreciate the opportunity to become acquainted with the individual who affects the musical lives of their children.

Parents organizations can be a great source of assistance for the busy music educator. They can, of course, help in supervising and chaperoning students on trips made by the performing groups. Parents can also aid in publicizing events and in building greater audience support for concert performances. When necessary, parents can serve a very productive role in providing financial assistance to music-education programs through their fund-raising efforts.

Some music educators believe that parents booster organizations, or students participating in the music program, should not be involved in raising funds in support of that program. They feel that, if the program is worthwhile, the school district should support it. This idealistic position cannot be successfully defended during years of budget cuts and program reductions. If parents have come to associate a certain quality with the music-education program, they are very often willing to realistically support that program by limited fund-raising efforts. It is not the position of this writer that the organization of parents groups and their associated raising of funds be undertaken in situations where school districts are willing to totally support the music-education programs. In cases where that type of school-district support does not exist, however, music educators would be failing their obligation to their students and the total music-education program if they were to neglect parental support and fund-raising as a source of moral and financial support.

The amount of physical and financial assistance that parents can provide for the music educator and the music-education program is limited only by the ingenuity of that educator.

Type of parents organizations

Parents booster organizations exist in three separate formats with associated variations. Such groups may call themselves "Music Boosters," "Band Parents," "Symphony Society," or a variety of other names. Regardless of the title or structure of the group, its primary function remains the same, that is, to provide support and assistance to the students for which it was organized.

The "one-shot" temporary parents organization. Booster organizations are often organized on a temporary basis and are then dissolved when a particular project has been completed. Generally, the sole purpose of such an organization is to raise funds for a trip, concert wear, or some major instrument or equipment purchase. When a booster group is organized temporarily, it must still be structured with officers, boards, and committees, the same as a permanent support group. The amount of administrative effort required for such a group is by necessity more intense than an organization with a more permanent framework. Planning meetings might be held weekly, and as the project develops perhaps daily attention is required.

This type of support group is acceptable in a situation where a sufficient music budget is provided by the school district, but an unanticipated circumstance arises that demands a level of funding beyond that which the school district can provide. A presidential inaugural invitation or selection for a performance at a national or state convention of music educators are just two of many situations where a need for increased funding could occur.

Some school administrations prohibit the initiation of a music booster group, but they are likely to support such an organization if it is to be active on a temporary basis with a specific goal in mind. It is not unusual for music parents to organize on a temporary basis, find that they enjoy the interaction that occurs in such groups, and vote, with the blessings of the music educators and administrators, to become a permanent booster organization. The level of involvement on the part of music educators is generally greater with temporary booster groups that it is with those more permanently structured.

Single-performing-group booster clubs. Unfortunately, most of the music booster organizations in the United States support only one school performance group, and that performance group is generally the school band.

For some unknown reason, choral and orchestra directors have not seen the need to establish a parent support organization as part of their individual programs. Booster organizations are discussed, if in a somewhat limited fashion, in nearly all undergraduate instrumental-music-methods textbooks. The same topic is rarely, if ever, discussed in textbooks written for choral-music-methods classes.

Permanent music parents organizations meet on a regular monthly basis, and their activity level is somewhat determined by the activity level of the school group with which they are associated. One thing is certain, no booster organization will function intact if it doesn't have adequate leadership and specific annual goals to meet. This doesn't necessarily mean that a particular educator must provide total leadership for such an organization, but he or she must provide direction and assistance in establishing yearly goals. When this action is taken by music educators, the leadership within the group will in all likelihood increase.

The comprehensive music booster organization. By far the most beneficial and educationally sound music support group is an organization designed to meet the needs of all music education taking place in a given school. Membership includes the parents of many student musicians in the school. An organization of this type supports the band, choral, and orchestra programs on a basis determined by the needs of each performing group. This level of support can extend into the junior-high-school program as well. It takes skilled and cooperative music educators to combine their talents and efforts in a comprehensive support organization for music education. Part of the inherent difficulty in such a group is trying to balance any fund-raising efforts among affected performing groups. If the members are unable to effectively balance their support for performing groups, they often turn into a booster group with a single focus and purpose. Fortunate are the music educators who have a music parents organization that is active and effective in the support of the total music-education program. Should a serious crisis ever arise that will drastically affect the music department in a negative manner, there is a large support force already in place that can be a positive voice for the total music program.

Organizing a Parents Booster Club

Prior to organizing a parents booster club, music educators should feel comfortable with the idea of working and associating with parents and other community members. Music educators should in no way feel threatened by the thought of working with individuals outside the school environment. Music teachers are the "in-residence" authorities on the subject in the entire community, and parents, with very few exceptions, have respect for someone who is sharing that knowledge with their children. Music educators need to be prepared to spend extra time and extra effort when initiating a parents organization, particularly at the outset. In the long run, however, a properly functioning support group will annually save a director countless hours.

A music educator must feel that a booster group will be a definite aid to the program and that such an organization will provide assistance in achieving goals and objectives established for the program by that music educator. Once the above determinations have been satisfied, the music educator is ready to proceed.

Check with school officials. School officials need to understand the purpose of a booster club. Carefully prepare a parents-organization proposal to present to those school administrators. List the reasons a music parents organization is needed to support the music program and the potential benefits to that program by the development of such a parent organization. It might also be wise to use area schools that have booster groups as examples in support of the request.

A music educator must be prepared to defend adequately a request to organize a booster group, even though once an administrator offers a negative response to a proposal, it may be very difficult to get that "no" changed to a "yes." If a proposal is well-prepared, researched, and documented, most administrators will see the long-term benefits to the music program and through that program, to the entire school.

Visit with parent leaders. It is easy to determine the influential community leaders with children involved in the music program. Music educators would do well to visit several of these parents personally concerning plans for a booster organization. Much of the information prepared for school administrators can be shared with them. Enlist their support because they will very likely be the early leaders of the booster club.

Visit with area music educators. Music educators from nearby schools can often be of assistance in providing information and practical advice regarding structure, format, and benefits that can be of use in building a new music parents support group. It is entirely possible that the president or some other officer from an area booster club would be willing to come to the first organizational meeting of a new club to discuss what the area club does to support their music program and why.

Write a letter. With the blessing of school officials and the support of several parents, the music educator can now draft a letter to be sent to all music parents and other community leaders that are potential supporters. A sample letter is provided in Figure 10.1. The letter needs to be short, but at the same time it must provide enough information to whet the interest of the reader. Include the starting and estimated ending time of the meeting. As with overly long public-school concerts, busy parents have no time for marathon meetings.

The meeting. The extent to which a music educator plans the organizational meeting will have a direct effect on the outcome of the meeting. Parents are willing to give of their time in support of a program that is guided by an individual who is upbeat, excited, and who can provide a degree of leadership through his or her organizational abilities. A short tape or slide show of a recent or proposed trip or event would certainly be in order, as would a few words of support from a school administrator, if one can be encouraged to attend the meeting. After the purpose and function of the group has been explained, as seen through the eyes of the music educator, the bulk of the

Figure 10.1. Sample letter for initial contact concerning a new parents organization.[1]

```
Dear Parents and Friends,

I have called a meeting for parents of music students and other
interested people to discuss the possibility of starting a music
booster organization. I am sure that we all share the common goal of
providing the best possible music program for our students. Such an
organization can be extremely helpful in achieving that goal. The
purpose of a music parents organization would be to promote and
support the entire music program and its activities in the Bea Flat
school system.

                DATE:  Monday, September 14, 1987

                TIME:  7:30 PM

                PLACE: High School Music Room

                AGENDA:  1.  Introductory remarks by Superin-
                             tendent Smart.
                         2.  Need for and purpose of a music
                             parents organization--Mr. Kleff.
                         3.  Open discussion.
                         4.  Election of officers.
                         5.  Date, time and place of next meeting.

Come to the meeting and let us hear your ideas. Refreshments will be
served.

                                Sincerely,



                                John C. Kleff
                                Music Instructor
```

remaining meeting time can be spent in open discussion, perhaps led by one of the parent leaders with whom the project was discussed in the early planning stages. Election of officers follows the discussion, and the meeting closes with setting the date, time, and place of the next meeting.

Constitution. All music parents organizations must draft a constitution or charter that outlines the function, structure, and intent of the organization. A sample constitution is presented in Figures 10.2 and 10.3. The "constitution" is presented only to initiate action on the part of the reader, not as the sum total of what should be included as part of a document governing all music booster organizations. Music educators are advised once again to check with their colleagues for ideas regarding this important facet of booster-club development. It must also be kept in mind that as the direction and scope of parents organizations change, as they very often do, the constitutions of these groups must be updated to keep pace with such changes.

Parents groups and political pressure. It is the right and perhaps the duty of parents to be involved in some manner in the policies established by the school district. It is parents' tax dollars that support, to a great extent, the daily operation of the school. They should be concerned and they should be involved. It is a grave error, however, for any music parents organization to officially become actively and politically involved as a pressure group to affect change in school policy. The booster group can serve as a forum for discussion of school philosophy and policy that affects the music program, but it must refrain in all but the most dire of circumstances to act as an official source of pressure for political change within the school system. A well-organized, active, and viable music booster organization can send a strong and positive message to school officials regarding the degree of parental and community support for a particular music program. Only when a situation becomes life-threatening for a music program is the active involvement of a booster club as a pressure group justified.

A recommended structure for a booster club

Membership. Booster-club membership does not necessarily need to be restricted to parents of student musicians. Businesses associated with the music-education program should be invited and encouraged to become involved in some way with club activities. Having a child involved in the music program automatically makes that parent a member. If the club is only associated with the orchestra, parents of every string student in the school, from grade school through high school, are members of the booster club. The same holds true for the choir and band as well. If the group is a comprehensive, all-school-music booster organization, the parents of *all* music students are considered members.

Structure. The usual panel of officers is elected, and they in turn select a board of at least thirty members who indicate a willingness to become actively involved in the organization. The board meets monthly. Various project committees are made up of members of the organization at large and are chaired by a board member. Separate standing committees can

Figure 10.2. A sample of articles of constitution for a music parents organization.[2]

Constitution

Article I — Identification

The name of this organization is_____. Our fiscal year runs from August 1 through July 31.

Article II — Objectives

The objectives of_____, a nonprofit organization, are:

Section 1. To arouse and maintain an enthusiastic interest in the various phases of the music department of_____ High School.

Section 2. To lend all possible support, both moral and financial, to the total music program in the school and to provide social and other programs and awards for music personnel.

Section 3. To cooperate with those in charge of the music department, school administration, and the school board to the end that this department be brought to and kept at the highest possible degree of efficiency; to build and maintain an organization that will help promote the general activities of the_____music department.

Article III — Membership

Section 1. The membership of this organization shall not be limited. Anyone interested in furthering the aims of the organization shall be eligible to join.

Section 2. Annual dues shall be specified and approved by the membership.

Article IV — Officers

The officers of the organization shall be a president, vice-president, recording secretary, corresponding secretary, treasurer, and music director of the_____High School.

Article V — Meetings

The regular meetings of the organization shall be held at 7:30 PM on the first Tuesday of each month from September through May. Special meetings may be called by the president.

Article VI — Amendments

The constitution and bylaws may be amended by a majority vote of the members present at any regular meeting. The amendments must have been presented at the preceding regular meeting of the organization and the membership notified of such amendments.

Article VII — Quorum

Ten members shall constitute a quorum for the purpose of conducting meetings.

Figure 10.3. A sample of constitutional bylaws for a music parents organization.[3]

Bylaws

Article I   —   Duties of Officers

Section 1. The president shall preside over all of the organization's meetings, appoint all committees, and be an ex-officio member of all committees.

Section 2. The vice-president shall assume all the duties of the president in his or her absence.

Section 3. The recording secretary shall keep all records of all meetings.

Section 4. The corresponding secretary shall be responsible for all of the organization's correspondence and retain the stamp for bulk mail.

Section 5. The treasurer shall receive all funds accrued by the organization, deposit the same in a federally insured bank, and make disbursements as directed by the organization. He or she shall keep a full and correct account of all money received and expended and make monthly reports at the regular meeting of the organization.

Section 6. The music director shall act as liaison between the _____, band personnel, and school authorities.

Article II   —   Executive Board

Section 1. The executive board shall be composed of the organization's officers, the past president, and such committee chairmen as deemed necessary by the president at the beginning of his or her term.

Section 2. The executive board shall supervise the affairs of the organization.

Section 3. Elected officers and chairpersons shall not hold the same office for more than two (2) consecutive years.

Article III   —   Elections

Section 1. A nominating committee of two (2) members of the executive board and three (3) members from the general membership shall be appointed by the president at the February meeting. The past president shall act as chairman with no vote.

Section 2. Nominations may be made from the floor after the report of the nominating committee at the March meeting.

Section 3. Officers are to be elected by ballot at the April meeting, or if a single slate is presented, the secretary is to cast one ballot.

Section 4. Elected officers will be installed at the May meeting, but official duties will not be assumed until July 31 to allow booster activities to be completed.

Section 5. Any elective officer's post that becomes vacant shall be filled by appointment by the executive board to fill the unexpired term, except the president's office, which shall be filled by the vice-president.

Article IV

If the _____ shall at any time disband, any monies in the treasury shall be turned over to the Music Department of the _____ High School.

Article V

No expenditure that adds to the physical properties of the school shall be authorized until first approved by the school board.

handle fund-raising, publicity, concert attendance, awards, membership, and community events. Numerous other committees can be established by the board as the need arises, with the chairman of the committee in charge of keeping accurate records of committee work and providing progress reports to the panel of officers and the board.

The thirty-to-forty-member board concept is offered because of the low percentage of parents that are willing to be involved on a long-term basis in such a project. But almost everyone is willing to give a little of themselves over a short period of time and in doing so are freed from the obligation of monthly meetings and active participation.

Activities. Activities of the booster organization can and should include the printing and distribution of a newsletter to the membership three or four times annually. Included in the newsletter could be such information as a calendar of events, individual school activities, feature activities, club projects, and news of other innovative projects. Fund-raising in support of the music-education program need not be the major consideration of such a parents organization, but very often it will be. Other projects can be to boost concert attendance for school and community cultural events, support music-budget requests, support and assist Music in Our Schools Month, organize music-classroom visitations, and encourage community musical efforts. It must be kept in mind that a music teacher's obligation to the school is to *teach*. The organization of a booster club and the eventual assuming of responsibility for a variety of activities by that club can allow the dedicated and concerned music educator to devote maximum effort to his or her students.

Determining a name. Some common titles for school music booster groups were mentioned earlier and would certainly be satisfactory for this organization. The author, however, suggests a title such as "Friends of Music," because it promotes an image of professionalism that carries beyond the doorstep of the local school and promotes a feeling of comprehensiveness. No matter what the title of a music parents organization is, the parents themselves must make that determination. The title of the group provides a degree of identity to the group, and that fact should be taken into consideration when selecting a name for the organization.

Music educators willing to try this structure and format for a music parents organization will find themselves with a streamlined, effective, and efficient organization with which to deal. Always keep in mind the importance of a charter or constitution. It is a requisite for group stabilization. The membership makeup and leadership of a booster organization may change, but its scope and direction remain intact when the group is guided by a charter or constitution.

A final thought concerning booster-club organization: Far too often music educators overlook a tremendously important asset to any booster group—that is, the fathers of music students. Music educators should make every effort to solicit and promote the involvement of the male members of a community's musical families. They often possess the banking, business, publicity, and promotional skills necessary to the successful operation of a music parents organization.

Fund-Raising

Much has already been said about budget reductions fueling a need for increased fund-raising by public-school music departments, other entities within the school, and in some cases, the school district itself. Funds raised by students and/or their parents should be used only for budget benefits that the school district does not supply. In many cases funds that are raised are used for travel purposes. Concert wear, large equipment items, awards, music camp scholarships, clinicians, and guest conductors are often paid for by money raised through the efforts of a performing organization or their support group. However, even in times of the tightest budget restrictions, the school district still has the distinct obligation to provide new and replacement equipment, equipment maintenance and repair, festival and contest fees, music and instruction books, and printing. In situations where even the above basic obligations of the school district to the music program cannot be met, resourceful music educators generally find some way in which to maintain a program's integrity for the mutual benefit of the students and community.

Need for fund-raising? Prior to the initiation of any successful fund-raising campaign, a genuine need for that campaign must be established. Neither parents nor students are motivated toward achieving a financial goal unless a genuine need for fund-raising is demonstrated. Some teachers feel that by simply declaring a need to raise funds, the declaration will touch off frantic activity. Set financial goals and demonstrate the need to meet those goals.

Approval for fund-raising. It is always wise to keep administrators informed of any fund-raising project to be undertaken by the music department. When a project involves students, permission should be received from the appropriate school official(s). Fund-raising projects undertaken solely by a parent support group generally do not need administrative approval, but informing school officials of such action is a courtesy and a good administrative practice on the part of the music educator.

Getting organized. In most successful fund-raising campaigns, many people are involved. Project leaders must be selected; chairmen of various aspects of the project are an important ingredient of success. Several of these chairmen are project chairman (a winning and positive attitude), publicity chairman (energy, time, writing ability), civic chairman, and sales chairman (the last two are perhaps the most important).

As one would imagine, the project chairman oversees the total project and coordinates the efforts of the other chairmen. The publicity chairman is responsible for getting news releases to the media and for any advertising associated with the campaign. The civic chairman coordinates a committee, the members of whom will visit every civic and service organization in the community. Such organizations are always in search of programs for their meetings, and with enough advance notice, an informational program can be developed about the group doing the fund-raising and how the proceeds of the drive will be used.

The sales chairman works closely with the music educator in selecing fund-raising products and activities and in developing the campaign approach. A successful organizational plan will see five or six student musicians and their respective families grouped into teams under the leadership of a team captain. Five or six team captains are grouped under an area chairman, and all area chairmen report directly to the sales chairman. This type of organizational structure is effective in the world of business and industry and can be used, at its simplist level, to administrate a brief but intense fund-raising effort.

Activity guidelines. Music-department projects should entail only limited student involvement. Fund-raising campaigns that involve a great deal of student time are generally not successful, and, if they are, are difficult to justify from an educational standpoint. A one-week campaign with one month of preparation time preceding the effort is usually sufficient. Students and parents alike thrive on the intensity of a short campaign and the feeling that there's a job to be done.

Fund-raising project considerations. When selecting a product for sale, the product should return a minimum profit level of 40 percent, and more ideally, a profit of 50 percent. Sell a product that is useful, not something that people buy just to support the group. Music educators are encouraged to pick a product that both they and their group approve. Enthusiasm sells! It's difficult for individuals to communicate enthusiasm if they don't like the product. Fund-raising company representatives are willing to provide samples of their products. Comparison shop for similar products to compare both quality and price.

Check the competition. Become aware of other school, church, and civic organizations that schedule annual fund-raising campaigns. A sure way to ensure fund-raising failure and perhaps create feelings of ill will is to schedule a music department fund-raising effort in direct conflict with other school or community campaigns.

Music educators are cautioned to be aware of "too much of a good thing." If the profit levels appear to be unusually high or if a salesman paints a picture similar to "fish jumping into the boat," the product or project probably *is* too good to be be true. It generally works best to select products that have sold well in the past, but allow plenty of time between campaigns. If a sales item was successful in previous years but suddenly fails, don't necessarily blame the campaign approach. Seek out a different product.

Five questions that need to be answered by a music educator seeking a fund-raising product are: (1) Do the customers get something of value for their money? (2) Is it a better value than they can get somewhere else? (3) Is a service being provided? (4) Is there a need for the service or product? (5) Is the service or product unique? How a music educator is able to answer those questions can directly influence product or project selection.

Some consumable products can be sold several times annually on a telephone reorder basis. The simplicity of a telephone reorder campaign is often attractive to music educators, participants, and customers alike. Food products, if they are of high quality, are particularly appealing for that reason.

Preselling a product is an advantage for student salesmen that must be considered. They need not take samples with them when making sales. A brief description of the product, perhaps in the form of a brochure and an explanation of what the profit will be used for are generally sufficient to sell a quality product. The customer pays for the product when it is ordered. After the shipment arrives at the school, students can deliver presold orders in a very short period of time. A classic example of this technique is the millions of boxes of Girl Scout cookies that have been sold throughout the years.

Activity guidelines. Keep the campaign short, and if selling a product, be sure it is backed by a solid program of sales and distribution through a professional consultant who will actually come into a music educator's school. There are enough fund-raising representatives who are willing to call on individual schools to explain their programs and products that it is simply not necessary for music educators to take the risk of dealing with fund-raising campaigns on a mail-order basis. Develop an advertising budget. The public must be prepared in advance for a major fund-raising drive to succeed. Annual, successful United Way campaigns are a positive example of advance advertising. Developing a theme or logo is another means of building an identity for a successful effort.

Many campaigns providing products for use in fund-raising also have prize programs designed to motivate students toward and beyond their sales goals. If such a plan is not part of a campaign's fund-raising program, a music educator may wish to initiate one at the local level. By the same token, just because a prize program happens to be available through a company does not necessarily mean that a music educator must adopt that portion of the program. In some cases, a higher profit percentage can be negotiated in lieu of the motivational prize program.

Student "accounts."   One of the problems with any fund-raising program associated with music education has been the equitable dispersion of benefits in direct proportion to the amount of effort invested by student participants. This problem is particularly true when travel is involved. Students, parents, and teachers alike have been concerned with the inequity of a system that allows students who put forth very little effort toward achieving a group's financial goal to receive the same benefits for their efforts as other students who achieved or exceeded the goal that was established for them. An approach that has been developed by a number of successful music educators, and is recommended for use by this author, is to establish an individual "account" for each member of a performing group. Profits raised by individual students as part of a fund-raising campaign or series of campaigns are credited to each individual's "account." For example, perhaps an invitation to perform at a national convention has been received by a high-school choral director. The total cost of the trip for meals, lodging, and transportation is $42,000. Perhaps the school district was able to provide $4,000 in the form of a special allocation, and gifts from local businesses and service clubs total $2,000. With a choir enrollment of eighty-four students, and with a total of $36,000 yet to be raised, the resulting cost-per-pupil figure is approximately $430.

A series of fund-raising projects are then designed to allow students to easily meet that cost-per-pupil goal. When the predetermined funding deadline arrives, those students with full funding in their "accounts" make the trip at no additional expense to themselves or their families. Those students with deficiencies in their "accounts" must make up the difference between their "account" balance and the $430 cost per pupil for the trip.

When sufficient advance notice is provided to students and their parents that such a procedure is being followed, there is no confusion as to how money is allocated, and all parties can agree that the system provides parity for all involved in the project. The old "all for one and one for all" system in which every member of a group contributed his or her efforts to whatever level is adequate to support a project is certainly an alternative to the preceding system. The "account" system, however, removes much of the pressure from the music educator to maintain equity, and the danger that hard feelings may replace exuberance upon successful completion is eliminated.

Fund-Raising Ideas

Music educators are encouraged to read periodical literature associated with their performance areas to keep abreast of new fund-raising ideas. Another source of ideas is the efforts of colleagues. Music educators are always happy to be able to share their fund-raising successes and failures with one another.

The following products and projects are offered as examples of items and ideas that have proven to be successsful for music educators through the year. A major concern to bear in mind when making decisions regarding a fund-raising project is maintaining the integrity of the music program and promoting credibility, which will establish standards for future fund-raising projects.

Sales. For a group of energetic members of the educational society in this country who have promoted the sale of everything from birthday calendars to toilet paper, the following list may appear to be rather mundane. The items on the list, however, do carry with them a degree of historical sense in assisting music educators in meeting their financial goals. When selecting a product, the past success of that product can, and perhaps should be, a determining factor.

Candy can be considered the original fund-raising product for musical groups. Whether offered in bars or boxes of candies or wafers, the mouth-watering color photographs arouse the taste buds of candy lovers across the United States. Candy sales still account for a major portion of annual revenue raised by school music groups today. Candy is a popular fund-raising product when funding requirements are not extremely large.

Popcorn, light bulbs, candles, Christmas ornaments, cleaning agents, and shampoo sales have increased significantly in recent years. Part of this success lies in the fact that these products have long shelf lives and are not perishable. These and similar products can earn hundreds and perhaps several thousands of dollars in a disciplined campaign and are quite successful within those parameters. Such products, along with candy products, are usually provided on a consignment basis, allowing the music educator to return unsold, unopened cartons of merchandise.

Sausage and cheese products as fund-raisers have become quite popular with music educators in the last ten years. The success of these items perhaps lies in the fact that the quality of the product has been maintained, and the

American public has grown more attracted to that type of product. The total funding potential for sausage and cheese products remains somewhat higher than previously mentioned items because they are consumable food items and also make attractive and welcome gift packages.

Citrus-fruit and pizza sales have become the foundation for many school music programs that need to raise tens of thousands of dollars annually. Both products must be presold and delivered to the customers upon receipt of the shipment at the school. The goal of most music educators involved in the sale of citrus and pizza products is to create sales sufficient to allow them to place truckload orders. This effort, of course, pays dividends through reduced freight costs. Citrus-fruit and pizza products are also attractive as fund-raisers because they have the potential to develop a clientele for reorder purposes, along with the potential to raise thousands of dollars in annual revenue in support of music programs. Frozen-fish sales have also been successful for many music educators and are certainly worthy of consideration if a geographic area dictates that such food items be purchased in a frozen state.

Magazine sales are another source of substantial income that can be earned on an annual basis. Nearly every household in America subscribes to at least one, and often several, magazines. But the recent development of multimillion dollar prizes associated with clearing house companies' promotion of magazine sales has made the sale of magazines at the school level less attractive as a fund-raising agent.

School administrators are often reluctant to allow fund-raising efforts that permit large sums of money to leave that community. For example, if a school band raises $20,000 through the sale of some product, that means that another $20,000 to $25,000 leaves that community as income for a company in some distant state. Such administrators encourage local promotions if fund-raising is a necessity. Once again, music educators must always receive administrative approval prior to initiating a fund-raising campaign.

Nonproduct projects. Any number of fund-raising projects can be developed that do not necessarily involve the sale of a product. Very often such projects are annual affairs, and once established, build a faithful clientele. Other nonproduct projects can earn large amounts of money for a music program, but their success very often depends largely upon promotional efforts.

Examples of successful projects that can result in varying amount of financial gain include an annual pops concert with a guest artist. Through creative organization, promotion, and performance, such a project can become an anticipated annual event. Turkey suppers and "soup and pie" dinners have become popular fund-raisers in smaller communities across the country, with the food donated by parents and supportive community members. Meals of this nature often precede a concert and help increase the audience for the performance. School carnivals and "big-name" entertainment can be very successful money makers, but require somewhat of an "up front" investment and hold an element of financial risk for the sponsor. Auctions of some unique nature have a proven history of financial success with little or no investment and provide profits of nearly 100 percent when auction items are donated by community members and local businesses.

With the high level of interest in running in the 1980s, mini-marathons (6K and 10K races) have become a popular and fun way to raise money. Local assistance in organizing the event and helping with locating sponsors is often available through a local track or athletic club. Some music groups are able to secure the concession and refreshment contract with the local school system. Such an arrangement can provide thousands of dollars in annual income. Community paper drives also hold a great deal of potential for substantial income for music groups, but difficulty is often encountered in getting music students actively involved in such a project.

Rent-a-kid programs and car washes are sources of quick funding that require a minimum of student and teacher effort. Pledges may be generated from the public on the number of cars to be washed in one day. Caution is urged when soliciting pledges that contributors understand the approximate amount of their financial obligation when the car wash is completed. One publicized car wash "scheme" has music students securing pledges from the citizenry at the rate of $.01 per car to be washed by that group. What appears to be a rather insignificant sum mushrooms when the one hundred-member ensemble washes a total of five thousand cars in twenty or more locations in a city. The amount of the pledge then becomes a total of $50, far more than any benefactor would have imagined, and this can be the source of hard feelings between the group raising the funds and the individual making the pledge. The public deserves to understand in advance the extent of money pledged.

Raffles. In schools and communities where raffles are permitted, they can be a source of substantial funding. They involve a minimum of effort distributed over a month-long period. There are numerous ways in which to operate a raffle project, but perhaps the most successful is one in which a variation of the previously established "account" method is used—that is, a fixed dollar amount to be raised per student is established, and the student and their parents have the option of selling or *buying* the raffle tickets. Five-dollar raffle ticket prices are suggested rather than the usual $1 per ticket, particularly if the prize to be awarded is at least $1,000 cash. If the figure of $200 per student is established, forty $5 tickets must be sold as opposed to 200 of the $1 tickets. The $5 price makes the process much more expedient. If some students are only able to sell twenty of the tickets, then either they or their parents understand that they must purchase the remaining twenty tickets. This type of project can be especially productive when older students are involved. A crucial aspect in preparing for this type of raffle is that students and parents understand their role in the project. Similar efforts have resulted in tens of thousands of dollars raised in the period of one month.

When music program fund-raising projects are conducted by parent booster organizations, it is still the responsibility of the music teacher to oversee the entire process. These responsibilities include providing a source of informational leadership for the group and providing a sincere rationale for a fund-raising project. Music educators must also be prepared to answer honestly all questions and doubts about club projects and to provide leadership in screening and selecting quality fund-raising projects.

Whether fund-raising projects involve parents or students alone, the results of the project and the quality of the experience for the participants is determined by the music educator's integrity, dedication, and administrative abilities.

The reader must understand that the intention of this chapter is not to necessarily advocate fund-raising by music students, their parents, or both. Nor is it advocating the establishment of music parents organizations where none presently exist. The purpose is, however, to provide prospective and young music educators with enough information and support material to allow them to deal with one or both subjects as effectively and professionally as possible should the need arise. A poorly structured parents organization is far worse than no support group at all, and inadequately administered, unsuccessful fund-raising projects reflect negatively on the music program and the music educator in charge of that program.

Summary

It is difficult to discuss parents organizations without including the subject of fund-raising. Both topics are becoming very visible in music-education programs across the United States. If the trend to reduce the funds allocated by schools for music education continues, there is a strong likelihood that the number of music parent support groups—and their role in financially assisting music programs—will increase significantly. Parents organizations can provide strong support for school music education not only financially but in other ways. For example, they can become a viable influence in the arts at the community level. It would appear that a comprehensively structured organization provides the greatest overall support for the total music program. When organizing a booster club, music educators are encouraged to seek administrative approval and to keep school officials well informed of group activities. Music parents organizations need to be governed by a charter or constitution to maintain the scope and direction of the group.

Fund-raising on the part of school music programs and their support groups has become a big business in the United States. As with the initiation of a booster group, music educators are encouraged to seek the approval of school officials prior to beginning any fund-raising campaign. Any successful fund-raising effort must be accompanied by a solid organizational base. The establishment of several chairmanships in conjunction with a project removes a great deal of the burden from music educators and allows them the opportunity to be more effective in administrating the project. There are numerous techniques for raising funds for school music groups. Music educators should test-market products for potential sale and consult with colleagues for nonproduct ideas for raising money. To maintain a high intensity level of all participants, fund-raising campaigns should be short and efficient. Music educators need to explore expedient and equitable ways in which to distribute moneys raised through the efforts of students and/or their parents. Regardless of the nature or scope of any project, its ultimate success depends directly on the administrative and organizational skills of the music educator associated with it.

Suggested Activities

1. Using the model constitution presented in Figures 10.2 and 10.3, draft a set of constitutional articles and bylaws for a mythical "Friends of Music" parents organization as it was described in this chapter.
2. Discuss fund-raising with a local music educator with some experience in such projects and determine a "best" and a "worst" actual fund-raising experience. Discuss in class.
3. Review twelve consecutive recent issues of a music-education periodical and determine the total number and variety of different products offered for sale. Discuss in class.
4. Invite a fund-raising company consultant to class and discuss the "do's" and "don't" of any sales-oriented fund-raising projects.
5. Invite an area booster-club president or other officer to class to explain the structure and purpose of the club, student benefits derived, level of adult participation, and other pertinent information he or she feels would be of benefit to the class. Compile a list of questions to ask the club officer prior to the scheduled visit.
6. By researching periodical literature, determine ten additional ideas for fund-raising projects not presented in this chapter.
7. Through your own investigative efforts, determine the most popular fund-raising product in your own geographical area. Why is it so popular? What, if any, negative aspects can be associated with the sale of that product for fund-raising purposes.

References and Suggested Reading

Bessom, Malcom E., Alphonse M. Tatarunis, and Samuel L. Forcucci. *Teaching Music in Today's Secondary Schools*. New York: Holt, Rinehart and Winston, 1974.

Daggett, Ron. "Organizing a Parent Booster Club." *The Instrumentalist*, May 1979.

Garvey, William H. "Marketing: Common Sense Plus." *The Instrumentalist*, August 1979.

Hoffer, Charles R. *Teaching Music in Secondary Schools*. Belmont, Calif.: Wadsworth Publishing Company, 1966.

Toward Broader Horizons

11

Historical Influences on Music Education

U ndergraduate students in music education rarely have an opportunity to study with any depth the people and events that have contributed historically to their chosen career field. In most music schools in this country, the study of the history of music education is reserved for graduate study. Prospective music educators need to have a basic understanding of their specialty's evolution prior to entering the profession. To see their chosen career as a true profession, they must approach it to a certain degree from a historical perspective. Having done so, music educators are in a better position to understand why school districts support music education to the extent they do, and they become more aware of how such an extensive system as public-school music education actually came into existence.

This chapter is an attempt to acquaint the reader with the events and circumstances, as well as the pioneering individuals, that contributed to the goal of the Music Educators National Conference, "Music for every child, every child *for* music." That 1923 statement by Karl Gehrkens, subsequently adopted as the MENC motto, is as close to reality now as at any time in history. Knowledge of the historical "roots" of music education can lead to a feeling of professional pride and allow young music educators to administer music-education programs with confidence, safe in the knowledge that their chosen career field has a three-hundred-year history of distinguished achievement.

Early Foundations of Music Education

The Bay Psalm Book

The Puritans who settled in Boston brought to this country a book of psalms called the *Ainsworth Psalter*. There were no melodies included and over the years it became increasingly difficult for the colonists to remember the tunes. In 1640 three colonial ministers prepared a metrical, revised version of the psalms entitled the *Bay Psalm Book,* which was the second book published in America—the Bible was the first—and is an indication that music in the seventeenth century was not insignificant. The publication of the *Bay Psalm Book* marked the beginning of American-made songbooks.

The *Bay Psalm Book* went through numerous editions and was published in many countries. It went through twenty-six different editions in this country by 1774 and probably seventy in all, including both European and American versions. The number of tunes in the book rarely exceeded five or six until the late seventeenth century. The ninth edition, in 1698, was the first edition with notation and had bars only at the end of each line. This very crudely printed book is the oldest existing printed music in America.

In 1721, Rev. Thomas Walter produced a singing book, which was the fourth book published in America, entitled *The Grounds and Rules of Music*

Explained, or an Introduction to the Art of Singing by Note. Walter's book is said to be the first printed music in America to have bar lines. It was written in choral style and some tunes had three parts.

The singing school

Singing in the church before the middle of the eighteenth century was uncultivated and was said to be "distressing to the ear." Rev. Walter said, "It sounded like 500 different tunes roared out at the same time."[1] From 1620 to 1700 the musical sensitivity of the colonial people was dulled by the terrible state of singing in this country. The early colonial times saw little part singing, and if members did possess books, they were certainly not able to read them. During the 1600s, many churches allowed only the "saved" to sing, with the congregation joining in on the "amens." When the entire membership was allowed to sing, the pastor would sing a line and the congregation would answer in rote fashion. This was called the "lining out" method.

The development of singing schools was a direct result of the desire to improve singing in church, and it gave public-school music its first methods and all of its first teachers. Singing schools were basically instructional sessions organized by the clergy or other individuals possessing some degree of musical skills. The schools rarely lasted over twenty-four sessions and the students paid the instructor a prearranged fee. For example, an advertisement in an early Ohio paper promoted a singing school for a fee of $1 for thirteen nights, two hours per night, and the students had "to bring their own wood and candles."[2]

The first recorded singing school was in Boston in 1717. From 1720 to 1775 the primary concern of the singing school was not the theory of music, but rather to get people to sing the melody correctly and to approximate the correct rhythm. By 1800, the movement had found its way to Maine, the Carolinas, and Georgia, but singing by note was still not universally adopted.

The advent of note singing as brought about by the singing school was the first great step toward attempting "music for all." The singing-school movement deserves full recognition as the first effective medium to bring such education to the layman.

Everything about the singing school is characteristically American. For example, it was supported by fees paid by the participants, not through the use of tax moneys, and the music taught was popular and socially useful. The singing school remained eclectic, never adopting one method, but using bits and pieces from all available materials. Singing schools also produced their own textbooks and music, thus creating an element of independence. Singing schools promised both musical and moral benefits for their students. As the schools improved singing, for instance, they also provided an element of recreation for the young. Those particular aims are still a force in music education today.[3]

The decline of the popularity of singing schools began around the middle 1800s. Contributing to the decline was an increase in singing societies and other musical societies. Also, students began traveling to Europe to study privately with European teachers or to study in America with European-trained teachers. Another influence on the decline of the singing school was the growth of music programs in public-school curriculums.

In its time, the singing school was as universal and as much a part of daily life as the country store or the post office. The singing school undoubtedly laid the foundation for the high level and rapid rise of music within this country. At the time singing schools were being organized, Bach had already completed much of his vast offerings of choral and instrumental music in Europe. Handel and Haydn began and ended their productive musical careers while Americans were still learning to sing psalm tunes. The foundation laid by the singing-school movement played a significant role in the progress of music in this country.

Singing societies

The early singing schools and singing societies were almost synonymous with one another. The singing school, however, primarily taught people *how* to sing, and the singing societies provided opportunities for musical performance. In this country, the oldest singing society still in existence is the Stoughlan Musical Society in Stoughlan, Massachusetts, which was organized in 1786. One of the greatest and most influential societies of its time was the Handel and Haydn Society of Boston. Organized in 1815, this singing society was dedicated to the performance of music composed by the two great masters from whom the society took its name.

Singing societies were important in that they provided an outlet for musical talent and, through their performances, set standards for musical attainment. Additionally, they were able to bring outstanding musical works before the public, and in doing so provided impetus to the singing-school movement.

The Pestalozzian principles

John Heinrich Pestalozzi was born in Zurich, Switzerland, in 1746, the son of a middle-class surgeon. Almost all pre–Civil War vocal music in American public schools was guided and patterned according to Pestalozzian principles of teaching. Pestalozzi ranks high as an individual who inspired and greatly influenced American education. He was probably the first person to insist that music be included in the course of study in public schools.

Pestalozzi was not so much interested in rote instruction; he believed that it was important for students to appreciate the differences in melody, rhythm, harmony, and dynamics. He felt that they should eventually be able to translate notation and characters into a familiar language, as if they were reading the letter characters of a language.

Pestalozzi's educational principles were adopted for music instruction by Lowell Mason. A detailed study of Lowell Mason's contributions to the progress of music education appear later in this chapter. In 1834 Mason wrote a book, printed in the United States, that was the first formulation of modern principles of teaching music. What follows is Mason's incorporation of the seven Pestalozzian principles from his *Manual for Instruction*.

1. To teach sounds before signs—to make the child sing before he learns the written notes or their names.
2. To lead him to observe, by hearing and imitating sounds, their resemblances and differences, their agreeable and disagreeable effects, instead of explaining these things to him—in short, to make him active instead of passive in learning.
3. To teach but one thing at a time—rhythm, melody, expression being taught and practiced separately before the child is called to the difficult task of attending to all at once.
4. To make them practice each step of each of these divisions, until they are master of it, before passing to the next.
5. To give the principles and theory after practice and as an induction from it.
6. To analyze and practice the elements of articulate sound in order to apply them to music.
7. To have the names of the notes correspond to those used in instrumental music.[4]

Mason's adaptation of Pestalozzi's educational principles was the first formulation of principles for teaching music in this country.

Conference/convention movement

Musical conventions began to appear in the early 1800s and were designed to provide training for those teachers who conducted singing schools. They generally lasted two or three days. The first recorded convention of this kind took place in Concord, New Hampshire, in 1829.

The Boston Academy of Music was founded in 1832 by the mayor of Boston, Samuel E. Elliot, and some of his associates. By 1834 it had become the focal point of the convention movement. Lectures at the 1834 convention presented the method of teaching music as outlined in the *Manual of the Boston Academy of Music*. This event was so successful that participants voted to return the following year, a trend that continued for eighteen years. Due to the enthusiasm and efforts of Mason, another of the academy's founders, the annual gathering became a source of significant influence for years to come.[5] In 1840 the group adopted as its name the National Music Convention.

As one might expect, a controversy developed between those individuals who wanted to maintain a lecture approach to the convention and those who wanted the performance of great works to be the main emphasis of the event. A compromise was realized and a second organization resulted, the American Musical Convention, which maintained a format similar to earlier conventions.

The convention movement spead as associates of the Boston Academy of Music traveled away from that city to hold conventions in the West. The format and curriculums of the conventions continued to diversify. Lectures were developed on a variety of musical topics, such as singing-class pedagogy. Those supervisors attending the conventions spent a great deal of time in a rehearsal setting, and the sessions always closed with a concert. Also included in convention curriculums were such topics as sight singing, reading of new music, trying new methods, and performing new works by the great masters.

As time went on, conventions became very commercial. Convention directors became heavily involved in the promotion and sale of their own musical materials; conductors circulated their own methods texts; and publishers were able to sell merchandise that had previously gone unsold. Convention critics questioned whether the sessions were held for commercial or musical purposes. In spite of this criticism, the people who attended went home with new ideas on teaching music and revitalized enthusiasm for the instruction of music in their own communities.

In 1906, Philip C. Hayden invited music supervisors from the Midwest to a meeting in Keokuk, Iowa, to observe and provide feedback for a rhythm-based approach to note reading. Those attending the 1907 Keokuk Conference were totally unaware that they were marking one of the milestones in school music history. Over one hundred supervisors attended, and of those, sixty-nine became permanent members of the conference.

At this time, no one considered the possibility that the organization would become permanent. At that time, the music section of the National Education Association was regarded as the official representative of school music teachers. In 1910, at a meeting in Cincinnati attended by 150 members, the name of the organization was established as the Music Supervisors National Conference. By 1920, conference membership had risen to a total of nearly 2,000 music instructors. At their 1915 meeting in Kansas City, over 3,000 music educators attended.[6]

In 1926, a National High School Orchestra was organized to perform for the conference. The orchestra was made up of school musicians from over thirty states, consisting of 246 players from 121 different schools. Joseph Maddy, later of Interlochen Arts Academy fame, conducted the orchestra.

At their meeting in 1934, the conference members voted to change their name to Music Educators National Conference. Thus, an organization originally made up of supervisors became an organization representing every aspect of music as taught in public schools. Music education has gained recognition as part of the school curriculum largely because of the work of the Music Educators National Conference. This organization of sixty-nine members in 1907 has grown to a total membership of nearly 57,000 (10,500 of them college students), a significant voice for music education throughout America.

The publishing industry

As the influence of the singing schools gradually spread to the public schools, publishers in this country were quick to realize a new market was being established for educational materials. From 1850 to 1860, over sixty-five music books were published. Sales of music books in the nineteenth century totaled millions of books, very few of which were used in the public schools, but all had some indirect effect on the music-education movement. Just one example of a successful publishing effort was *Carmina Sacra,* a popular 1841 effort of Lowell Mason, which sold over 400,000 copies in a ten-year period.

Between 1840 and 1880, the Oliver Ditson Company bought the rights to more and more music books and by the late nineteenth century it had become the largest publisher of tune books in the country. The John Church Company in Cincinnati, Ohio, became the largest music-book publisher in the Midwest.

In 1861, the Oliver Ditson Company published a book by Joseph Bird in which the author strongly disagreed with Lowell Mason's rote-learning approach. His book, *Vocal Music Reader,* was the first step in the multiple book, or series, concept. When music was introduced in the elementary schools of Boston in 1864, the need for a graded series of instructional books was created. Lowell Mason, who was instrumental in making music part of the curriculum of the Boston schools, published his first in a series of music books, entitled *Song Garden,* in 1864. The second book in the series was published in 1864 as well, with the third and final book appearing in 1866.[7]

Hosea Edson Holt also became disenchanted with the rote approach to teaching vocal music. He took charge of the elementary-school music program in the Boston schools in 1859 and developed the *Normal Music Course,* which was a series of five graded books first published in 1863. The Silver Burdette Company purchased the rights two years later and began their publishing efforts with Holt's series.

Luther Whiting Mason's series, entitled the *National Music Course,* was written between 1870 and 1875. Because it set the standard for similar books for the next fifty years, this series will be discussed in greater detail in the next section of this chapter. The *National Music Course,* along with the *Normal Music Course,* became the most popular of all the music series published between 1850 and 1900.

During the latter part of the nineteenth century, competition between publishing companies was intense. They soon discovered it was to their distinct advantage to offer institute classes whereby classroom teachers could be trained in the use of their published materials. For example, in 1887, the Ginn Company initiated institute classes on Mason's *National Music Course,* with the author and eight of his associates as faculty. The Silver Burdett Company offered institutes, beginning in 1889, that promoted Holt's opposing view on teaching music presented in his *Normal Music Course.* Such institutes grew very popular, as well as extremely profitable.

National Music Course

Luther Whiting Mason's series for elementary music instruction enjoyed a fifty-year period of popularity. It was published by Edwin Ginn and consisted of seven books, five readers, and two supplementary texts. Mason included charts as instructional visual aids. The music incorporated into the series was taken largely from German folk tunes and became so popular that it was translated into German and used in that country. The *National Music Course* was the first completely planned method and was adopted by the Japanese government after Mason's visit to that country. School music in Japan came to be known as "Mason-song." In this country, that *National Music Course* was by far the most popular and progressive book of Mason's time.

Modern Music Series

Published in 1898, the *Modern Music Series* was the result of a joint effort by Robert Foresman, who did the planning and general psychology of the series, and Eleanor Smith, who did much of the editing, translating of verses, and song-writing. The Silver Burdette Company acquired the rights to the series in 1901. It became very popular, especially in the Midwest, and it introduced a new era in music education and established new instructional standards. The pedagogy of the series was experimental and suggestive and left much of the teaching process up to the imagination and skill of the teacher. The primary assertion of the *Modern Music Series* was that if a song contained all the elements necessary for a reading technique, the song must be of the highest quality. In this respect, the series was definitely a pioneer.

Contests and festivals

The role that contests and festivals played in advancing the cause of school music is of unquestionable importance, particularly for instrumental music.

Little documentation exists regarding contests in the nineteenth century. One of the earliest known events was a convention of fifteen cornet bands in Portage, Wisconsin, in 1877. That same year eight brass bands competed before large audiences in Port Huron, Michigan. Each band was judged on the basis of its parade marching and concert performance. In 1897, at a choral competition in Ottawa, Kansas, a $400 first prize was awarded to the winning choir.[8]

In 1912, the first contest devoted to a competition between public-school musicians was held—the All-Kansas Music Competition Festival. The early Kansas contests included competitions for organ, piano, voice, strings, wind instruments, and girl's glee clubs.

The entire contest movement greatly appealed to the energetic and competitive American citizenry. The states of Kansas, Missouri, and North Dakota were frontrunners in the contest movement. The Welsh immigrants residing in the above states brought with them their inherent love of music and the *eisteddfods,* a concept on which early music contests in this country were based. The North Dakota contest, which was organized in 1919, grew so large by 1921 that elimination contests became necessary. In 1922, six hundred students from forty-four schools participated in the finals of the North Dakota event.

The first national contest was held in Chicago, June 4 through June 6, 1923. This contest gave a national focus to school bands and brought them to a position of prominence during that time. The original contest was organized by a Chicago music dealers' association with some help from the Conn instrument manufacturing company. The thirty bands that participated ranged in size from twenty-five to eighty-five members.

The first national competition was greatly criticized by the participating schools because there was only one adjudicator, the adjudication standards were different from those being used at the state level, and there were no required pieces and no size or instrumentation requirements.

The success of the first "band tournament" caught the attention of the instrument manufacturing industry. Prior to this time, industry leaders saw little future in the sales of instruments to schools. In fact, some manufacturers considered projects aimed at school sales to be "wasteful." The success of the 1923 contest was a turning point in the industry's history.

Since the market for musical instruments for professional and amateur adult bands was greatly reduced by the end of World War I, instrument manufacturers determined that the survival of the industry was directly related to the development of a new market large enough to sustain mass production. Thousands of former military musicians assumed teaching positions as band directors at the close of the war, creating a tremendous increase in the number of band programs in schools throughout this country.

The industry decided to support financially a national contest. A 1924 event was planned, complete with a repertoire list that accentuated many school bands' inadequate instrumentation. An effort was made to assure that the scope of the contest was truly national by securing participating bands from every section of the country.

Interest in the Schools Band Contest of America grew rapidly during the late 1920s. Railroads offered reduced fares for participants, and communities throughout the country raised funds to support a trip to Chicago for the local school band. The band became a great source of community pride. Even during the Depression years, only one Schools Band Contest was cancelled. This national contest accepted orchestras in 1926, and the event eventually became so large that competitions for band and orchestras had to be held on alternate years.

The national contest played a large role in the success of instrumental music in the public schools, and it was a natural public-relations vehicle for those programs. Another result of the national contest was that state and national associations for instrumental teachers were developed as a forum to discuss problems associated with the contest movement and as a medium to raise performance standards. They also dealt with instrumentation problems. The one-half woodwind and one-half brass instrumentation concept was a source of controversy as soon as it was introduced. As a result, a "blue ribbon" committee was established to develop a standard instrumentation for school bands. Members of the panel included John Philip Sousa, Edwin Franko Goldman, and Herbert L. Clark, and the resulting instrumentation became the standard for American bands to this day.[9]

By 1940 the contest movement served a total of 10,000 bands and orchestras, 7,500 vocal and instrumental ensembles, and 15,000 instrumental soloists, a total of over a half-million student participants.[10] The advent of World War II saw the end of the national contest, but the effects of the contest movement established the meteoric rise in stature of instrumental music in public schools throughout the United States.

Early Leaders and Educators

Lowell Mason

The individual who is believed by many music educators to have made the greatest contribution to the advancement of music education in the public schools is Lowell Mason. He was the first teacher of school music in the United States and the first supervisor of vocal music in the Boston schools.

Mason was born in Medfield, Massachusetts, in 1792, the son of a hat manufacturer and part-time mechanic. During the early years of his life, he learned to play a variety of musical instruments. When he was twenty he moved to Savannah, Georgia, where he took a full-time position in a bank, but he still found time to organize a band and direct church choirs. While in Savannah, Mason became involved with the Handel and Haydn Society of Boston and composed a collection of church music for them, which they published. He didn't want his name associated with the publication because he still wanted to be known as a banker, not a musician.

The Handel and Haydn Society encouraged him to accept an appointment with three Boston churches so that he could become more involved in the society. In 1827, he was elected president of the Handel and Haydn Society and made sweeping innovations designed to improve the quality of its performances.[11]

In 1833, influenced by Mason's work, the mayor of Boston and some of his associates established the Boston Academy of Music to give greater scope to Mason's efforts. This was the first school of music pedagogy in the United States.

In 1837, Mason began teaching music classes, without pay, in elementary schools in Boston. In 1838, he was appointed supervisor of music with an annual budget of $130 for each school he supervised. Of this fee, $90 went to training teachers and $20 to piano rental. There is some disagreement as to how long Mason served as supervisor of music, but recent information indicates that he was dismissed in 1845. The school board accused him of showing religious favoritism in selecting his teaching associates.[12]

After severing relations with the Boston schools, Mason immersed himself in writing, lecturing, and teaching at the Boston Academy of Music, activities that resulted in his being recognized as an outstanding proponent of music education. Mason was definitely America's first important public-school music educator. Some of his accomplishments follow:

1. Revised music-instruction materials according to the Pestalozzian principles.
2. Collected innumerable psalm, hymn, and school music books.
3. Taught so successfully that he had few peers.
4. Organized and instructed educational conventions.
5. Originated the study of the rudiments of music in American public schools.
6. Worked for improved singing schools.
7. Established a precedent for the type of song material to be included in nineteenth-century church song books.[13]

John Tufts

Almost a century after the Mayflower's arrival in New England a Boston bookseller offered for sale a book by a relatively obscure, forty-two-year-old minister, Rev. John Tufts. *Introduction to the Singing of Psalm Tunes* was the first American textbook. Its sale marked the beginning of organized music education in the United States. For notation, Tufts used only F, S, L, M (fa, sol, la, and mi), and note lengths were indicated by various punctuation signs following each note. There were thirty-seven tunes on twelve pages. Tufts called his approach "learning to sing by rule."[14]

The New England singing-school movement was developed from Tufts' book. By 1744 it had gone through eleven editions, and it was still in use in the nineteenth century. After Tufts, there was no musical step of comparable magnitude until Lowell Mason came on the scene in the early part of the nineteenth century.

Tufts was unknown when his book was published; for that reason, early advertisements of *Introduction to the Singing of Psalm Tunes* did not include his name. Tufts can be considered a pioneer in the movement to improve church singing, and his work left a permanent mark on our culture.[15]

William Billings

William Billings was the first native, self-taught American composer to meet the challenge of the advent of singing by note. In 1770 (the year Beethoven was born; Bach had been dead for twenty years) Billings' first work appeared: *The New England Psalm Singer or the American Chorister.* One of his best works was a collection called the *Singing Master's Assistant,* published in 1778.

Fuging tunes were not Billings' creation, but he was so successful at using them that many people through the years have thought that fuging tunes were his own discovery. Billings' music is important because it appeared at a time when singing the old union psalms was going out of style, and his tunes were easy to memorize.

Billings was as much a force in America's democratic upheaval as was the Boston Tea Party, because he aroused a musical response from the people. One of his tunes, "Chester," was called the "Battle Hymn of the Revolution"; it was the only tune the Continental pipes used when on the march. A devoted patriot and a friend of Samuel Adams, Billings was very popular in his time.

He was blind in one eye and had a withered arm, legs of different lengths, and a rasping voice that added color to his slovenly appearance. Although highly respected, his deformities are thought to have occasionally made him the brunt of practical jokes.[16]

While little of his music is alive today, Billings made a lasting contribution to our musical life through his activities, which included forming singing societies and church choirs. He improved the quality of church performances by introducing the pitch pipe and advocated the use of the violincello in church music, a move considered daring at that time. He brought New England's musical interest to life.

Charles Aiken

The most striking pioneer figure in music-education history, with the exception of Lowell Mason, is Charles Aiken. In 1839, Aiken met Reuben

Mussey, a famous surgeon who was also a fine cellist. Mussey influenced the initiation of a singing class in the basement of a Presbyterian church in Cincinnati. Aiken taught temperance songs and used the new movable "Do" system of instruction in that school. All types of laymen took classes, free of charge, and learned music using techniques based on the teaching methods of Lowell Mason.

Aiken went to Europe to study and gather facts about the German schools and their music-education techniques. His seventy-page report had an immediate effect on music education in Vermont and Ohio, and subsequently that of the entire nation.

In 1842, Aiken taught music without a salary in the Cincinnati schools. During the following years, he continued to instruct public-school students, but did a great deal of teaching outside the school. Aiken was appointed superintendent of music for the Cincinnati schools in 1871 and was totally responsible for getting music into the elementary grades of that city. In addition to teaching and administration, he assisted in the writing of several texts and edited *The High School Choralist*. During the eight years he served as the superintendent of music, Aiken made numerous improvements in the system, such as establishing a means of systematizing music instruction—using exams to measure and improve instruction—and he wrote the first edition of the multivolume *Cincinnati Music Readers*. These books used the works of the great masters, and were considered to be remarkable for their time.[17]

Aiken retired in 1879. His son, Walter H. Aiken, who was considered a brilliant choral director, was appointed superintendent of music in Cincinnati in 1900. He was active in music education for a period of fifty-four continuous years. The work of the father and son combined amounts to eighty-six years of service to the students and public of Cincinnati.

Luther Whiting Mason

Luther Whiting Mason, a distant relative of Lowell Mason, began teaching in Cincinnati in 1857. He initiated a thorough study of available music instruction books, including the materials of Johann Nageli, an associate of Pestalozzi in Swiss and German schools. He published a translated version of the materials that had formed the basis of Lowell Mason's song books written for young voices. Luther Mason became known for his rote-note approach to music instruction.

In 1864, Mason accepted a position in Boston to organize and teach elementary music. In doing so, he established a precedent for elementary music instruction, because prior to this time, it had only been offered at what we know as the junior-high-school level.

He recognized a pressing need for teaching materials at the elementary school and wrote the *National Music Course*, a series that became very popular nationwide. Luther Whiting Mason is considered the founder of school-music methodology. Not only was his *National Music Course* the first series of its kind to receive national recognition, but it became the prototype of most music instruction books that followed. Mason is recognized for his formulation of instructional materials for early grades.[18]

Frances Elliot Clark

Born in 1860 in Angola, Indiana, Frances Elliot Clark studied organ and voice at a singing school With only an eighth-grade education, she passed the necessary exams and began teaching in 1884. During the summers she attended Tri-state Normal College. There she studied voice, sang in choirs, and became recognized as soprano soloist. For training as a music supervisor, she attended the Ginn Institute in Detroit, Michigan, where she learned the note-rote approach.

In 1891, Clark accepted a position in Monmouth, Illinois. It was here that she developed the abilities that would take her to the top of her profession. She became very active in women's music clubs, both locally and on the national level. In 1896, she moved to Ottumwa, Iowa, a town with a history of excellent music programs. There she was able to organize three choirs, the best of which was said to be able to read and sing such music as the *Messiah* and *Elijah*. She recognized the need to relate the history of music to performance. Although there were no books on the subject, she developed ten-minute talks about opera, Bach's life and works, as well as the lives and works of other recognized composers. Her efforts represented one of the first attempts at including music appreciation in public-school instruction.[19]

Clark left Iowa in 1903 to accept a music supervisor's position in Milwaukee, Wisconsin. Music was highly regarded in Milwaukee, but there was little of it in the public schools. In the grade schools Clark organized a new and very successful music-education program, which included ear training and music in kindergarten classes.

Clark was vice-president of the music section of the National Education Association when she presided over the 1907 meeting of the soon-to-be Music Supervisors National Conference in Keokuk, Iowa. She offered guidance and provided stability during the early meetings, which were at times somewhat confrontational.

Clark's greatest contribution to music education was her early recognition of the educational value of the "talking machine." By 1906 records were being pressed, and Clark was excited by the educational value of the machines, though many others considered it only a toy. She arranged for the first demonstration of a Victor Talking Machine as a teaching tool for grade-school children from Milwaukee. The school principals in attendance were very impressed and immediately ordered some of the machines for their respective schools.

Clark later joined the Victor Talking Machine Company, where she organized an educational department. This company published its first educational catalog in 1911, and by 1924 it was classified into subjects by grade and contained almost three thousand selections. The use of the Victrola spread throughout the country and became one of the all-time greatest teaching aids for the instruction of music, bringing good music within the reach of every child.[20]

Will Earhart

Will Earhart was one of the first people to expand the high-school curriculum beyond choral music. He established classes in harmony, music appreciation, and various instruments, as well as forming an orchestra and a band. He is particularly known for his contribution to the music-appreciation movement. Earhart wanted his students to know about a composer, his place of origin, his successes, and his place in the world. He wanted them to understand musical form. Earhart's music-appreciation-course efforts in Richmond, Indiana, were later accepted by many as a model.

Earhart organized an orchestra in Richmond, Indiana, in 1898 and was an enterprising and innovative leader prior to World War I in organizing orchestras where they had not previously existed. In 1921, he conducted a performance of an orchestra made up of members of the Music Supervisors National Conference in St. Joseph, Missouri. This concert led to the formation of a committee on instrumental instruction by the Music Supervisors National Conference in 1922.[21]

Sterrie Weaver

Sterrie Weaver was born in New London, Connecticut, in 1853. He studied music at evening singing schools, later attended the New England Conservatory, and eventually studied music education in Germany. In the late 1800s, he became music supervisor of three schools in Connecticut. He also found time to edit the periodical *The Music Courier*.[22]

In 1900, Weaver opened a school to train music supervisors and had a great influence on music education in a short period of time. He successfully applied the scientific method to the problem of reading music, and through his addresses, articles, and personal actions he encouraged others to take a more scientific approach to their work. When he died in 1904, his work was just becoming nationally known.

Weaver stood out among his contemporaries. Edward Birge points out his distinctness:

> Like the prophet Elijah of old, he suddenly appeared on the scene
> of school-music, delivered his message, completed his work, and
> suddenly departed. His character was strong, self-reliant and ruggedly
> honest. His personality was simple, and vibrant with energy and deep
> feeling. His intellect was keen and penetrating, and he was born

a teacher. It was his mission to evolve a method of teaching sight reading which was devoid of all the paraphernalia of the period, and to prove that every child can be taught to read music.[23]

Birge concludes that Weaver was the first exponent of tests and measurements in music sight reading. "This stands out as his main contribution to school music and, in the writer's opinion, the main contribution of the period." [24]

Philip C. Hayden

Born in Brantford, Ontario, in 1854, Philip Hayden studied at New York University for one year and Oberlin College for five years. He served as supervisor of music in Quincy, Illinois, and Keokuk, Iowa. He taught music in public schools for a total of thirty-five years.

Hayden founded the *School Music* magazine in 1900 and published a series of articles about his method of teaching music through a progressive series of rhythmic forms. In 1906, he sent a letter to thirty Midwest music supervisors inviting them to Keokuk for a meeting and an opportunity to observe and investigate his work. The response was so great that, in January 1907, *School Music* published a nationwide invitation, this time signed by twenty-six music supervisors who indicated their belief in the value of such a meeting at Keokuk. They pledged their attendance and requested that their colleagues from across the country join them. Hayden had originally hoped that at least fifteen supervisors would attend. In the end, over a hundred music supervisors from around the nation participated in the first meeting of what was to become the Music Educators National Conference.

Contemporary Music Education

The contemporary period in music education began in the mid-1950s. Music education found itself caught up in the sweeping changes occurring throughout the American educational system. In 1957, the Ford Foundation began to explore the relationship of the arts to American society. (In several curricular areas at this time, change was initiated and nurtured by industrial philanthropic foundations.)

What follows is a brief survey of five important projects and seminars that have influenced music education in the past thirty-five years. Together they represent the movement toward quality contemporary music education. For more in-depth study, readers are encouraged to refer to Michael L. Mark's *Contemporary Music Education*.

Young Composers Project

Between 1959 and 1962 thirty-one American composers were placed in school systems across the country through sponsorship of the Ford Foundation. The young musicians, all under thirty-five years of age, served as composers in residence for students in their representative schools. The composers were paid a stipend of $5,000 per year to write music for special performance media, with specific experience and proficiency levels in mind, and with assurances that their music would be studied, and in all likelihood, performed.

Contemporary Music Project

In 1963 the Ford Foundation awarded a grant to the Music Educators National Conference to organize the Contemporary Music Project for Creativity in Music Education. Through the project an additional forty-six composers in residence were placed in public schools by 1968.

The five-fold purpose of the Contemporary Music Project, as stated in the proposal accepted by the Ford Foundation, follows:

1. To increase the emphasis on the creative aspect of music in public schools.
2. To create a solid foundation or environment in the music-education profession for acceptance, through understanding, of the contemporary-music idiom.
3. To develop a close relationship and better understanding between members of the composition and music-education professions.
4. To cultivate taste and discrimination on the part of music educators and their students for the quality of contemporary music used in the schools.
5. To discover, whenever possible, creative talent among students.[25]

In addition to continuing the Young Composers Project (retitled Composers in Public Schools), the Contemporary Music Project sponsored numerous workshops and seminars across the country. The Seminar on Comprehensive Musicianship, held on the campus of Northwestern University in April 1965, was intended to develop and implement means of improving the college and university training of musicians, and to determine the subsequent effect of that training on public-school music-education curriculums. The seminar established basic principles for comprehensive musicianship, and while relatively few colleges have integrated comprehensive musicianship into their teacher-training programs, that concept has had a great impact on elementary- and secondary-school performing ensembles.

Pilot projects were the third result of the Contemporary Music Project and were also sponsored in cooperation with public-school systems. Objectives of the pilot projects were to (1) identify suitable approaches in the presentation of contemporary music, (2) experiment with various techniques for providing creative musical experiences for children, (3) identify contemporary music suitable for use with students at several grade levels, and (4) provide in-service training for teachers.[26]

The Contemporary Music Project ended in 1973. It gave direction, issued challenges, developed contemporary methods and materials, and created an atmosphere of open-mindedness toward change and innovation on the part of the music-education profession.

The Yale Seminar

From June 17 to June 28, 1963, thirty-one musicians, teachers, and other scholars gathered on the campus of Yale University to consider the problems facing music education in this country. Concern had developed among leading music educators that, though students participating in large ensembles in public schools were enjoying the audience appreciation of their performances and the satisfaction derived from striving for high contest and festival ratings, they were perhaps missing out on the musical aspects of the experience. In other words, educators were starting to ask, "Have they really learned anything about music?" It was the task of those individuals gathered for the Yale Seminar to examine the kindergarten through twelfth-grade music-education curriculum from several previous decades in an attempt to learn why public-school music programs in this country had failed to produce a musically active and literate public.

The seminar found that music-classroom materials were lacking in relevance and that student exposure to both non-Western and early Western music was being neglected amost entirely. Music teachers were also failing to share music from the jazz, popular, and folk idioms with their students.

The seminar noted that weak musical arrangements were being used by both large and small ensembles. The same problem existed with the songbook series used by many general-music-classroom teachers. They concluded that the music selected for use in music programs directly reflected the skill level of the teachers involved as well as their lack of interest and/or ability to work to improve the listening and hearing skills of their students.

Instrumental music was found to have been successful in contributing to the overall musical growth in this country, but the seminar expressed concern that vocal music repertory appeared to be primarily aimed at audience appeal and was being programmed so as to offend the least possible number of listeners. Basically, the seminar concluded that materials used in music-education classrooms and rehearsals had not changed appreciably in the previous thirty years.

The recommendations of the Yale Seminar included the following:

1. The basic goal of the K-12 music-education curriculum should be to develop musicality through performance, movement, creativity, and listening.

2. The music-education repertory should be broadened to include jazz, folk, and contemporary popular music.
3. A sequence of guided listening to worthwhile music should be developed.
4. Performance activities should include large ensembles for which an authentic and varied repertory would exist and that small-ensemble participation by student musicians should be of particular importance.
5. Advanced theory and literature courses should be available to students who could most benefit from them.
6. Performing musicians, composers, and scholars should be brought into schools to provide students with insights as to how professionals think and work.
7. Music programs in the public schools need to take greater advantage of community and national human and material resources.
8. Audiovisual aids and individualized instruction programs need to be developed and used in music-education classrooms.
9. A plan must be developed to train and retrain teachers so as to enable curriculum revision to be successfully implemented.[27]

The recommendations resulting from the Yale Seminar were already present in some existing school-music programs, but other programs have benefited from them. School music repertory has improved significantly, although artificial and synthetic music is rapidly influencing that repertory. Whether that influence will eventually be judged positive or negative has yet to be determined. The training of music teachers has improved in this country, due in part to upgraded state-certification requirements and to the fact that higher-education institutions have improved efforts to provide their students with the proper tools to become good teachers.

The Manhattanville Project

The Manhattanville Music Curriculum Project was initiated in 1965 and was based on a grant from the United States Office of Education. The project drew its name from the fact that it originated at the Manhattanville College of the Sacred Heart in Purchase, New York.

The primary objective of this project was to develop a music curriculum and associated methods and materials for a sequential music-education program, grades K-12. Some experimental music-education programs were already in existence in this country; therefore the project began with an exploratory study of ninety-two of those programs, which were located in thirty-six different states. Fifteen of the experimental programs were selected for in-depth study.

The Manhattanville Music Curriculum Project was divided into three phases. Phase I involved determining student-learning potential, studying problems relating to curriculum reform, and drafting a series of classroom procedures. Phase II involved refining information gained from studies and organizing that information into a workable curriculum. Phase III entailed the refinement and field testing of the music curriculum developed as a result of the study. It also investigated separate curriculums for early childhood education; addressed the problem, the need for, and the approach to teacher retraining; and developed a testing instrument for the assessment of the level of completion of program objectives.

The MMCP approach to music instruction was used in a small number of schools over a period of time. The most common use in today's schools is the adaptation by traditional music programs of its strengths, namely its emphasis on creativity and compositional activities.

The lack of a high level of implementation and application of the resultant MMCP curriculum is more than likely because it required teachers to work within a framework far removed from traditional music education. Proponents of the MMCP approach to music instruction were largely unsuccessful in convincing administrators and parents that music education need not necessarily justify itself based on performance. The informal, self-motivated approach that is a requisite of the MMCP approach corresponds closely to the philosophical foundation of open education, a philosophy that has not to date gained wide acceptance in educational circles in this country.

The Tanglewood Symposium

Convened at Tanglewood, Massachusetts, in July and August 1967, the Tanglewood Symposium was a venture sponsored by the Theodore Presser Foundation, the Berkshire Music Center, and Boston University of Fine and Applied Arts. The symposium brought together scientists, sociologists, musicians, labor leaders, educators, corporate and foundation representatives, and government leaders. The symposium was titled "Music in American Society," and its purpose was to discuss and define the role of music education in contemporary American society. As a group, symposium participants were to make recommendations to improve and make more efficient the instruction of music education in this country.

Committees were formed and addressed the following:

1. The wide divergence between "school music" and what children listen to away from school.
2. How higher personal income levels, along with increased leisure time, provided more opportunity to participate in and enjoy the arts.
3. The need to recognize the value and necessity of the study of African and Asian music during this country's struggle for racial equality.
4. Why contemporary or "new" music is aesthetically valid.
5. The importance of music education's role in helping students "know" a musical work as opposed to "appreciating" a musical work.
6. The need for the music-education profession to anticipate future social conditions and develop different kinds of teaching and performance

techniques, as well as being prepared to work with more sophisticated students.

7. The role of music education in adult education.
8. The need to explore the roles of such individuals involved in the process of music as the creators, distributors, consumers, and educators.

Recommendations resulting from the Tanglewood Symposium included the following:

1. Elementary music-education curriculums should place more emphasis on such elements of musical experience as (a) understanding many types of music through listening and performance, (b) studying music by singing, playing, and movement, (c) arranging and composing music, and (d) being able to understand and use musical notation.
2. All junior-high-school students should be required to take one general music class.
3. All senior-high-school students (even those is performance groups) should be required to take one arts course.
4. Social musical instruments should be taught at all levels.

Another committee recommendation was that a means should be established to identify potential future music educators while they are still in high school and that the MENC should prepare a set of materials that could assist high-school counselors in such an identification process.

The most important result of the Tanglewood Symposium was that it established a unified and eclectic philosophy of music education for an emerging society. It not only recommended that all kinds of music be accepted into the curriculum, but also recognized that all types of music have aesthetic validity and should therefore be offered as ends in themselves.

Summary

This chapter has been devoted to a survey of the people and events that have affected the development of music education as a viable part of America's public-school curriculum. It is interesting to note that the early development of music education in this country was "people" oriented, with easily identifiable leaders making valuable contributions. In the first forty or fifty years of this century, conventions, contests, and the music industry assumed a role of increased significance. In the last one-third of the evolving cycle of music education, projects, seminars, and conferences have assumed leadership responsibilities, along with the emergence of the Music Educators National Conference as a stronger and more unified voice for all of music education.

It was not the intent of this chapter to provide an in-depth study of the history of music education in the United States. A comprehensive investigation of the topic justifiably belongs at the graduate level. It is the author's most sincere desire that the historical survey presented in this chapter will engender the reader's interest and promote further study of the development of music education. Both present and future music teachers can look with pride at the history of the music-education movement, aware that their profession has an honorable three-hundred-year history of outstanding and dedicated achievement.

Suggested Activities

1. Research the attendance at the first Keokuk Conference, select an individual not previously discussed in this chapter, and report to the class that person's contributions to the history of music education.
2. Determine the three ministers responsible for the compilation of the *Bay Psalm Book* and report to the class their motivation for the project.
3. Compare the lives and contributions to the education movement of John Tufts and the Rev. Thomas Walters.
4. Select a significant twenty-five-year period in the history of music education and compare it with what was taking place musically in Europe during the same period. What was the status of education in general in both locales? What were the social and political factors associated with the status of music and music education in the United States and Europe during the same twenty-five year period?
5. Interview a "veteran" music educator regarding the format of contemporary music conventions and compare them with the music conventions during the time of Lowell Mason.
6. Research and present a report to the class on how music education in this country was affected by the 1957 Soviet launch of the first space satellite.
7. Research and report to the class about what is known as the "shaped note" or "buckwheat" music notation system.
8. Conservatories played quite an important role in the progress of music education in the nineteenth and early twentieth centuries in the United States. Compare the early music-conservatory concepts and approach to education with the programs used in music education in today's colleges and universities.
9. Discuss in class the effect the National Band Contest movement had on the vocal music programs in this country.
10. Examine the guidelines for teaching music established by Pestalozzi. Which, if any, of the guidelines are still in use today?
11. Compile a report to be submitted in class on the development and purpose of the "Normal School" in the United States and how it affected music education.

12. Develop a half-hour instructional project based on Manhattanville Music Curriculum Project principles and present it to the class.

13. Assemble a panel of local music educators for the purpose of discussing their views as to the direction music education has taken in the last ten years. Prepare a list of questions in advance.

References and Suggested Reading

Abeles, Harold F., Charles L. Hoffer, and Robert H. Klotman. *Foundations of Music Education*. New York: Schirmer Books, 1984.

Birge, Edward Bailey. *History of Public School Music in the United States*. Washington, D.C.: Music Educators National Conference, 1928.

Britton, Allen P. "Music Education: An American Specialty." In *Perspectives in Music Education*. Washington, D.C.: Music Educators National Conference, 1966.

Fitzgerald, R. Bernard. "The Contemporary Music Project for Creativity in Music Education." In *Perspectives in Music Education*. Washington, D.C.: Music Educators National Conference, 1966.

Howard, John Tasker. *Our American Music*. New York: Thomas Y. Crowell, 1939.

———, and George Kent Bellows. *A Short History of Music in America*. New York: Thomas Y. Crowell, 1967.

Keene, James. *A History of Music Education in the United States*. Hanover, N.H.: University Press of New England, 1982.

Lowens, Irving. *Music and Musicians in Early America*. New York: Norton, 1964.

Mark, Michael L. *Contemporary Music Education*, 2d ed. New York: Schirmer Books, 1986.

Sunderman, Lloyd Frederick. *Historical Foundations of Music Education in the United States*. Metuchen, N.J.: Scarecrow Press, 1971.

Toward a Philosophy
of Music Education

M usic educators have struggled for years in the attempt to establish some type of comprehensive philosophy for their profession. At this point in time the effort has yet to be totally successful. The reference sources that appear at the end of this chapter indicate the volume of printed material available regarding philosophy and music education. Those same sources provide much of the insight and resulting information that appear in this chapter.

The most common approach toward the development of a philosophy of music education has been to relate music education to one of the more traditional educational philosophies, such as Idealism, Realism, or Pragmatism. This practice, while offensive to some music educators and philosophers, is perhaps the most effective procedure presently available to music educators.

Bennett Reimer, Charles Leonhard, and Abraham Schwadron are the most active and vocal exponents of a comprehensive philosophy of music education. All three men are prolific writers and lecturers on the topic of the philosophy of music education and are highly respected for their views on the subject. Reimer, Leonhard, and Schwadron argue that a comprehensive philosophy should be based on aesthetic theories. They feel that only through a serious study of aesthetics are music educators able to develop the background necessary to enter into a productive partnership with educational philosophers, one in which the philosophers could assist the music educators in examining their beliefs and principles. The music educators, in turn, could provide new data and concepts for the philosophers. Reimer, in his book *A Philosophy of Music Education,* has provided music educators with a model for associating music education with several aesthetic theories. Reimer's book is the most in-depth effort yet to relate aesthetic theories to music education and should be on the "must read" list of all serious students of music-education philosophy.

Leonhard defines a philosophy of music education as a "system of basic beliefs which underlies and provides a basis for the operation of the musical enterprise in an educational setting. A philosophy should serve as the source of insight into the total music program and should assist music teachers in determining what the musical enterprise is all about, what it is trying to accomplish and how it should operate."[1] Developing a philosophy of music education must involve building a theory that relates to the meaning and value of music and the role of music in life.

A contemporary rationale for the necessity of a philosophy is that it's important to understand the purpose of human life. In medieval times, philosophy was referred to as the total of all knowledge represented by the arts and sciences. Educational philosophy today can be both speculative and prescriptive, and, as previously mentioned, music teaching in general is aligned with prevailing educational philosophies. The two main streams of philosophical thought in American education are Pragmatism and Realism. Most educational beliefs appear to be associated with one or the other, or a philosophy somewhere in between. Pragmatism has profoundly affected music-education texts and methods in the last fifty years. The idea of "learning by doing" dominates twentieth-century music-education thought as it relates to music methods. A more detailed presentation of the effects of traditional educational philosophies on music education appears later in this chapter.

The Need for a Philosophy of Music Education

Successful music-education programs have always attempted to achieve a balance between student concerns and what music educators deem to be important subject-matter concerns. Unfortunately, there are also many examples where the balance was never reached, or for that matter even sought. Some music programs present the knowledge of music without an actual musical experience, while others provide extensive opportunities for students to make music without allowing them the opportunity to develop an understanding of *why* they are doing it. A solid philosophical approach to music education should not permit such unbalanced teaching.

The development of that solid philosophical approach must begin at the undergraduate level. This is a demonstrated weakness in higher education as it pertains to the training of music-education teachers. In a survey of all colleges and universities who hold membership in the National Association of Schools of Music, the author learned that only 18 out of 247 responding schools (7.3 percent) offered an undergraduate course in music-education philosophy. Of the remaining colleges and universities, 68.5 percent indicated that a unit on music-education philosophy was offered as part of a music-education methods class. Numerous other institutions indicated that this topic was reserved for graduate courses. That information is the prime motivating factor for the inclusion of this chapter in a book dealing with the administration of school music-education programs.

It is absolutely critical that college students preparing to enter the music-education profession develop an understanding of the importance of their career field. This is the time in an individual's life that the need for self-justification is the highest, as he or she is preparing to become a contributing member of society. Students need to develop a meaning for their professional lives. They need a mission! This need is especially true in music education, because the value of the career field is often not fully understood by its own members and is generally even less understood by professionals in related fields. "The individual who has a clear notion of what his aims are as a professional, and who is convinced of the importance of these aims, is a strong link in the chain of people who collectively make a profession."[2] The profession will become more solid, more secure, to the degree that music educators are able to formulate a persuasive, forceful, and compatible philosophy.

Individuals need to feel their chosen profession is important and that they can enrich society. If a person cannot develop a feeling of career respect or if he or she feels such work is of little worth to society, the resulting contributions will be of questionable value. "The understanding a person has about the value and nature of his profession inevitably affects his understanding of the value and nature of his life."[3]

In addition, music educators can turn to their philosophical foundations for appropriate solutions to problems when they arise. A responsible, well-tested philosophy enables the music educator to react rationally and confidently to a problematic situation rather than in a spontaneous and perhaps reckless manner.

A philosophy supplies the most important and specific objectives of music education. As Reimer points out:

> It is the function of a philosophy to provide broad objectives under which specific behaviors and behavior-clusters can be chosen intelligently and influenced effectively. Without the synthesizing, directing force of a philosophy, education can only be indiscriminate and diffuse. Every aspect of the teaching and learning of music is similarly influenced by a philosophy. If problems of method, of program, of organization and administration, of evaluation, even of research are to be dealt with in ways which are relevent to the nature and value of music education, that nature and value must clearly be understood. A philosophy, then, provides the foundation on which the entire structure of music education rests.[4]

Problems in the organization and administration of a music-education program can be facilitated, accommodated, and guided by an individual's basic philosophy of music education. Such a philosophy is of the utmost benefit in decision-making. Decisions based on a philosophical foundation are made quickly; they are made with ease and confidence.

A philosophy of music education can and should evolve from a large variety of experiences and be in keeping with contemporary social philosophies, as well as dedicated to the developmental growth of students and teachers alike. Such a philosophy must have survived the test of practice and time, in addition to being able to withstand current debate and examination.

A strong philosophy of music education is not totally acquired from academic investigation. It is also developed through classroom experience and administrative opportunities. It must be flexible to adjust to changing times; as situations change, certain characteristics of one's philosophical position will mature and adjust to the change. Music-education philosophy is founded on mistakes as well as successes.[5]

The academic preparation for developing a philosophy of music education is of great importance, and as mentioned earlier, it is in somewhat of a state of neglect in this country's institutions of higher education. Classwork at the undergraduate level can and should build a foundation for philosophical principles and serve as the framework for the future "on the job" developmental processes.

Schools of Philosophy

Music educators today generally feel that present-day philosophies relating to music education stem from and are based on traditional philosophies of education. Rightly or wrongly, this relationship has resulted from the lack of any other basic source that can serve as a philosophical foundation for music education. Reimer, Schwadron, and Leonhard have all voiced a need to base music-education philosophy on the study of aesthetics and aesthetic theories, and Reimer's book is a brilliant effort in that direction. However, the majority of music education philosophies are closely tied to traditional education philosophy. For that reason, a general presentation of traditional philosophy is included here. It is important as well for music educators to have some understanding of the philosophical evolution of their profession.

What follows are descriptions of several educational philosophies, their application to education in general, and more specifically to music education.

Idealism

An idealist believes that reality is governed by a permanent, uniform, and absolute spiritual mind and that physical objects are simply imperfect representations of the ideas they donate. For example, the pencil an individual may have in hand is only an imperfect representation of the "ideal" pencil. Idealism does not greatly concentrate upon ideals for living, but rather upon *ideas* as the necessary elements of reality.

Idealists feel that objects of the so-called external exist only as they enter minds or ideas. For example, it is not so much that a tree or painting has reality, but it is an *idea* of a tree or painting that is conceived within the mind.[6]

Strengths of idealism. The greatest strength of Idealism is its conscious, intellectual approach to reality. Another strength possessed by Idealists is the stability of the philosophy. What is true is true, always was true, and always will be true. Idealism is more systematic than other philosophies.[7]

Weaknesses of idealism. Although "what is true is true" according to idealism, it is difficult to arrive at what truths are. Idealists have difficulty accounting for new developments and changes. Logic has proven to be a less precise philosophical tool than Idealists like to admit. For example, people often tend to make judgments according to personal values rather than on the basis of logical reasoning.

Idealism and education. The process of education is very serious and very purposeful for the idealist. The idealist music teacher feels his or her personality is both an inspiration and a model for student imitation and makes a conscious effort toward personality development. The idealist tends to teach aspects of music that are considered to be of great and lasting worth. The *Messiah*, Beethoven's symphonies, Tchaikovsky's *Romeo and Juliet,* and the piano music of Brahms are all examples of music that would qualify for inclusion into a music-education curriculum based on idealism. "Foremost in promoting the development of such cultural taste, the idealist holds to the mutual companionship of mind and feelings, for true taste and aesthetic enjoyment require exposure, objective mastery, and finally understanding."[8] The objective is to arouse an emotional response by means of exposure, followed by studies of the characteristics of the music and the implications of the composers' and students' own socioeconomic backgrounds. In fact, music's expression of meaning beyond itself is contained in writings of Susanne Langer and John Dewey. They feel that music arouses or expresses feelings without the need for words. One may listen to a piece of music and find it sad; another may find the same piece pensive. This is not important! What is important, however, is that the music has expressed something to each.

The idealist teacher primarily uses the discussion method in the classroom setting and presents what he or she feels are worthy models of creative work for student imitation, as well as stimulation of student interest and initiative. The idealist teacher has a strong interest in evaluating the level of student learning and is concerned that students gain a comprehensive understanding of classroom work and the ability to apply that knowledge. The capacity of the student to grasp the "big picture" of the material studied is also of great importance to the idealist.

The idealist teacher sees discipline as a part of teaching, not as an end in itself, but rather as a pattern of behavior that will eventually benefit the student. The idealist attempts to show students the effect of misconduct on the rest of the class. The teacher asks the misbehaving student what would happen if everyone behaved in a similar manner. Infractions of discipline are therefore seen as demonstrations of selfishness in ignoring the obligations to fellow class members and members of the community.[9]

Realism

Realism is a belief in the reality of matter, independent of human opinions and desires. When compared with idealism, the realist's position is more material and less spiritual. Realists feel that all physical things or objects are real in themselves and exist independently of the perceiver. For example, if there were no human perceivers, the objects would still exist and still be real.

Plato felt that to understand an object or concept is to comprehend its form and structure, which is the basis for the theory that education should have a central core of subject matter that will help students experience the physical and cultural structure of the world in which they live. Realists consider liberal education to be the focal point of all education. Liberal education refers to education that pertains to a wide range of subjects and activities, such as mathematics, science, literature, and the arts. The educational approach to these activities as seen by the realists is theoretical rather than applied as in pragmatism. The realist is interested in knowledge as it relates to all mankind.[10]

Strengths of realism. The principal strength of realism is its practicality. Realists take what they have and work with it. They don't spend time wondering if a wall in front of them is the "real" wall, but they know if they bump into it, the result will be real. Realism deals with reality as it can best be known.

Weaknesses of realism. The practicality that is the primary strength of realism is also one of its weaknesses. Knowledge of reality as perceived through the senses is subject to error. Realism relies on the opinion of experts, and this creates the problem of who should decide, and what will happen if the experts disagree. A case in point is that there is much disagreement in music education. Determining the correct embouchure, the best way to teach rhythm, the value of music contests, and the content of music-theory courses are examples of such disagreement. The problems surrounding the inclusion of jazz studies in this country's college curriculums is another example.

Realism and education. To the realist, ordered and organized forms are similar to mathematical relationships; thus, musical works of profound structure and design qualify as artistic products. Pedagogically the study of construction precedes the emotional dimension of a musical work. The realist feels that playing an instrument is important for the development of mature appreciation and cultural taste.

Realists believe in teaching what the authorities in an academic discipline feel is worth knowing, and they place a great deal of emphasis on direct experience, such as actually singing a song rather than talking or reading about it. The realist teacher likes the objectivity of the scientific method and uses an objective approach to learning. Realists tend to see students objectively or impersonally, and they are not concerned with personality or character development. Realist teachers are primarily interested in the acquisition of specific information and skills considered necessary to function in society. For example, a piano teacher might have a student learn all the Beethoven concertos because they are seen as essential repertoire for successful concert pianists.

Realists have no respect for the "inspirational value" of history because history is something to be viewed by objectivity. They favor the "whatever works" policy as an objective means of transmitting knowledge to students. Realists see lecturing and reading as part of the learning process and are quick to include computers and individualized instruction methods in the classroom approach. Realist teachers see themselves as central to the educational process. If they cannot provide a given piece of information, they will tell the students where to find it.

Realists tend to be impatient with distracting behavior. They feel that "life is too short for fooling around." The realist teacher feels that children should be taught to live by absolute moral standards. Acquiring good habits is essential because virtue does not come automatically. It must be learned.[11] The idea of accepting what can be known and working with that knowledge as best one can seems defensible, practical, and reasonable.

Pragmatism

Dating back to the sixth century B.C., pragmatism did not come into its own until the nineteenth and twentieth centuries, and then it primarily flourished in America. It is, therefore, a philosophy generally regarded as being indigenous to the United States, although it is deeply rooted in the British tradition of "We know what we experience."

Charles Sanders Peirce, William James, and John Dewey were leading exponents of the pragmatic point of view. Pragmatism is concerned with questions of practical usefulness. Pragmatists feel, for example, that ideas, beliefs, and attitudes are important, particularly for their formation and functioning in social interaction. Thus, pragmatism assumes that the principal function of knowledge is to guide action.

Pragmatists uphold the value of examining particulars in order to see how those particulars might work in practice, and they feel that all things are in a state of flux, creating a need for experimentation. Dewey proposed five steps of thinking: activity, awareness of the problem, observation of the data, formulation of a hypothesis, and testing of the hypothesis. This scientific method of gaining knowledge is the basis of pragmatic philosophical thought. Pragmatists believe that the only knowledge that really matters results from successful testing of hypotheses.

Pragmatists greatly emphasize education and feel that the function of the school is not merely to prepare students for life, but to also provide a suitable environment for actual experiences.

Strengths of pragmatism. One of the great strengths of pragmatism is the dedication to the process of uncovering the truth and determining reality through the application of the scientific method. Pragmatism is not burdened with the problem of "who is the expert." The process, not persons, determines the truth, and the meaning of an idea resulting from that process lies in its consequences after it has been put into operation.[12]

Weaknesses of pragmatism. Perhaps the greatest weakness of pragmatic thought is its devotion to a relatively simple means of determining truth. Pragmatism tends to work well in small, controlled situations, but many questions in life are too large and unwieldy to withstand experimental examination. Unfortunately, the scientific method cannot answer questions of *value* any better than can logical thinking. Pragmatism provides information that can be useful in making decisions, but pragmatism cannot distinguish which is the *right* decision. Without lasting values and goals, teachers have little guidance as to what should be taught.[13]

Pragmatism and education. Pragmatists tend to place a great deal of importance on learning how to acquire skills and gather information. Because what needs to be learned is always changing, the pragmatic educational emphasis is on the process rather than the product. To music teachers, pragmatism says that consistency is needed between the subject and the manner in which it is taught. For example, to study the instruments of the orchestra, orchestral music must be studied as well. Pragmatism views teachers as agents who share with the young techniques for living, not only knowledge.[14]

The pragmatist teacher is interested in the nonmusical result of music study. He or she feels, for example, that it's acceptable if music study contributes to improved student citizenship and health, even if that's not a part of the subject matter. The pragmatist provides classroom opportunities for social interaction and believes that group work is an important ingredient in the teaching approach. That same teacher wants the facts presented in class to be useful to the student. Pragmatist teachers want their students to be active in the classroom rather than merely passive listeners. Those same teachers are constantly alert to the need for change and are ready to adapt to new situations as they arise.

The pragmatist teacher is less interested in evaluation than is the idealist or realist. This teacher is not so much concerned with the content that has been learned, but rather *how* the material was learned. The strict conventional idea of discipline is not of great importance to pragmatist teachers, but pointless high jinks or unusual disruptive behavior is not tolerated. To the pragmatist, the *results* of the learning experience assume the greatest importance. For this reason, pragmatists have at times been accused of being too lenient in structuring classroom activities.

Pragmatist music teachers feel that music education is not a product taken home after leaving school like a bag of groceries, but rather a process that goes on partly in school and partly in all informed social communications and liaisons occurring throughout a lifetime.

Experimentalism/Instrumentalism

Experimentalism, formerly known as Instrumentalism, stems from the writing and work of John Dewey and is characteristically twentieth-century American in origin. The experimental philosophy is closely related to Pragmatism in that experimentalists believe in learning by doing and in the importance of direct experience.

The experimentalist wants an active school with active learners. Experimentalist teachers have the responsibility to organize, select, and direct learning activities toward meaningful goals, but they also feel that they must arouse student interest, so that students are led to knowledge that will help them deal with the problems of life. Such teachers stress thinking through problems rather than memorizing meaningless answers and feel that human relationships are developed in a democratic classroom atmosphere.

A variation of this philosophy has been used for many years in an attempt to justify music programs in public schools; music education, it has been argued, benefits students in ways that are essentially unrelated to music. Phrases such as "music education contributes to better health," "develops wholesome conduct and good citizenship," as well as "promotes good work habits" are examples of statements often offered in support of music education. Such declarations "may convince some reluctant administrator to more fully support the music-education program, but those values can't stand close scrutiny because they are not directly related to music and not unique to music. In fact, many other areas of the curriculum are in a position to make a more powerful contribution to these values than is music."[15] Bennett Reimer cites writings of Susanne Langer and John Dewey when he challenges music educators to put aside their nonmusical objectives and look to aesthetic qualities for a foundation on which to build a philosophy of music education.[16]

Aesthetics and Music Education

It was mentioned earlier in this chapter that a new and comprehensive philosophy of music education must relate to the study of aesthetics and to aesthetic theories. The purpose of this section is to clarify the meaning of "aesthetics," what is meant by "aesthetic experience," and what constitutes "aesthetic education."

Aesthetics. *The Harvard Dictionary of Music* defines musical aesthetics as the study of the relationship of music to the human senses and intellect. Schwadron interprets aesthetics as the "philosophy or study of the beautiful, resulting in the establishment of criteria which help one to determine whether or why one particular composition is beautiful while another is not."[17]

Aesthetic experience. According to Reimer, an aesthetic experience includes some level of involvement with expressive qualities rather than simply with symbolic designations. He believes that an example of how this "aesthetic attitude" is cultivated are the elaborate steps taken to create an encouraging atmosphere in concert halls, theaters, and museums—in other words, providing a setting that makes people receptive to an aesthetic experience.[18]

Charles Leonhard and Robert W. House feel that the aesthetic experience can be any experience that has qualities of both undergoing and doing and involves a balance between struggle and fulfillment. They point out that ordinary experiences have two components—the practical and the intellectual. They use the following example to make their point. A farmer who transforms uncultivated land into a field undergoes a practical experience. At the same time, the experience involves an intellectual process. He determines the need for a crop and reflects on how to best clear and plow the field. He uses his knowledge, based on years of farming experience, concerning climate, soil, and the market to determine which crop to plant and when to plant it. "He is conscious of the results of his efforts, can conceive of the finished product and anticipates the consummation of his experience. These constitute the aesthetic element of his experience."[19] Leonhard and House continue, "An experience is aesthetic when resistance, tension, excitement and emotion are transformed into a movement toward fulfillment and completion."[20]

In the simplest terms, an aesthetic experience can also be expressed as "an individual's response to something beautiful." The key word here is "individual's." What could be an aesthetic experience for one person may be something entirely different for another. Reimer uses the analogy of four men viewing the same scene from a lookout point along a mountain road. All look at the same scene, but each one perceives something different and reacts accordingly.

The first viewer, a geologist from a nearby university, notes the interesting examples of glacial movement and wonders if he should bring his graduate seminar class to the location to view the scene. The second man, a farmer (undoubtedly the one who just cultivated the previously unbroken land), looks at his field below, worries about the lack of moisture and decides he should begin raising chickens instead of farming. The third man is a clergyman who is awed by the grandeur of the scene, and because he sees this as an instance of divine creation, begins to recite a prayer. The fourth person to view the scene is a music educator. Reimer, with tongue somewhat in cheek, describes the probable reaction:

> The music educator (aesthetic to the core) perceives the interplay of
> colors, of shapes, of the texture of the clear sky against the roughness
> of forest and sparkle of water, of the mass of mountains against the
> horizon, framing the entire valley. The perceived aesthetic qualities
> of the scene are enjoyed for their intrinsic loveliness. The scene is
> felt to be beautiful—to give a sense of pleasure, of signficance, of

immediately present import. "How lovely," he thinks. And in wordless absorption he "loses himself" in the qualities presented to his vision. His experience is aesthetic.[21]

The above summary is an accurate example of how individuals who bring different backgrounds and points of reference to the same experience will most naturally react in varied and somewhat unpredictable manners. How boring it would be to exist in a world where everyone reacted in a similar manner to parallel experiences or sets of circumstances.

Aesthetic education. It has been substantiated that an aesthetic experience is not founded on universal material responses, but rather developed in abstract fashion through education. In music, if the aesthetic experience occurs as an interaction between the listener and the musical work, the resulting experience depends largely on the preparation of the listener to perceive the aesthetic, as well as the capability of the object to produce the aesthetic. It is in the cultivation of attitudes and the application to the learning process of the experiences that occur through contact with aesthetic objects that education makes its contribution. And finally, aesthetic education "aims toward the fullest possible sharing of the expressive power in the aesthetic qualities of things."[22]

Building a Philosophy of Music Education

Four traditional philosophies of education have been explored in this chapter, along with their respective implications for music education. It is tempting to consider taking the best points of each philosophical view and combining them into the "perfect" philosophy—an eclectic philosophy. Some philosophers caution against this practice and suggest rather that music educators explore in-depth each philosophy to find the one that comes closest to their actual beliefs and classroom practices. Teachers are then encouraged to build from that accepted philosophic viewpoint and adopt the entire doctrine as theirs, thus creating teaching techniques and a classroom environment based on that philosophy. Those same philosophers urge such a course of action, because in times of trouble or program justification it is difficult, if not impossible, to fall back on a philosophy developed eclectically. They believe that a single, educationally sound philosophy is a far more practical and defensible approach for music educators to follow in developing an individual philosophy of music education.

Undergraduate education of prospective music teachers can only provide students with a basic foundation on which to build a philosophy of music education. The first several years of young music educators' professional lives are spent experimenting with and sorting out the multitude of methods and teaching procedures presented to them as college or university undergraduate music students. They will retain the practices that work for them and discard those that don't; thus, each will formulate his or her own "philosophy of music education." Perhaps the least desirable course a music educator could take is to select a particular philosophical approach to teaching in advance of classroom involvement and then attempt to *become* that type of teacher without the benefit of the actual teaching experience. If the foundation is properly and carefully laid at the undergraduate level, the prospective music educator will find many options available as he or she builds a philosophy of music education based on experience as well as theory.

There are some educational philosophers who believe it's perfectly legitimate and logical to build a single philosophy based on the exploration of several. As Kneller states, "This is the way of the eclectic, and it is a reasonable first step toward the building of a systematic philosophy of education."[23] Some music educators and prospective music educators will be attracted in different ways by all forms of the traditional philosophies presented in this chapter. If one is to develop an eclectic philosophy, however, caution must be exercised to ensure that each element selected is related logically to the rest. Kneller feels that all philosophies start eclectically. Each reader will have to begin by selecting from the philosophies he or she has read and, based on life's experiences, draw upon those ideals that best represent the reader's own thoughts and feelings.[24]

Whichever method is used to build a philosophy of music education, it is necessary as well to consider building from the aesthetic theory approach discussed earlier in this chapter. Music educators need to examine their lives to determine what purpose they have in life, what it is they value most highly, what they consider to be worthwhile knowledge, and do they *really* "love" children. Whatever the outcome, the self-analysis cannot help but be beneficial. In any walk of life, individuals must have philosophies of their own to understand where they are going. If a teacher or educational administrator cannot develop a philosophy of education, students will have no alternative but to follow aimlessly or put youth's important questions to someone else.[25]

Music in the School Curriculum

Through the development of a personal philosophy of music education, a music educator is in an authoritative position to examine the place of music in the curriculum of today's schools. When asked as part of a job-application process to articulate, either verbally or in writing, their philosophy of music education, music educators must necessarily respond with what they believe is the place of music in the school curriculum. This response can be carefully shaped by one's personal philosophy, regardless of that philosophy's stage of development. School administrators are not so much concerned with whether or not a prospective teacher relates to the Realistic or Pragmatic schools of philosophical thought, for example, but rather how the music educator views the role of music education in that particular school system.

In 1959, at a meeting in Atlantic City, New Jersey, the American Association of School Administrators passed a resolution that stated:

> We believe in a well-balanced school curriculum in which music . . .
> and the like are included side by side with other important subjects
> such as mathematics, history and science. It is important that pupils,
> as a part of general education, learn to appreciate, to understand,
> to create, and to criticize with discrimination those products of the
> mind, the voice, the hand, and the body which give dignity to the
> person and exalt the spirit of man.[26]

The entire joint statement of the Music Educators National Conference and the American Association of School Administrators appears in *Perspectives in Music Education,* an MENC publication. This statement should be required reading for every undergraduate or graduate music-education student. Music-education curriculums to this day are being structured and justified on the basis of that joint statement. What follows is an example of a response to school administrators concerning the role of music education in the school's curriculum.

> *The music education program in the curriculum of today's schools* should
> provide every student with the opportunity to develop the following
> goals: intellectual, technical, aesthetic, and social. These goals repre-
> sent a basic minimum for performers and nonperformers alike. The
> school should attempt to achieve as much depth and understanding
> in these skills as the resources of the school and community will per-
> mit.
>
> *Intellectual.* Students should possess an awareness of the logical orga-
> nization of musical works and develop the ability to listen attentively
> and follow with understanding their performance. The ability should
> be developed to appreciate good standards of musical performance
> and to value such artistic principles as unity and coherence, variety
> and contrast, and structural balance and architecture.
>
> *Technical.* Students should be able to use the singing voice as a means
> of self-expression and develop the ability to make music on instru-
> ments, either in exploration or as part of in-depth study. Students
> should be able to read musical notation and use that ability to partici-
> pate in group and community singing. Children of all ages should be
> given many opportunities to explore music through composition.
>
> *Aesthetic.* Students should develop a sharpened sense of beauty in
> sound through the cultivation of musical listening abilities, so that

the musical listening experience can be meaningful, creative, aesthetically significant, and satisfying. Students should be provided the opportunity to develop an awareness of the products of their musical heritage relating directly to human aesthetic history. Student consciousness should be aroused concerning the level of aesthetic and cultural values present in their own communities.

Social. A sense of belonging should be achieved by student participants, as well as a feeling of identification through association with successful performance groups. The social qualities of music need to be recognized. Both listening to and making music lead to enjoyable associations with people of like interests. Students need to become aware of the contributions artists of America, as well as other countries, have made to their own cultural enjoyment.

The preceding statement of the place of music education in today's schools can result from a philosophy of music-education development and is offered as a model approach to a music-education curriculum. This model is offered only as an example of a curriculum declaration that falls in line with the previously mentioned joint statement of the Music Education National Conference and the American Association of School Administrators.

Developing a philosophy is a demanding, yet necessary, process that frees the teacher's imagination and allows the mind to be applied systematically to issues of importance. Kneller sums up the whole process in a most direct manner. "An educator who does not use philosophy is inevitably superficial. A superficial educator may be good or bad—but, if good, less good than he could be, and if bad, worse than he need be."[27]

Summary

It has been the intent of this chapter to provide the reader with a "down to earth" and understandable approach to developing a philosophy of music education. Exploring philosophical foundations *can* be made enjoyable as well as rewarding. Philosophy of *anything* has been approached with a great deal of apprehension through the years by undergraduate college and university students. This simply need not be the case. The information included in Chapter Twelve can only serve as introductory material to a somewhat more complex, yet not overwhelming, effort to accommodate the need for a philosophy of music education. The author hopes that this chapter will whet the appetite of music educators and prospective music educators to examine in greater depth their involvement in music education—what they do, how they do it, and, perhaps more important, *why* they do it.

If music educators are to administer with success programs as complex as music-education programs, the development of individual music-education philosophies is not an option, it is a mandate. Through investigation of the traditional schools of educational philosophy, as well as examination of aesthetic theories, the music educator is most likely to satisfy that mandate.

Suggested Activities

1. Carefully examine the suggested "program in the curriculum of to-day's schools" provided on pages 283–284 of this chapter. Briefly list the suggested requirements that support each goal and determine which traditional philosophy is compatible with each particular requirement and why.

2. Read the joint statement of the Music Education National Conference and the American Association of School Administrators and the position paper extract adopted by the National Association of Secondary School Principals that appear on pages 194-204 of the MENC publication *Perspectives in Music Education*. How are the two statements similar? Different? Discuss long-range implications of each as they affect philosophic thought.

3. How can you justify including music in a high-school curriculum? Draft a statement that would convince a school principal and parents.

4. Select two public-school or college music teachers you remember well and sketch their philosophic orientation according to classroom techniques and attitudes toward music and music students.

5. Think about music education as you know it in the last ten years. How do you feel it has improved? How has it failed? Make a comprehensive list of each.

6. List the ways in which your education has been most successful to this point and why. In what respect has it been less than successful and perhaps even frustrating?

7. Recall and describe in writing a learning experience that involved an aesthetic experience.

8. Discuss in writing the differences and resulting causes and effects of musical athletics and music aesthetics.

9. In less than two hundred words, respond in writing to the question "What is aesthetic education?"

10. Write a speech to be presented to a general meeting of parents and staff regarding what you do as a music educator, why you do it, and why the program is important to the school, and more specifically, to the student participants.

References and Suggested Reading

Abeles, Howard F., Charles L. Hoffer, and Robert H. Klotman. *Foundations of Music Education*. New York: Schirmer Books, 1984.

Broudy, Harry S. "Educational Theory and the Music Curriculum." *In Perspectives in Music Education.* Washington, D.C.: Music Educators National Conference, 1966.

Brown, L.M. *General Philosophy in Education.* New York: McGraw-Hill, 1966.

Buford, Thomas. *Toward a Philosophy of Education.* New York: Holt, Reinhart and Winston, 1969.

Dewey, John. *Art As Experience.* New York: Minton, Balch and Company, 1934.

———. *Democracy and Education.* New York: Macmillan; 1917. Paperback, 1963.

Glenn, Neal E., William B. McBride, and George H. Wilson. *Secondary School Music: Philosophy, Theory and Practice.* Englewood Cliffs, N.J.: Prentice-Hall, 1970.

Klotman, Robert H. *The School Music Administrator and Supervisor.* Englewood Cliffs, N.J.: Prentice-Hall, 1973.

Kneller, George F. *Introduction to Philosophy of Education.* New York: Wiley, 1964.

Korvall, Bonnie, ed. "Music in the School Curriculum." *In Perspectives in Music Education.* Washington, D.C.: Music Educators National Conference, 1966.

Langer, Susanne K. *Problems of Art.* New York: Charles Scribner's Sons, 1957.

Leonhard, Charles. "Philosophy of Music Education." *Music Educators Journal,* September–October 1965

——— and Robert W. House. *Foundations and Principles of Music Education.* New York: McGraw-Hill, 1972.

Meyer, Leonard B. *Emotion and Meaning in Music.* Chicago: University of Chicago Press, 1956.

———. *Explaining Music.* Los Angeles: University of California Press, 1973.

Reimer, Bennett. *A Philosophy of Music Education.* Englewood Cliffs, N.J.: Prentice-Hall, 1970.

———. "What Music Can Do." *Music Educators Journal,* September–October 1959.

Schwadron, Abraham. "Aesthetic Values and Music Education." *In Perspectives in Music Education.* Washington, D.C.: Music Educators National Conference, 1966.

———. *Aesthetics: Dimensions for Music Education.* Washington, D.C.: Music Educators National Conference, 1967.

Tait, Malcom, and Paul Haack. *Principles and Processes of Music Education: New Perspectives.* New York: Teacher College Press, Columbia University, 1984.

Notes

Chapter One

1. Robert House, *Administration in Music Education* (Englewood Cliffs, N.J.: Prentice-Hall, 1973), p. 3.
2. Stephen J. Knezevich, *Administration of Public Education, 3rd ed.* (New York: Harper and Row, 1975), pp. 37–38.
3. Keith D. Snyder, *School Music Administration and Supervision* (Boston, Allyn and Bacon, 1965), p. 34.
4. Knezevich, op. cit., pp. 88–89.

Chapter Two

1. Charles R. Hoffer, *Introduction to Music Education* (Belmont, Calif.: Wadsworth, 1983), p. 177.
2. Frederick J. Swanson, *Music Teaching in the Junior High School* (Englewood Cliffs, N.J.: Prentice-Hall, 1973), p. 267.
3. William J. Gnagey, *Motivating Classroom Discipline* (New York: Macmillan, 1981), p. 11.
4. Tim Lautzenheiser, "Action: The Key to Motivation," *The Instrumentalist,* October 1985, p. 49.
5. Ibid., p. 44.
6. This training program for prospective and current teachers is available from Windthyme, Inc., 728 South 153rd Circle, Omaha, Nebraska 68154. The total cost of the videotape, teachers manual, and student materials is $100.

Chapter Three

1. Polly Hansen, "School Instrumental Music Budgets—Our Ninth Annual Survey," *The Instrumentalist,* August 1985, pp. 44–49.
2. "The 1987 School Instrumental Music Budget Survey," *The Instrumentalist,* pp. 33–35.
3. Keith D. Snyder, *School Music Administration and Supervision* (Boston: Allyn and Bacon, 1965), p. 195.
4. Ibid., p. 197.

Chapter Four

1. Ed Solomon, "The Not-So-Silent Menace," *The Instrumentalist,* October 1986, p. 24.

Chapter Five

1. Richard H. Dempsey and Henry P. Traverso, *Scheduling the Secondary School* (Reston, Va.: National Association of Secondary School Principals, 1983). p. 3.
2. Ibid., p. 13.
3. Donald C. Manlove and David W. Beggs III, *Flexible Scheduling* (Bloomington: Indiana University Press, 1966), p. 23.
4. Ibid., pp. 9–21.
5. Dempsey and Traverso, op. cit., p. 22.
6. James B. Conant, *The American High School Today* (New York: McGraw-Hill, 1959), p. 48.
7. Ibid., p. 65.
8. Malcom E. Bessom, Alphonse M. Tatarunis, and Samuel L. Forcucci, *Teaching Music in Today's Secondary Schools* (New York: Holt, Rinehart and Winston, 1980), p. 348.

Chapter Six

1. Malcom E. Bessom, Alphonse M. Tatarunis, and Samuel L. Forcucci, *Teaching Music in Today's Secondary Schools* (New York: Holt, Rinehart and Winston, 1980), pp. 365–66.

Chapter Seven

1. William Whybrew, *Measurement and Evaluation in Music Education* (Dubuque, Iowa: Wm. C. Brown, 1972), p. viii.
2. James L. Mursell and Mabelle Glenn, *The Psychology of School Music Teaching* (New York: Silver Burdett, 1931), p. 326.
3. Whybrew, op. cit., p. 3.
4. Ibid., p. 6.
5. Ibid., p. 15.
6. Paul R. Lehman, *Tests and Measurements in Music* (Englewood Cliffs, N.J.: Prentice-Hall, 1968), p. 7.

7. Edwin Gordon, *The Psychology of Music Teaching* (Englewood Cliffs, N.J.: Prentice-Hall, 1971), p. 7.
8. Lehman, op. cit., p. 8.
9. Ibid., p. 14.
10. Ibid., pp. 10-15.
11. James O. Froseth, "Using MAP Scores in the Instruction of Beginning Students in Instrumental Music," *Journal of Research in Music Education,* Spring 1971, p. 96.
12. Ibid., pp. 98-105.
13. Lehman, op. cit., p. 7.
14. Paul R. Lehman, "Review of Primary Measures of Music Audiation," *Mental Measurements Yearbook,* edited by James V. Mitchell. (Lincoln: University of Nebraska Press, 1986), p. 1205.

Chapter Eight

1. Donald Ivey, "Can We Afford to Deceive Ourselves?" *Perspectives in Music Education* (Washington, D.C.: Music Educators National Conference, 1966), p. 543.

Chapter Ten

1. Ron Daggett, "Organizing a Parent Booster Club," *The Instrumentalist,* May 1979, pp. 24-27.
2. Ibid.
3. Ibid.

Chapter Eleven

1. Lloyd Frederick Sunderman, *Historical Foundations of Music Education in the United States* (Metuchen, N.J.: Scarecrow Press, 1971), p. 19.
2. Ibid., p. 20.
3. Allen P. Britton, "Music Education: An American Specialty," *Perspectives in Music Education* (Washington, D.C.: Music Educators National Conference, 1966), pp. 15-16.
4. Edward Bailey Birge, *History of Public School Music in the United States* (Washington, D.C.: Music Educators National Conference, 1928), p. 38.
5. Ibid., p. 25.
6. James Keene, *A History of Music Education in the United States* (Hanover, New Hampshire: University Press of New England, 1982), p 249.

7. Ibid., p. 189.
8. Ibid., p. 294.
9. Ibid., p. 304.
10. Ibid., p. 305.
11. Ibid., p. 48.
12. Sunderman, op. cit., p. 50.
13. Ibid., p. 54.
14. Irving Lowens, *Music and Musicians in Early America* (New York: Norton, 1964), p. 39.
15. John Tasker Howard and George Kent Bellows, *A Short History of Music in America* (New York: Thomas Y. Crowell, 1967), p. 47.
16. Ibid., p. 46.
17. Keene, op.cit., p. 170.
18. Birge, op.cit., p. 98.
19. Keene, op.cit., p. 246.
20. Ibid., p. 254.
21. Birge, op.cit., pp. 261–263.
22. Ibid., p. 124.
23. Ibid., p. 124.
24. Ibid., p. 127.
25. Michael L. Mark, *Contemporary Music Education, 2nd ed.* (New York: Schirmer Books, 1986), p. 37.
26. Ibid., pp. 29–36.
27. R. Bernard Fitzgerald, "The Contemporary Music Project for Creativity in Music Education," *Perspectives in Music Education* (Washington, D.C.: Music Educators National Conference, 1966), p. 491.

Chapter Twelve

1. Charles Leonhard, "Philosophy of Music Education," *Music Educators Journal*, September–October 1965, p. 59.
2. Bennett Reimer, *A Philosophy of Music Education* (Englewood Cliffs, N.J.: Prentice-Hall, 1970), p. 4.
3. Ibid.
4. Ibid., p. 11.
5. Robert H. Klotman, *The School Music Administrator and Supervisor* (Englewood Cliffs, N.J.: Prentice-Hall, 1973), p. 5.
6. L.M. Brown, *General Philosophy in Education* (New York: McGraw-Hill, 1966), p. 78.
7. Harold F. Abeles, Charles L. Hoffer, and Robert H. Klotman, *Foundations of Music Education* (New York: Schirmer Books, 1984), p. 35.
8. Abraham Schwadron, *Aesthetics: Dimensions for Music Education* (Washington, D.C.: Music Educators National Conference, 1967), p. 49.
9. George F. Kneller, *Introduction to Philosophy of Education* (New York: Wiley, 1964), p. 38.

10. Neal E. Glenn, William B. McBride, and George H. Wilson, *Secondary School Music: Philosophy, Theory and Practice* (Englewood Cliffs, N.J.: Prentice-Hall, 1970), p. 30.
11. Abeles et al., op.cit., p. 44.
12. Abeles et al., op.cit., p. 42.
13. Ibid., p. 43.
14. Ibid.
15. Leonhard, op.cit., p. 59.
16. Bennett Reimer, "What Music Can Do," *Music Educators Journal,* September–October 1959, pp. 29–32.
17. Abraham Schwadron, "Aesthetic Values and Music Education," *Perspectives in Music Education* (Washington, D.C.: Music Educators National Conference, 1966), p. 187.
18. Reimer, *A Philosophy of Music Education,* p. 76.
19. Charles Leonhard and Robert W. House, *Foundations and Principles of Music Education* (New York: McGraw-Hill, 1972), p. 93.
20. Ibid.
21. Reimer, *A Philosophy of Music Education,* p. 77.
22. Ibid., p. 72.
23. Kneller, op.cit., p. 127.
24. Ibid.
25. Ibid., p. 128.
26. Bonnie Korvall, ed., "Music in the School Curriculum," *Perspectives in Music Education* (Washington D.C.: Music Educators National Conference, 1966), p. 195.
27. Kneller, op.cit., p. 128.

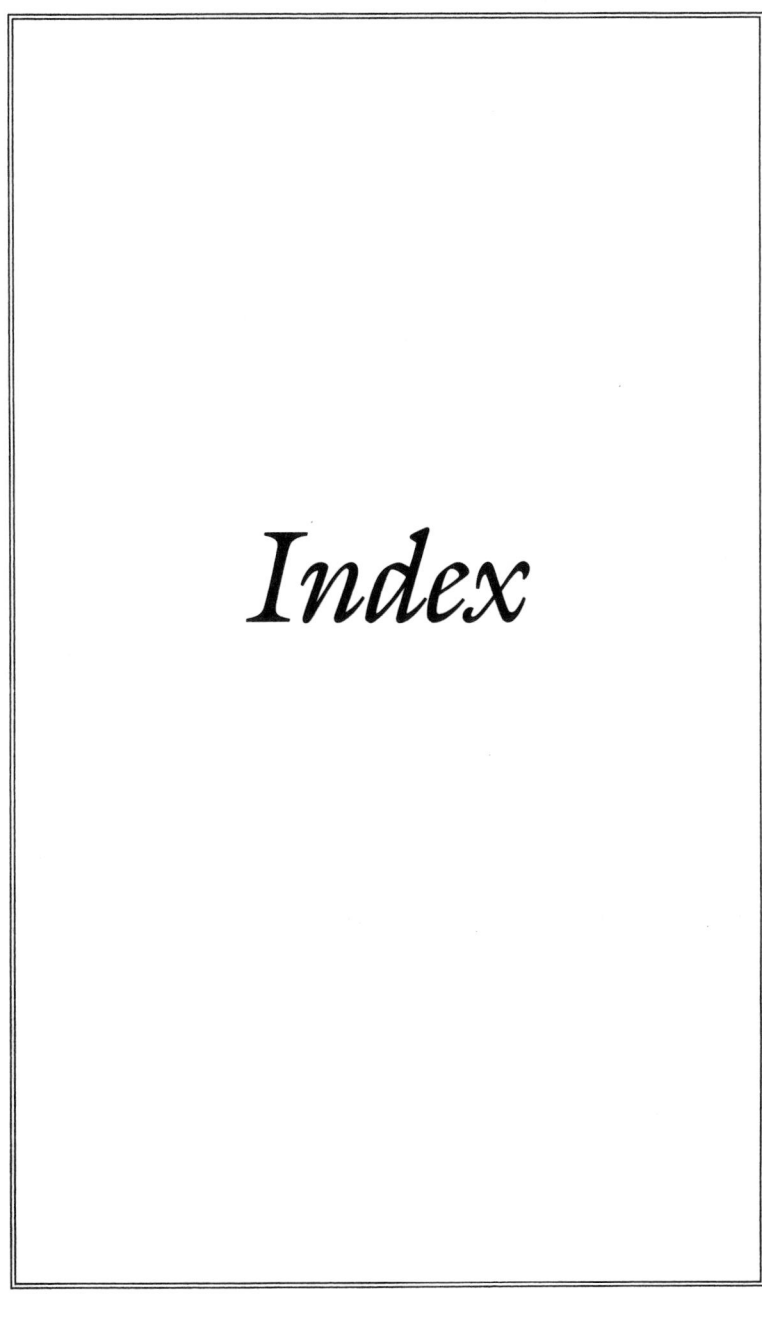

Index